T0344745

THIS IS YOUR **PASSBOOK**® FOR ...

CARPENTER

NATIONAL LEARNING CORPORATION®

passbooks.com

PASSBOOK® SERIES

THE *PASSBOOK® SERIES* has been created to prepare applicants and candidates for the ultimate academic battlefield – the examination room.

At some time in our lives, each and every one of us may be required to take an examination – for validation, matriculation, admission, qualification, registration, certification, or licensure.

Based on the assumption that every applicant or candidate has met the basic formal educational standards, has taken the required number of courses, and read the necessary texts, the *PASSBOOK® SERIES* furnishes the one special preparation which may assure passing with confidence, instead of failing with insecurity. Examination questions – together with answers – are furnished as the basic vehicle for study so that the mysteries of the examination and its compounding difficulties may be eliminated or diminished by a sure method.

This book is meant to help you pass your examination provided that you qualify and are serious in your objective.

The entire field is reviewed through the huge store of content information which is succinctly presented through a provocative and challenging approach – the question-and-answer method.

A climate of success is established by furnishing the correct answers at the end of each test.

You soon learn to recognize types of questions, forms of questions, and patterns of questioning. You may even begin to anticipate expected outcomes.

You perceive that many questions are repeated or adapted so that you can gain acute insights, which may enable you to score many sure points.

You learn how to confront new questions, or types of questions, and to attack them confidently and work out the correct answers.

You note objectives and emphases, and recognize pitfalls and dangers, so that you may make positive educational adjustments.

Moreover, you are kept fully informed in relation to new concepts, methods, practices, and directions in the field.

You discover that you arre actually taking the examination all the time: you are preparing for the examination by "taking" an examination, not by reading extraneous and/or supererogatory textbooks.

In short, this PASSBOOK®, used directedly, should be an important factor in helping you to pass your test.

CARPENTER

DUTIES AND RESPONSIBILITIES
Under supervision, does rough, finish and general carpentry work; performs related work.

EXAMPLES OF TYPICAL TASKS
Install, repair and replace flooring, steel or wood partitions, window frames and sashes, door frames and doors, and other related components of buildings and structures. Install, repair and replace board walks, fences, and screens. Build and repair tool boxes, movable and fixed sash, doors and wooden office furniture, playground, park and school equipment. Builds and rebuilds track cabs. Be familiar with, use and operate both hand and powered woodworking equipment. Builds and repairs various types of fire ladders. Work from plans and sketches. Keep job and other records. May supervise assigned personnel.

TESTS
The written test will be of the multiple-choice type and may include questions on use of tools and equipment; knowledge of materials and hardware; plan reading and specifications; knowledge of framing and details; determination of materials, labor, equipment and safety gear necessary for the job; fabrication of forms, frames and special shapes by using hand tools, power tools and machinery; installation of partitions, cabinets, work stations, doors and windows; working with wood, metal, sheetrock, plastic (such as plexiglass, lexan, formica); erection of scaffolds, ramps, platforms and structures; working on wood and metal stick framing and sheathing; preparation of footings, forms and panels for concrete work; lay out and installation of stairs, ceilings, floors and molding; supervision and safety and other related areas.

HOW TO TAKE A TEST

I. YOU MUST PASS AN EXAMINATION

A. WHAT EVERY CANDIDATE SHOULD KNOW

Examination applicants often ask us for help in preparing for the written test. What can I study in advance? What kinds of questions will be asked? How will the test be given? How will the papers be graded?

As an applicant for a civil service examination, you may be wondering about some of these things. Our purpose here is to suggest effective methods of advance study and to describe civil service examinations.

Your chances for success on this examination can be increased if you know how to prepare. Those "pre-examination jitters" can be reduced if you know what to expect. You can even experience an adventure in good citizenship if you know why civil service exams are given.

B. WHY ARE CIVIL SERVICE EXAMINATIONS GIVEN?

Civil service examinations are important to you in two ways. As a citizen, you want public jobs filled by employees who know how to do their work. As a job seeker, you want a fair chance to compete for that job on an equal footing with other candidates. The best-known means of accomplishing this two-fold goal is the competitive examination.

Exams are widely publicized throughout the nation. They may be administered for jobs in federal, state, city, municipal, town or village governments or agencies.

Any citizen may apply, with some limitations, such as the age or residence of applicants. Your experience and education may be reviewed to see whether you meet the requirements for the particular examination. When these requirements exist, they are reasonable and applied consistently to all applicants. Thus, a competitive examination may cause you some uneasiness now, but it is your privilege and safeguard.

C. HOW ARE CIVIL SERVICE EXAMS DEVELOPED?

Examinations are carefully written by trained technicians who are specialists in the field known as "psychological measurement," in consultation with recognized authorities in the field of work that the test will cover. These experts recommend the subject matter areas or skills to be tested; only those knowledges or skills important to your success on the job are included. The most reliable books and source materials available are used as references. Together, the experts and technicians judge the difficulty level of the questions.

Test technicians know how to phrase questions so that the problem is clearly stated. Their ethics do not permit "trick" or "catch" questions. Questions may have been tried out on sample groups, or subjected to statistical analysis, to determine their usefulness.

Written tests are often used in combination with performance tests, ratings of training and experience, and oral interviews. All of these measures combine to form the best-known means of finding the right person for the right job.

II. HOW TO PASS THE WRITTEN TEST

A. NATURE OF THE EXAMINATION

To prepare intelligently for civil service examinations, you should know how they differ from school examinations you have taken. In school you were assigned certain definite pages to read or subjects to cover. The examination questions were quite detailed and usually emphasized memory. Civil service exams, on the other hand, try to discover your present ability to perform the duties of a position, plus your potentiality to learn these duties. In other words, a civil service exam attempts to predict how successful you will be. Questions cover such a broad area that they cannot be as minute and detailed as school exam questions.

In the public service similar kinds of work, or positions, are grouped together in one "class." This process is known as *position-classification*. All the positions in a class are paid according to the salary range for that class. One class title covers all of these positions, and they are all tested by the same examination.

B. FOUR BASIC STEPS

1) Study the announcement

How, then, can you know what subjects to study? Our best answer is: "Learn as much as possible about the class of positions for which you've applied." The exam will test the knowledge, skills and abilities needed to do the work.

Your most valuable source of information about the position you want is the official exam announcement. This announcement lists the training and experience qualifications. Check these standards and apply only if you come reasonably close to meeting them.

The brief description of the position in the examination announcement offers some clues to the subjects which will be tested. Think about the job itself. Review the duties in your mind. Can you perform them, or are there some in which you are rusty? Fill in the blank spots in your preparation.

Many jurisdictions preview the written test in the exam announcement by including a section called "Knowledge and Abilities Required," "Scope of the Examination," or some similar heading. Here you will find out specifically what fields will be tested.

2) Review your own background

Once you learn in general what the position is all about, and what you need to know to do the work, ask yourself which subjects you already know fairly well and which need improvement. You may wonder whether to concentrate on improving your strong areas or on building some background in your fields of weakness. When the announcement has specified "some knowledge" or "considerable knowledge," or has used adjectives like "beginning principles of…" or "advanced … methods," you can get a clue as to the number and difficulty of questions to be asked in any given field. More questions, and hence broader coverage, would be included for those subjects which are more important in the work. Now weigh your strengths and weaknesses against the job requirements and prepare accordingly.

3) Determine the level of the position

Another way to tell how intensively you should prepare is to understand the level of the job for which you are applying. Is it the entering level? In other words, is this the position in which beginners in a field of work are hired? Or is it an intermediate or advanced level? Sometimes this is indicated by such words as "Junior" or "Senior" in the class title. Other jurisdictions use Roman numerals to designate the level – Clerk I, Clerk II, for example. The word "Supervisor" sometimes appears in the title. If the level is not indicated by the title, check the description of duties. Will you be working under very close supervision, or will you have responsibility for independent decisions in this work?

4) Choose appropriate study materials

Now that you know the subjects to be examined and the relative amount of each subject to be covered, you can choose suitable study materials. For beginning level jobs, or even advanced ones, if you have a pronounced weakness in some aspect of your training, read a modern, standard textbook in that field. Be sure it is up to date and has general coverage. Such books are normally available at your library, and the librarian will be glad to help you locate one. For entry-level positions, questions of appropriate difficulty are chosen – neither highly advanced questions, nor those too simple. Such questions require careful thought but not advanced training.

If the position for which you are applying is technical or advanced, you will read more advanced, specialized material. If you are already familiar with the basic principles of your field, elementary textbooks would waste your time. Concentrate on advanced textbooks and technical periodicals. Think through the concepts and review difficult problems in your field.

These are all general sources. You can get more ideas on your own initiative, following these leads. For example, training manuals and publications of the government agency which employs workers in your field can be useful, particularly for technical and professional positions. A letter or visit to the government department involved may result in more specific study suggestions, and certainly will provide you with a more definite idea of the exact nature of the position you are seeking.

III. KINDS OF TESTS

Tests are used for purposes other than measuring knowledge and ability to perform specified duties. For some positions, it is equally important to test ability to make adjustments to new situations or to profit from training. In others, basic mental abilities not dependent on information are essential. Questions which test these things may not appear as pertinent to the duties of the position as those which test for knowledge and information. Yet they are often highly important parts of a fair examination. For very general questions, it is almost impossible to help you direct your study efforts. What we can do is to point out some of the more common of these general abilities needed in public service positions and describe some typical questions.

1) General information

Broad, general information has been found useful for predicting job success in some kinds of work. This is tested in a variety of ways, from vocabulary lists to questions about current events. Basic background in some field of work, such as sociology or economics, may be sampled in a group of questions. Often these are principles which have become familiar to most persons through exposure rather than through formal training. It is difficult to advise you how to study for these questions; being alert to the world around you is our best suggestion.

2) Verbal ability

An example of an ability needed in many positions is verbal or language ability. Verbal ability is, in brief, the ability to use and understand words. Vocabulary and grammar tests are typical measures of this ability. Reading comprehension or paragraph interpretation questions are common in many kinds of civil service tests. You are given a paragraph of written material and asked to find its central meaning.

3) Numerical ability

Number skills can be tested by the familiar arithmetic problem, by checking paired lists of numbers to see which are alike and which are different, or by interpreting charts and graphs. In the latter test, a graph may be printed in the test booklet which you are asked to use as the basis for answering questions.

4) Observation

A popular test for law-enforcement positions is the observation test. A picture is shown to you for several minutes, then taken away. Questions about the picture test your ability to observe both details and larger elements.

5) Following directions

In many positions in the public service, the employee must be able to carry out written instructions dependably and accurately. You may be given a chart with several columns, each column listing a variety of information. The questions require you to carry out directions involving the information given in the chart.

6) Skills and aptitudes

Performance tests effectively measure some manual skills and aptitudes. When the skill is one in which you are trained, such as typing or shorthand, you can practice. These tests are often very much like those given in business school or high school courses. For many of the other skills and aptitudes, however, no short-time preparation can be made. Skills and abilities natural to you or that you have developed throughout your lifetime are being tested.

Many of the general questions just described provide all the data needed to answer the questions and ask you to use your reasoning ability to find the answers. Your best preparation for these tests, as well as for tests of facts and ideas, is to be at your physical and mental best. You, no doubt, have your own methods of getting into an exam-taking mood and keeping "in shape." The next section lists some ideas on this subject.

IV. KINDS OF QUESTIONS

Only rarely is the "essay" question, which you answer in narrative form, used in civil service tests. Civil service tests are usually of the short-answer type. Full instructions for answering these questions will be given to you at the examination. But in case this is your first experience with short-answer questions and separate answer sheets, here is what you need to know:

1) Multiple-choice Questions

Most popular of the short-answer questions is the "multiple choice" or "best answer" question. It can be used, for example, to test for factual knowledge, ability to solve problems or judgment in meeting situations found at work.

A multiple-choice question is normally one of three types—

- It can begin with an incomplete statement followed by several possible endings. You are to find the one ending which *best* completes the statement, although some of the others may not be entirely wrong.
- It can also be a complete statement in the form of a question which is answered by choosing one of the statements listed.
- It can be in the form of a problem – again you select the best answer.

Here is an example of a multiple-choice question with a discussion which should give you some clues as to the method for choosing the right answer:

When an employee has a complaint about his assignment, the action which will *best* help him overcome his difficulty is to
- A. discuss his difficulty with his coworkers
- B. take the problem to the head of the organization
- C. take the problem to the person who gave him the assignment
- D. say nothing to anyone about his complaint

In answering this question, you should study each of the choices to find which is best. Consider choice "A" – Certainly an employee may discuss his complaint with fellow employees, but no change or improvement can result, and the complaint remains unresolved. Choice "B" is a poor choice since the head of the organization probably does not know what assignment you have been given, and taking your problem to him is known as "going over the head" of the supervisor. The supervisor, or person who made the assignment, is the person who can clarify it or correct any injustice. Choice "C" is, therefore, correct. To say nothing, as in choice "D," is unwise. Supervisors have and interest in knowing the problems employees are facing, and the employee is seeking a solution to his problem.

2) True/False Questions

The "true/false" or "right/wrong" form of question is sometimes used. Here a complete statement is given. Your job is to decide whether the statement is right or wrong.

SAMPLE: A roaming cell-phone call to a nearby city costs less than a non-roaming call to a distant city.

This statement is wrong, or false, since roaming calls are more expensive.

This is not a complete list of all possible question forms, although most of the others are variations of these common types. You will always get complete directions for answering questions. Be sure you understand *how* to mark your answers – ask questions until you do.

V. RECORDING YOUR ANSWERS

Computer terminals are used more and more today for many different kinds of exams.

For an examination with very few applicants, you may be told to record your answers in the test booklet itself. Separate answer sheets are much more common. If this separate answer sheet is to be scored by machine – and this is often the case – it is highly important that you mark your answers correctly in order to get credit.

An electronic scoring machine is often used in civil service offices because of the speed with which papers can be scored. Machine-scored answer sheets must be marked with a pencil, which will be given to you. This pencil has a high graphite content which responds to the electronic scoring machine. As a matter of fact, stray dots may register as answers, so do not let your pencil rest on the answer sheet while you are pondering the correct answer. Also, if your pencil lead breaks or is otherwise defective, ask for another.

Since the answer sheet will be dropped in a slot in the scoring machine, be careful not to bend the corners or get the paper crumpled.

The answer sheet normally has five vertical columns of numbers, with 30 numbers to a column. These numbers correspond to the question numbers in your test booklet. After each number, going across the page are four or five pairs of dotted lines. These short dotted lines have small letters or numbers above them. The first two pairs may also have a "T" or "F" above the letters. This indicates that the first two pairs only are to be used if the questions are of the true-false type. If the questions are multiple choice, disregard the "T" and "F" and pay attention only to the small letters or numbers.

Answer your questions in the manner of the sample that follows:

32. The largest city in the United States is
    A. Washington, D.C.
    B. New York City
    C. Chicago
    D. Detroit
    E. San Francisco

1) Choose the answer you think is best. (New York City is the largest, so "B" is correct.)
2) Find the row of dotted lines numbered the same as the question you are answering. (Find row number 32)
3) Find the pair of dotted lines corresponding to the answer. (Find the pair of lines under the mark "B.")
4) Make a solid black mark between the dotted lines.

VI. BEFORE THE TEST

Common sense will help you find procedures to follow to get ready for an examination. Too many of us, however, overlook these sensible measures. Indeed, nervousness and fatigue have been found to be the most serious reasons why applicants fail to do their best on civil service tests. Here is a list of reminders:

- Begin your preparation early – Don't wait until the last minute to go scurrying around for books and materials or to find out what the position is all about.
- Prepare continuously – An hour a night for a week is better than an all-night cram session. This has been definitely established. What is more, a night a week for a month will return better dividends than crowding your study into a shorter period of time.
- Locate the place of the exam – You have been sent a notice telling you when and where to report for the examination. If the location is in a different town or otherwise unfamiliar to you, it would be well to inquire the best route and learn something about the building.
- Relax the night before the test – Allow your mind to rest. Do not study at all that night. Plan some mild recreation or diversion; then go to bed early and get a good night's sleep.
- Get up early enough to make a leisurely trip to the place for the test – This way unforeseen events, traffic snarls, unfamiliar buildings, etc. will not upset you.
- Dress comfortably – A written test is not a fashion show. You will be known by number and not by name, so wear something comfortable.
- Leave excess paraphernalia at home – Shopping bags and odd bundles will get in your way. You need bring only the items mentioned in the official notice you received; usually everything you need is provided. Do not bring reference books to the exam. They will only confuse those last minutes and be taken away from you when in the test room.
- Arrive somewhat ahead of time – If because of transportation schedules you must get there very early, bring a newspaper or magazine to take your mind off yourself while waiting.
- Locate the examination room – When you have found the proper room, you will be directed to the seat or part of the room where you will sit. Sometimes you are given a sheet of instructions to read while you are waiting. Do not fill out any forms until you are told to do so; just read them and be prepared.
- Relax and prepare to listen to the instructions
- If you have any physical problem that may keep you from doing your best, be sure to tell the test administrator. If you are sick or in poor health, you really cannot do your best on the exam. You can come back and take the test some other time.

VII. AT THE TEST

The day of the test is here and you have the test booklet in your hand. The temptation to get going is very strong. Caution! There is more to success than knowing the right answers. You must know how to identify your papers and understand variations in the type of short-answer question used in this particular examination. Follow these suggestions for maximum results from your efforts:

1) Cooperate with the monitor

The test administrator has a duty to create a situation in which you can be as much at ease as possible. He will give instructions, tell you when to begin, check to see that you are marking your answer sheet correctly, and so on. He is not there to guard you, although he will see that your competitors do not take unfair advantage. He wants to help you do your best.

2) Listen to all instructions

Don't jump the gun! Wait until you understand all directions. In most civil service tests you get more time than you need to answer the questions. So don't be in a hurry. Read each word of instructions until you clearly understand the meaning. Study the examples, listen to all announcements and follow directions. Ask questions if you do not understand what to do.

3) Identify your papers

Civil service exams are usually identified by number only. You will be assigned a number; you must not put your name on your test papers. Be sure to copy your number correctly. Since more than one exam may be given, copy your exact examination title.

4) Plan your time

Unless you are told that a test is a "speed" or "rate of work" test, speed itself is usually not important. Time enough to answer all the questions will be provided, but this does not mean that you have all day. An overall time limit has been set. Divide the total time (in minutes) by the number of questions to determine the approximate time you have for each question.

5) Do not linger over difficult questions

If you come across a difficult question, mark it with a paper clip (useful to have along) and come back to it when you have been through the booklet. One caution if you do this – be sure to skip a number on your answer sheet as well. Check often to be sure that you have not lost your place and that you are marking in the row numbered the same as the question you are answering.

6) Read the questions

Be sure you know what the question asks! Many capable people are unsuccessful because they failed to *read* the questions correctly.

7) Answer all questions

Unless you have been instructed that a penalty will be deducted for incorrect answers, it is better to guess than to omit a question.

8) Speed tests

It is often better NOT to guess on speed tests. It has been found that on timed tests people are tempted to spend the last few seconds before time is called in marking answers at random – without even reading them – in the hope of picking up a few extra points. To discourage this practice, the instructions may warn you that your score will be "corrected" for guessing. That is, a penalty will be applied. The incorrect answers will be deducted from the correct ones, or some other penalty formula will be used.

9) Review your answers

If you finish before time is called, go back to the questions you guessed or omitted to give them further thought. Review other answers if you have time.

10) Return your test materials

If you are ready to leave before others have finished or time is called, take ALL your materials to the monitor and leave quietly. Never take any test material with you. The monitor can discover whose papers are not complete, and taking a test booklet may be grounds for disqualification.

VIII. EXAMINATION TECHNIQUES

1) Read the general instructions carefully. These are usually printed on the first page of the exam booklet. As a rule, these instructions refer to the timing of the examination; the fact that you should not start work until the signal and must stop work at a signal, etc. If there are any *special* instructions, such as a choice of questions to be answered, make sure that you note this instruction carefully.

2) When you are ready to start work on the examination, that is as soon as the signal has been given, read the instructions to each question booklet, underline any key words or phrases, such as *least, best, outline, describe* and the like. In this way you will tend to answer as requested rather than discover on reviewing your paper that you *listed without describing*, that you selected the *worst* choice rather than the *best* choice, etc.

3) If the examination is of the objective or multiple-choice type – that is, each question will also give a series of possible answers: A, B, C or D, and you are called upon to select the best answer and write the letter next to that answer on your answer paper – it is advisable to start answering each question in turn. There may be anywhere from 50 to 100 such questions in the three or four hours allotted and you can see how much time would be taken if you read through all the questions before beginning to answer any. Furthermore, if you come across a question or group of questions which you know would be difficult to answer, it would undoubtedly affect your handling of all the other questions.

4) If the examination is of the essay type and contains but a few questions, it is a moot point as to whether you should read all the questions before starting to answer any one. Of course, if you are given a choice – say five out of seven and the like – then it is essential to read all the questions so you can eliminate the two that are most difficult. If, however, you are asked to answer all the questions, there may be danger in trying to answer the easiest one first because you may find that you will spend too much time on it. The best technique is to answer the first question, then proceed to the second, etc.

5) Time your answers. Before the exam begins, write down the time it started, then add the time allowed for the examination and write down the time it must be completed, then divide the time available somewhat as follows:

- If 3-1/2 hours are allowed, that would be 210 minutes. If you have 80 objective-type questions, that would be an average of 2-1/2 minutes per question. Allow yourself no more than 2 minutes per question, or a total of 160 minutes, which will permit about 50 minutes to review.
- If for the time allotment of 210 minutes there are 7 essay questions to answer, that would average about 30 minutes a question. Give yourself only 25 minutes per question so that you have about 35 minutes to review.

6) The most important instruction is to *read each question* and make sure you know what is wanted. The second most important instruction is to *time yourself properly* so that you answer every question. The third most important instruction is to *answer every question*. Guess if you have to but include something for each question. Remember that you will receive no credit for a blank and will probably receive some credit if you write something in answer to an essay question. If you guess a letter – say "B" for a multiple-choice question – you may have guessed right. If you leave a blank as an answer to a multiple-choice question, the examiners may respect your feelings but it will not add a point to your score. Some exams may penalize you for wrong answers, so in such cases *only*, you may not want to guess unless you have some basis for your answer.

7) Suggestions
   a. Objective-type questions
      1. Examine the question booklet for proper sequence of pages and questions
      2. Read all instructions carefully
      3. Skip any question which seems too difficult; return to it after all other questions have been answered
      4. Apportion your time properly; do not spend too much time on any single question or group of questions
      5. Note and underline key words – *all, most, fewest, least, best, worst, same, opposite,* etc.
      6. Pay particular attention to negatives
      7. Note unusual option, e.g., unduly long, short, complex, different or similar in content to the body of the question
      8. Observe the use of "hedging" words – *probably, may, most likely,* etc.
      9. Make sure that your answer is put next to the same number as the question
      10. Do not second-guess unless you have good reason to believe the second answer is definitely more correct
      11. Cross out original answer if you decide another answer is more accurate; do not erase until you are ready to hand your paper in
      12. Answer all questions; guess unless instructed otherwise
      13. Leave time for review

   b. Essay questions
      1. Read each question carefully
      2. Determine exactly what is wanted. Underline key words or phrases.
      3. Decide on outline or paragraph answer

    4. Include many different points and elements unless asked to develop any one or two points or elements
    5. Show impartiality by giving pros and cons unless directed to select one side only
    6. Make and write down any assumptions you find necessary to answer the questions
    7. Watch your English, grammar, punctuation and choice of words
    8. Time your answers; don't crowd material

8) Answering the essay question

Most essay questions can be answered by framing the specific response around several key words or ideas. Here are a few such key words or ideas:

M's: manpower, materials, methods, money, management
P's: purpose, program, policy, plan, procedure, practice, problems, pitfalls, personnel, public relations
    a. Six basic steps in handling problems:
      1. Preliminary plan and background development
      2. Collect information, data and facts
      3. Analyze and interpret information, data and facts
      4. Analyze and develop solutions as well as make recommendations
      5. Prepare report and sell recommendations
      6. Install recommendations and follow up effectiveness

    b. Pitfalls to avoid
      1. *Taking things for granted* – A statement of the situation does not necessarily imply that each of the elements is necessarily true; for example, a complaint may be invalid and biased so that all that can be taken for granted is that a complaint has been registered
      2. *Considering only one side of a situation* – Wherever possible, indicate several alternatives and then point out the reasons you selected the best one
      3. *Failing to indicate follow up* – Whenever your answer indicates action on your part, make certain that you will take proper follow-up action to see how successful your recommendations, procedures or actions turn out to be
      4. *Taking too long in answering any single question* – Remember to time your answers properly

IX. AFTER THE TEST

Scoring procedures differ in detail among civil service jurisdictions although the general principles are the same. Whether the papers are hand-scored or graded by machine we have described, they are nearly always graded by number. That is, the person who marks the paper knows only the number – never the name – of the applicant. Not until all the papers have been graded will they be matched with names. If other tests, such as training and experience or oral interview ratings have been given, scores will be combined. Different parts of the examination usually have different weights. For example, the written test might count 60 percent of the final grade, and a rating of training and experience 40 percent. In many jurisdictions, veterans will have a certain number of points added to their grades.

After the final grade has been determined, the names are placed in grade order and an eligible list is established. There are various methods for resolving ties between those who get the same final grade – probably the most common is to place first the name of the person whose application was received first. Job offers are made from the eligible list in the order the names appear on it. You will be notified of your grade and your rank as soon as all these computations have been made. This will be done as rapidly as possible.

People who are found to meet the requirements in the announcement are called "eligibles." Their names are put on a list of eligible candidates. An eligible's chances of getting a job depend on how high he stands on this list and how fast agencies are filling jobs from the list.

When a job is to be filled from a list of eligibles, the agency asks for the names of people on the list of eligibles for that job. When the civil service commission receives this request, it sends to the agency the names of the three people highest on this list. Or, if the job to be filled has specialized requirements, the office sends the agency the names of the top three persons who meet these requirements from the general list.

The appointing officer makes a choice from among the three people whose names were sent to him. If the selected person accepts the appointment, the names of the others are put back on the list to be considered for future openings.

That is the rule in hiring from all kinds of eligible lists, whether they are for typist, carpenter, chemist, or something else. For every vacancy, the appointing officer has his choice of any one of the top three eligibles on the list. This explains why the person whose name is on top of the list sometimes does not get an appointment when some of the persons lower on the list do. If the appointing officer chooses the second or third eligible, the No. 1 eligible does not get a job at once, but stays on the list until he is appointed or the list is terminated.

X. HOW TO PASS THE INTERVIEW TEST

The examination for which you applied requires an oral interview test. You have already taken the written test and you are now being called for the interview test – the final part of the formal examination.

You may think that it is not possible to prepare for an interview test and that there are no procedures to follow during an interview. Our purpose is to point out some things you can do in advance that will help you and some good rules to follow and pitfalls to avoid while you are being interviewed.

What is an interview supposed to test?

The written examination is designed to test the technical knowledge and competence of the candidate; the oral is designed to evaluate intangible qualities, not readily measured otherwise, and to establish a list showing the relative fitness of each candidate – as measured against his competitors – for the position sought. Scoring is not on the basis of "right" and "wrong," but on a sliding scale of values ranging from "not passable" to "outstanding." As a matter of fact, it is possible to achieve a relatively low score without a single "incorrect" answer because of evident weakness in the qualities being measured.

Occasionally, an examination may consist entirely of an oral test – either an individual or a group oral. In such cases, information is sought concerning the technical knowledges and abilities of the candidate, since there has been no written examination for this purpose. More commonly, however, an oral test is used to supplement a written examination.

Who conducts interviews?

The composition of oral boards varies among different jurisdictions. In nearly all, a representative of the personnel department serves as chairman. One of the members of the board may be a representative of the department in which the candidate would work. In some cases, "outside experts" are used, and, frequently, a businessman or some other representative of the general public is asked to serve. Labor and management or other special groups may be represented. The aim is to secure the services of experts in the appropriate field.

However the board is composed, it is a good idea (and not at all improper or unethical) to ascertain in advance of the interview who the members are and what groups they represent. When you are introduced to them, you will have some idea of their backgrounds and interests, and at least you will not stutter and stammer over their names.

What should be done before the interview?

While knowledge about the board members is useful and takes some of the surprise element out of the interview, there is other preparation which is more substantive. It *is* possible to prepare for an oral interview – in several ways:

1) Keep a copy of your application and review it carefully before the interview

This may be the only document before the oral board, and the starting point of the interview. Know what education and experience you have listed there, and the sequence and dates of all of it. Sometimes the board will ask you to review the highlights of your experience for them; you should not have to hem and haw doing it.

2) Study the class specification and the examination announcement

Usually, the oral board has one or both of these to guide them. The qualities, characteristics or knowledges required by the position sought are stated in these documents. They offer valuable clues as to the nature of the oral interview. For example, if the job involves supervisory responsibilities, the announcement will usually indicate that knowledge of modern supervisory methods and the qualifications of the candidate as a supervisor will be tested. If so, you can expect such questions, frequently in the form of a hypothetical situation which you are expected to solve. NEVER go into an oral without knowledge of the duties and responsibilities of the job you seek.

3) Think through each qualification required

Try to visualize the kind of questions you would ask if you were a board member. How well could you answer them? Try especially to appraise your own knowledge and background in each area, *measured against the job sought*, and identify any areas in which you are weak. Be critical and realistic – do not flatter yourself.

4) Do some general reading in areas in which you feel you may be weak

For example, if the job involves supervision and your past experience has NOT, some general reading in supervisory methods and practices, particularly in the field of human relations, might be useful. Do NOT study agency procedures or detailed manuals. The oral board will be testing your understanding and capacity, not your memory.

5) Get a good night's sleep and watch your general health and mental attitude

You will want a clear head at the interview. Take care of a cold or any other minor ailment, and of course, no hangovers.

What should be done on the day of the interview?

Now comes the day of the interview itself. Give yourself plenty of time to get there. Plan to arrive somewhat ahead of the scheduled time, particularly if your appointment is in the fore part of the day. If a previous candidate fails to appear, the board might be ready for you a bit early. By early afternoon an oral board is almost invariably behind schedule if there are many candidates, and you may have to wait. Take along a book or magazine to read, or your application to review, but leave any extraneous material in the waiting room when you go in for your interview. In any event, relax and compose yourself.

The matter of dress is important. The board is forming impressions about you – from your experience, your manners, your attitude, and your appearance. Give your personal appearance careful attention. Dress your best, but not your flashiest. Choose conservative, appropriate clothing, and be sure it is immaculate. This is a business interview, and your appearance should indicate that you regard it as such. Besides, being well groomed and properly dressed will help boost your confidence.

Sooner or later, someone will call your name and escort you into the interview room. *This is it.* From here on you are on your own. It is too late for any more preparation. But remember, you asked for this opportunity to prove your fitness, and you are here because your request was granted.

What happens when you go in?

The usual sequence of events will be as follows: The clerk (who is often the board stenographer) will introduce you to the chairman of the oral board, who will introduce you to the other members of the board. Acknowledge the introductions before you sit down. Do not be surprised if you find a microphone facing you or a stenotypist sitting by. Oral interviews are usually recorded in the event of an appeal or other review.

Usually the chairman of the board will open the interview by reviewing the highlights of your education and work experience from your application – primarily for the benefit of the other members of the board, as well as to get the material into the record. Do not interrupt or comment unless there is an error or significant misinterpretation; if that is the case, do not hesitate. But do not quibble about insignificant matters. Also, he will usually ask you some question about your education, experience or your present job – partly to get you to start talking and to establish the interviewing "rapport." He may start the actual questioning, or turn it over to one of the other members. Frequently, each member undertakes the questioning on a particular area, one in which he is perhaps most competent, so you can expect each member to participate in the examination. Because time is limited, you may also expect some rather abrupt switches in the direction the questioning takes, so do not be upset by it. Normally, a board member will not pursue a single line of questioning unless he discovers a particular strength or weakness.

After each member has participated, the chairman will usually ask whether any member has any further questions, then will ask you if you have anything you wish to add. Unless you are expecting this question, it may floor you. Worse, it may start you off on an extended, extemporaneous speech. The board is not usually seeking more information. The question is principally to offer you a last opportunity to present further qualifications or to indicate that you have nothing to add. So, if you feel that a significant qualification or characteristic has been overlooked, it is proper to point it out in a sentence or so. Do not compliment the board on the thoroughness of their examination – they have been sketchy, and you know it. If you wish, merely say, "No thank you, I have nothing further to add." This is a point where you can "talk yourself out" of a good impression or fail to present an important bit of information. Remember, *you close the interview yourself.*

The chairman will then say, "That is all, Mr. _____, thank you." Do not be startled; the interview is over, and quicker than you think. Thank him, gather your belongings and take your leave. Save your sigh of relief for the other side of the door.

How to put your best foot forward

Throughout this entire process, you may feel that the board individually and collectively is trying to pierce your defenses, seek out your hidden weaknesses and embarrass and confuse you. Actually, this is not true. They are obliged to make an appraisal of your qualifications for the job you are seeking, and they want to see you in your best light. Remember, they must interview all candidates and a non-cooperative candidate may become a failure in spite of their best efforts to bring out his qualifications. Here are 15 suggestions that will help you:

1) Be natural – Keep your attitude confident, not cocky

If you are not confident that you can do the job, do not expect the board to be. Do not apologize for your weaknesses, try to bring out your strong points. The board is interested in a positive, not negative, presentation. Cockiness will antagonize any board member and make him wonder if you are covering up a weakness by a false show of strength.

2) Get comfortable, but don't lounge or sprawl

Sit erectly but not stiffly. A careless posture may lead the board to conclude that you are careless in other things, or at least that you are not impressed by the importance of the occasion. Either conclusion is natural, even if incorrect. Do not fuss with your clothing, a pencil or an ashtray. Your hands may occasionally be useful to emphasize a point; do not let them become a point of distraction.

3) Do not wisecrack or make small talk

This is a serious situation, and your attitude should show that you consider it as such. Further, the time of the board is limited – they do not want to waste it, and neither should you.

4) Do not exaggerate your experience or abilities

In the first place, from information in the application or other interviews and sources, the board may know more about you than you think. Secondly, you probably will not get away with it. An experienced board is rather adept at spotting such a situation, so do not take the chance.

5) If you know a board member, do not make a point of it, yet do not hide it

Certainly you are not fooling him, and probably not the other members of the board. Do not try to take advantage of your acquaintanceship – it will probably do you little good.

6) Do not dominate the interview

Let the board do that. They will give you the clues – do not assume that you have to do all the talking. Realize that the board has a number of questions to ask you, and do not try to take up all the interview time by showing off your extensive knowledge of the answer to the first one.

7) Be attentive

You only have 20 minutes or so, and you should keep your attention at its sharpest throughout. When a member is addressing a problem or question to you, give him your undivided attention. Address your reply principally to him, but do not exclude the other board members.

8) Do not interrupt

A board member may be stating a problem for you to analyze. He will ask you a question when the time comes. Let him state the problem, and wait for the question.

9) Make sure you understand the question

Do not try to answer until you are sure what the question is. If it is not clear, restate it in your own words or ask the board member to clarify it for you. However, do not haggle about minor elements.

10) Reply promptly but not hastily

A common entry on oral board rating sheets is "candidate responded readily," or "candidate hesitated in replies." Respond as promptly and quickly as you can, but do not jump to a hasty, ill-considered answer.

11) Do not be peremptory in your answers

A brief answer is proper – but do not fire your answer back. That is a losing game from your point of view. The board member can probably ask questions much faster than you can answer them.

12) Do not try to create the answer you think the board member wants

He is interested in what kind of mind you have and how it works – not in playing games. Furthermore, he can usually spot this practice and will actually grade you down on it.

13) Do not switch sides in your reply merely to agree with a board member

Frequently, a member will take a contrary position merely to draw you out and to see if you are willing and able to defend your point of view. Do not start a debate, yet do not surrender a good position. If a position is worth taking, it is worth defending.

14) Do not be afraid to admit an error in judgment if you are shown to be wrong

The board knows that you are forced to reply without any opportunity for careful consideration. Your answer may be demonstrably wrong. If so, admit it and get on with the interview.

15) Do not dwell at length on your present job

The opening question may relate to your present assignment. Answer the question but do not go into an extended discussion. You are being examined for a *new* job, not your present one. As a matter of fact, try to phrase ALL your answers in terms of the job for which you are being examined.

Basis of Rating

Probably you will forget most of these "do's" and "don'ts" when you walk into the oral interview room. Even remembering them all will not ensure you a passing grade. Perhaps you did not have the qualifications in the first place. But remembering them will help you to put your best foot forward, without treading on the toes of the board members.

Rumor and popular opinion to the contrary notwithstanding, an oral board wants you to make the best appearance possible. They know you are under pressure – but they also want to see how you respond to it as a guide to what your reaction would be under the pressures of the job you seek. They will be influenced by the degree of poise you display, the personal traits you show and the manner in which you respond.

ABOUT THIS BOOK

This book contains tests divided into Examination Sections. Go through each test, answering every question in the margin. At the end of each test look at the answer key and check your answers. On the ones you got wrong, look at the right answer choice and learn. Do not fill in the answers first. Do not memorize the questions and answers, but understand the answer and principles involved. On your test, the questions will likely be different from the samples. Questions are changed and new ones added. If you understand these past questions you should have success with any changes that arise. Tests may consist of several types of questions. We have additional books on each subject should more study be advisable or necessary for you. Finally, the more you study, the better prepared you will be. This book is intended to be the last thing you study before you walk into the examination room. Prior study of relevant texts is also recommended. NLC publishes some of these in our Fundamental Series. Knowledge and good sense are important factors in passing your exam. Good luck also helps. So now study this Passbook, absorb the material contained within and take that knowledge into the examination. Then do your best to pass that exam.

———

EXAMINATION SECTION

CARPENTRY

EXAMINATION SECTION
TEST 1

DIRECTIONS: Each question or incomplete statement is followed by several suggested answers or completions. Select the one that BEST answers the question or completes the statement. *PRINT THE LETTER OF THE CORRECT ANSWER IN THE SPACE AT THE RIGHT.*

1. In a ratchet bit brace, the part that holds the bit is called the   1.____

    A.   vise   B.   chuck   C.   pawl   D.   cam ring

2. The BEST tool to use as a guide when scribing a line perpendicular to the side of a 2" x   2.____
    4" stud is a

    A.   T-square   B.   Try square
    C.   Batter board   D.   Parallel bar

3. Of the following planes, the *one* that does NOT have a double plane iron is the   3.____

    A.   block plane   B.   jack plane
    C.   fore plane   D.   smooth plane

4. Of the following files, the BEST one to use to sharpen a rip-saw is a   4.____

    A.   taper   B.   flat bastard   C.   mill   D.   half round

5. The size of auger bit to select in order to bore a 5/8" hole is   5.____

    A.   #5   B.   #8   C.   #10   D.   #12

6. The type of circular saw used for cutting grooves that are *wider* than the cut that can be   6.____
    made by ordinary saws is known as a

    A.   dado set   B.   rabbet set
    C.   scarf set   D.   dove tail set

7. Of the following saws, the *one* that should be used for cutting circular disks out of 5/8"   7.____
    plywood is a

    A.   circular saw   B.   buck saw
    C.   back saw   D.   band saw

8. The saw used in a miter box is a   8.____

    A.   compass saw   B.   coping saw
    C.   back saw   D.   hacksaw

9. Of the following, the BEST wood to use for the handle of a claw hammer is   9.____

    A.   pine   B.   hickory   C.   cypress   D.   elm

10. A 3" belt sander requires a 3 x 21 belt. The "21" refers to the belt's   10.____

    A.   grit number   B.   diameter
    C.   contact area   D.   length

11. In sharpening a paring chisel, a carpenter should grind the bevel at an angle of, *approxi-*   11.____
   mately,

    A.   5°   B.   15°   C.   25°   D.   35°

12. "Dressing" a saw has to do with   12.____

    A.   lowering the height of the teeth
    B.   removing burrs from the side of the teeth
    C.   lowering of the tooth gullets
    D.   tilting the file upward at the end of the stroke

13. To cut a 1/4-inch chamfer in a piece of wood two feet long, a carpenter should use a   13.____

    A.   chisel   B.   plane   C.   saw   D.   hone

14. To tighten a lag screw, a Carpenter should use a   14.____

    A.   mallet   B.   Phillips head screw-driver
    C.   wrench   D.   hammer

15. When boring a hole through a thin piece of wood, the bit that will LEAST splinter the   15.____
   backside of the wood is a(n)

    A.   center bit   B.   expensive bit
    C.   Foerstner bit   D.   countersink bit

16. Shown below is a sketch of a hinge.   16.____

The hinge is a(n)

    A.   T-hinge   B.   strap hinge
    C.   piano hinge   D.   offset hinge

17. A hinged strap with a slotted flap that passes over a staple and is secured by a padlock is   17.____
   known as a

    A.   hasp   B.   hamper   C.   harbinger   D.   hawk

18. To bend saw teeth to the proper angle, a carpenter should use a   18.____

    A.   saw screed   B.   saw tap   C.   saw bit   D.   saw set

19. A tool used to make a pilot hole for starting a screw in wood is a(n)   19.____

    A.   grommet   B.   cotter pin   C.   awl   D.   counter point

20. The tool to use to finish driving a nail into corners and moldings is a nail   20.____

    A.   set   B.   punch   C.   pin   D.   all

21. Of the following fasteners, the *one* that is LEAST often used in structural wood work is a   21.____

    A. lag screw   B. wood screw   C. nail   D. spike

22. When wood loses moisture, it shrinks in   22.____

    A. thickness and width and expands in length
    B. thickness and expands in width and length
    C. width and length and expands in thickness
    D. thickness, width, and length

23. Of the following types of commercial nails, the *one* that has the GREATEST withdrawal resistance is a   23.____

    A. cement-coated nail   B. galvanized nail
    C. chemically etched nail   D. spirally grooved nail

24. The grit number for a 1/0 sand paper is   24.____

    A. 200   B. 100   C. 80   D. 60

25. The length of a 6d nail is   25.____

    A. 1 3/4"   B. 2"   C. 2 1/4"   D. 2 3/4"

KEYS (CORRECT ANSWERS)

1.	B	11.	B
2.	B	12.	B
3.	A	13.	B
4.	A	14.	C
5.	C	15.	A
6.	A	16.	D
7.	D	17.	A
8.	C	18.	D
9.	B	19.	C
10.	D	20.	A

21.	B
22.	D
23.	D
24.	C
25.	B

TEST 2

Each question or incomplete statement is followed by several suggested answers or completions. Select the one that BEST answers the question or completes the statement. *PRINT THE LETTER OF THE CORRECT ANSWER IN THE SPACE AT THE RIGHT.*

1. The number of board feet in 15 pieces of lumber 2" x 10" by 12 feet long is   1._____

   A. 30   B. 300   C. 600   D. 900

2. When unpainted wood is left outdoors for a considerable time, the color of the wood *usually* changes to   2._____

   A. brown   B. gray   C. yellow   D. amber

3. When wood is to be in permanent contact with earth, it should be treated with   3._____

   A. creosote   B. tri-sodium phosphate
   C. sodium chloride   D. sal ammoniac

4. A panic bolt is *most frequently* installed on a   4._____

   A. window   B. door   C. roof scuttle   D. skylight

5. Of the following, the BEST reason for oiling plywood concrete forms is to   5._____

   A. lubricate the concrete during vibration
   B. allow forms to be removed easily
   C. decrease porosity of the plywood
   D. prevent seapage of rain water into the concrete in case it rains while the concrete is setting

6. Of the following species of wood, the *one* that is classified as a SOFT wood is   6._____

   A. chestnut   B. white ash   C. birch   D. cypress

7. S.S. glass means   7._____

   A. Smooth Surface glass   B. Silicone Surface glass
   C. Single Strength glass   D. Square Sides glass

8. Of the following types of wood, the *one* that is NOT coarsegrained is   8._____

   A. oak   B. pine   C. walnut   D. chestnut

9. The one of the following materials that does NOT contain wood is   9._____

   A. hardboard   B. compressed board
   C. particle board   D. masonite

10. Plywood sub flooring is used instead of 1" x 6" sub flooring MAINLY because it   10._____

    A. is more sound proof   B. is easier to install
    C. is more fire resistant   D. makes the floor more rigid

11. Wainscoting paneling would be installed on a   11._____

    A. wall   B. floor   C. ceiling   D. roof

12. According to the building code, galvanized wire staple fasteners in plywood may   12.____

    A.   not be used anywhere in buildings
    B.   be used on roofs only
    C.   be used on wall sheathing only
    D.   be used on roofs and wall sheathing

13. Galvanized nails are nails that are coated with   13.____

    A.   brass   B.   cadmium   C.   copper   D.   zinc

14. The tip of a Phillips screwdriver is   14.____

    A.   elliptical   B.   pointed   C.   flat   D.   concave

15. Putlogs are used PRIMARILY on   15.____

    A.   ladders   B.   scaffolds   C.   horses   D.   hatchways

16. The tapered end of a file that fits into a wood handle is called the   16.____

    A.   tip   B.   heel   C.   edge   D.   tang

17. Of the following bolts, the type which has a *round* head is the   17.____

    A.   machine bolt   B.   stud bolt
    C.   carriage bolt   D.   coupling bolt

18. A metal T-anchor would be used on a   18.____

    A.   door   B.   window   C.   joist   D.   stud

19. A lock that is surface mounted on the side of a door is known as a   19.____

    A.   rim lock   B.   tenon lock
    C.   mortise lock   D.   flange lock

20. Clapboards are *generally* used for   20.____

    A.   stair treads   B.   wood siding
    C.   window sills   D.   roof copings

21. Shown below is a sketch of the floor joists in a building.   21.____

The pieces of wood marked X are known as

    A.   bridging   B.   bracketing   C.   corbeling   D.   casing

22. A specification for a belt sander states that it is *UL* approved. The *UL* in the specification is an abbreviation of   22.____

    A. Universal Listing   B. Underwriters Laboratories
    C. Unlimited Liability   D. Use Limited

23. Shown below is a sketch of a wood joint.   23.____

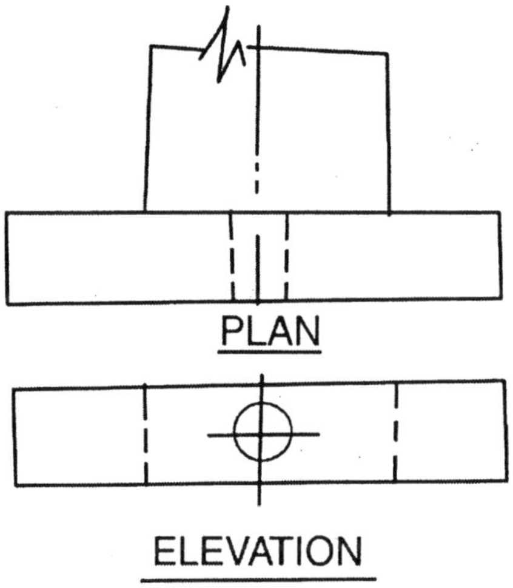

PLAN

ELEVATION

The wood joint is a

    A. peg tenon   B. plain dovetail butt
    C. dovetail half lap   D. blind housed tenon

Questions 24-25.

DIRECTIONS: Questions 24 and 25 refer to the wood form work for concrete shown in the sketch at the top of the next page.

24. The horizontal member X is known as a   24.____

    A. girt   B. soldier   C. pivot   D. waler

25. The horizontal member Y is known as a   25.____

    A. scab   B. ledger   C. kerf   D. putlog

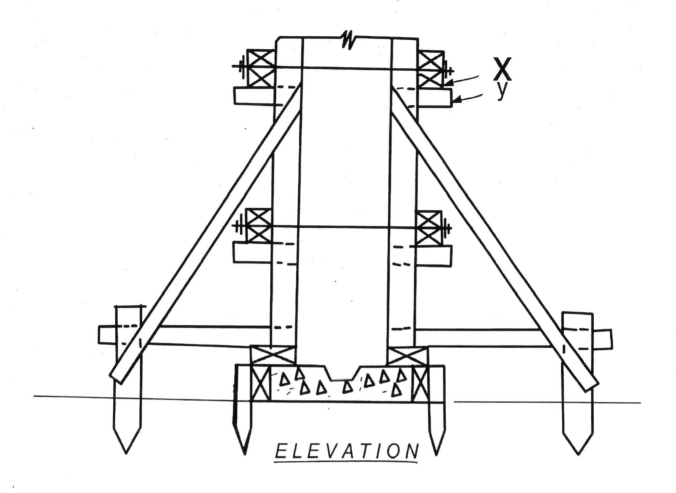

ELEVATION

KEYS (CORRECT ANSWERS)

1.	B	11.	A
2.	B	12.	D
3.	A	13.	D
4.	B	14.	B
5.	B	15.	B
6.	D	16.	D
7.	C	17.	C
8.	B	18.	C
9.	B	19.	A
10.	B	20.	B

21.	A
22.	B
23.	A
24.	D
25.	B

TEST 3

DIRECTIONS: Each question or incomplete statement is followed by several suggested answers or completions. Select the one that BEST answers the question or completes the statement. *PRINT THE LETTER OF THE CORRECT ANSWER IN THE SPACE AT THE RIGHT.*

Questions 1-3.

DIRECTIONS: Questions 1 through 3 refer to the wood truss shown in the sketch below.

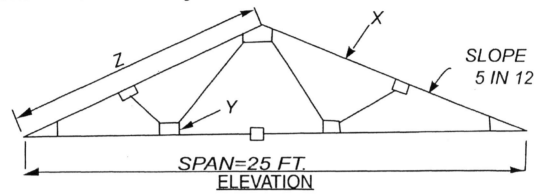

SPAN=25 FT.
ELEVATION

1.   The inclined member X is known as a   1.____

   A. ridge   B. rafter   C. brace   D. bridge

2.   The plate marked Y is known as a(n)   2.____

   A. gusset   B. batten   C. spacer   D. anchor

3.   The TOTAL distance Z is, *most nearly,*   3.____

   A. 13' 2 1/2"   B. 13' 4 1/2"
   C. 13' 6 1/2"   D. 13' 8 1/2"

4.   Shown in the sketch below is a bolted timber.   4.____

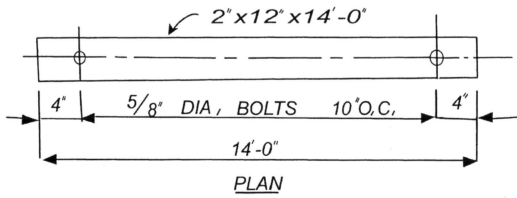

PLAN

The number of 5/8" diameter bolts required is

   A. 15   B. 16   C. 17   D. 18

5. Plywood sub flooring 5/8" thick has a Panel Identification Index of 42/20. The "20" indicates the

    A. maximum allowable load in pounds on a square foot of panel
    B. maximum permitted center to center distance in inches between floor joists
    C. weight of a cubic foot of panel
    D. minimum number of 8d nails required per panel

5.____

6. An identifying symbol *HDO* G-1 - DFPA - 19 - PS1 - 66 is stamped on the edge of a plywood panel. The *HDO* part of this code stands for

    A. Heavy Duty Outside
    B. High Density Oak
    C. High Density Overlaid
    D. Housing Development Organization

6.____

7. Floor plans showing the modification of partitions are drawn to a scale of 1/4" to a foot. If the length of a partition shown on the drawing scales 6 3/8", then the ACTUAL length of the partition would be, *most nearly,*

    A. 2.4' 6"   B. 25' 2"   C. 24' 4"   D. 25' 6"

7.____

Questions 8-9.

DIRECTIONS: Questions 8 and 9 refer to the DETAIL shown below.

8. The number of 3/8" bolts in the roof scuttle is

    A. 6   B. 8   C. 10   D. 12

8.____

9. In the DETAIL shown above, the number of 2" x 6" planks required is

    A. 7   B. 8   C. 9   D. 10

9.____

10. On an alteration drawing, the location of *new* partitions would be shown on a(n)

    A. floor plan   B. front elevation
    C. frame cross-section   D. end view

10.____

11. A drawing specifies "3-1x6-*Fas* - Wh. Oak S4S." *Fas* is an abbreviation for

    A. face all sides   B. finish all sides
    C. fabricate as specified   D. firsts and seconds

11.____

12.   12.____

In the trade mark shown above, the abbreviation DFPA means

    A.   Designers Fabricated Partition Authority
    B.   Douglas Fir Plywood Association
    C.   Developed Fabricated Plyscord Association
    D.   Durable Federal Product Authority

13.   A specification calls for *3/8" x 2"* steel lag screw. In the above specification, the *3/8"* refers   13.____
    to the

    A.   height of the head
    B.   root diameter of the thread
    C.   diameter of the body under the head
    D.   length of body under the head

14.   The following statement is taken from a specification scope of work: 14.____
      Except as otherwise specified, furnish, deliver and install all carpentry and millwork,
related work and equipment as required by the drawings and specified herein, including, but not necessarily limited to the following:
      All rough carpentry work where shown on the drawings, implied as necessary,
specified, or otherwise required including permanent and temporary grounds, blocking,
rough framing and *bucks,* nailing strips, furring, plates, under floor sleepers, and the
like.
In the above passage, *bucks* would refer to

    A.   doors   B.   windows   C.   scuppers   D.   hatchways

15.   A specification states the floowing: 15.____
        Blind nail T and G flooring.
In the above specification, the word *blind* means to

    A.   bend   B.   hide   C.   extrude   D.   offset

16.   Narrow strips of wood nailed upon walls and ceilings as a support for the wall or ceiling   16.____
    finish is known as

    A.   darbying   B.   batting   C.   heading   D.   furring

17.   A purlin is *most similar* in function to a   17.____

    A.   stud   B.   jamb   C.   joist   D.   batten

18.   If the riser for a stairway is 7 1/2" high, then the *number* of risers required for a flight of   18.____
    stairs 8' 9" high is

    A.   11   B.   12   C.   13   D.   14

19. The one of the following that is NOT a common type of wood joint is the

    A. scarf   B. dovetail   C. chamfer   D. butt

19.____

20. A flat hardwood board set on the floor in a doorway between rooms is called a

    A. mullion   B. jamb   C. jib   D. saddle

20.____

21. Shown below is a section of wall and flooring of a building.

21.____

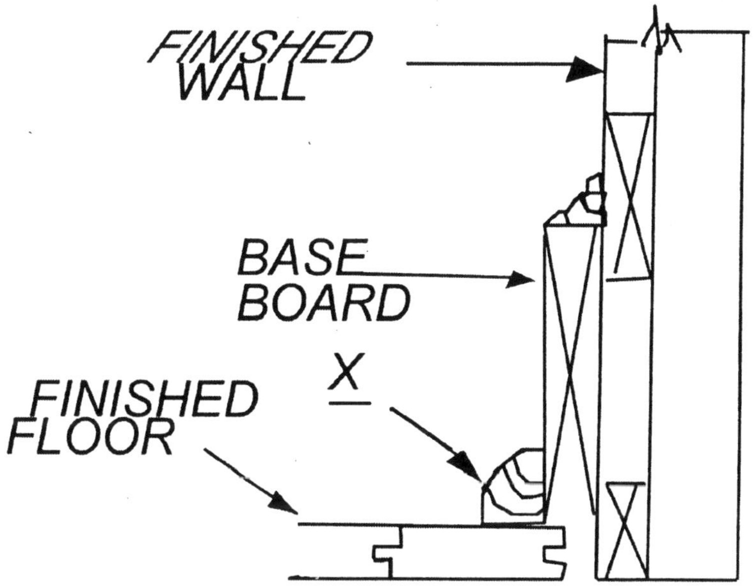

In the drawing shown above, the molding X represents a

    A. base mold   B. shoe mold   C. bed mold   D. lip mold

22. Shown below is a section through a door.

22.____

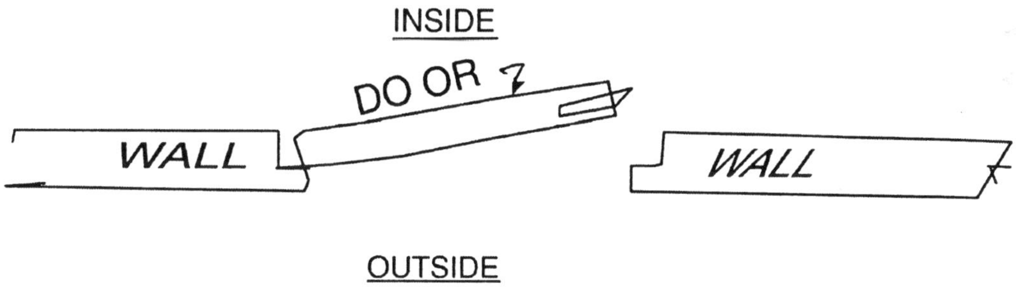

The hand of the door is

    A. left hand regular   B. left hand reverse
    C. right hand regular   D. right hand reverse

23. A 3/4" thick flooring is to be laid directly on joists.
Of the following, the BEST practice is to nail the flooring to

    A. every joist
    B. every third joist
    C. end joists only
    D. end joists and middle joist only

23.____

24. The margin which should be left all around between the edges of an 8" x 10" pane of glass and the sides of the rabbet in a wood sash is   24.____

   A. none   B. 1/16"   C. 3/16"   D. 5/16"

25. The *horizontal* wood member which supports the load over a window or door is known as a   25.____

   A. putlog   B. ledger   C. collar   D. lintel

_____

KEYS (CORRECT ANSWERS)

1.	B	11.	D
2.	A	12.	B
3.	C	13.	C
4.	C	14.	A
5.	B	15.	B
6.	C	16.	D
7.	D	17.	C
8.	D	18.	D
9.	D	19.	C
10.	A	20.	D

21.	B
22.	A
23.	A
24.	B
25.	D

_____

TEST 4

DIRECTIONS: Each question or incomplete statement is followed by several suggested answers or completions. Select the one that BEST answers the question or completes the statement. *PRINT THE LETTER OF THE CORRECT ANSWER IN THE SPACE AT THE RIGHT.*

1. Shown below is a section of a wood joint.

ELEVATION

The joint shown is a

   A. dove tail joint   B. double butt joint
   C. shiplap joint   D. serrated joint

1.____

2. In the construction of a wood frame building a metal shield is sometimes placed between the top of concrete piers and the wood girder resting on it. Of the following, the BEST reason for the metal shield is to

   A. spread the load over the pier
   B. protect the wood against termites
   C. insulate the building
   D. allow for expansion and contraction of the wood

2.____

3. Shown below is a section of wood molding.

The molding is a(n)

   A. reed   B. center bead   C. round   D. astragal

3.____

4. Wood is *most frequently* fastened to a concrete wall by a(n)

   A. clevis   B. expansion shield
   C. brad   D. spike

4.____

5. A bolt with a spring loaded part used for securing wood to a hollow wall is a(n)

   A. anchor bolt   B. stud bolt
   C. toggle bolt   D. toe bolt

5.____

6. The *number* of plane surfaces in a gambrel roof is

   A. two   B. three   C. four   D. five

6.____

7. The *vertical* members of a wooden door are known as   7.____

    A. rails   B. stiles   C. struts   D. sleepers

8. Driving nails at an angle to the surface of a vertical member in order to get adequate penetration into a horizontal member is known as   8.____

    A. clinch nailing   B. toe nailing
    C. French nailing   D. dog nailing

9. Collar beams are *most often* used on   9.____

    A. trusses   B. windows   C. girders   D. doors

10. On a double-hung wood window, the stool rests on the sill *and* a(n)   10.____

    A. mullion   B. rail   C. apron   D. stud

11. In a two-story wood frame building, a fascia would be found on the   11.____

    A. roof   B. stair   C. wall   D. floor

12. A baluster is a part of a   12.____

    A. roof   B. wall   C. door   D. stair

13. Stair treads rest on strips of wood nailed to the inside of stair stringers. These strips of wood are called   13.____

    A. shims   B. wedges   C. stubs   D. cleats

14. Shown at the top of the next page is a section through the exterior wall of a building. The member X represents a   14.____

    A. wall plate   B. ledger
    C. fire stop   D. girder

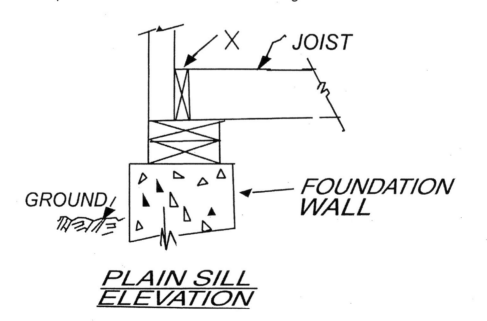

PLAIN SILL
ELEVATION

15. The molded projection which finishes the top of the wall of a building is a   15.____

    A. coronet   B. corolla   C. cornice   D. cupola

16. The BEST reason for *not* painting a wood ladder is that   16.____

    A. the paint may conceal cracks
    B. it saves money not to paint the ladder
    C. painted ladder rungs get very slippery when wet
    D. the wood used is difficult to paint and paint spalls readily

17. In case of a fire in the floor below in a building in which a carpenter is making alterations,   17.____
the BEST action for the carpenter to take is to

    A. walk quickly to the nearest stairway
    B. walk quickly to the nearest elevator
    C. collect all his tools and run to the nearest stairway
    D. open all the windows and run to the nearest stairway

18. Of the following, the one that should NOT be used as an improvised tourniquet is a   18.____

    A. leather belt   B. Venetian blind cord
    C. stocking   D. scarf

19. Of the following character traits, the BEST trait for a supervisor to have is   19.____

    A. optimism   B. rudeness   C. punctuality   D. decisiveness

20. Assume that you are acting in charge of a group of carpenters in the field installing parti-   20.____
tions. You receive a telephone call from the office that they need a carpenter in the shop
to do a rush job.
Of the following, the BEST action to take is to

    A. send the senior carpenter
    B. send the most capable carpenter
    C. ask for volunteers
    D. send the least capable carpenter

21. In assigning additional work to carpenters, a supervisor should FIRST consider the car-   21.____
penter's

    A. seniority   B. previous output
    C. current work load   D. attendance record

22. In checking the daily work of several carpenters at different locations, a good supervisor   22.____
should visit the men

    A. according to each man's seniority
    B. at random hours each day
    C. according to location of nearest man first and farthest man last
    D. according to priority of when jobs have to be completed

23. Of the following jobs, the *one* that usually requires WRITTEN orders instead of ORAL orders is a job where   23._____

    A. progress can be easily checked
    B. emergency exists
    C. a mistake will be of little consequence
    D. many details are involved

24. To obtain cooperation from subordinates, a supervisor should   24._____

    A. complain about it   B. practice it
    C. demand it   D. suggest it

25. The BEST way to *temporarily* store oily sawdust in a carpenter shop before discarding the sawdust is in a   25._____

    A. metal can with a perforated metal cover
    B. metal can without a cover
    C. metal can with an air-tight metal cover
    D. perforated metal can with an air-tight cover

KEYS (CORRECT ANSWERS)

1. C		11. A
2. B		12. D
3. D		13. D
4. B		14. C
5. C		15. C
6. C		16. A
7. B		17. A
8. B		18. B
9. A		19. D
10. C		20. B

21. C
22. B
23. D
24. B
25. C

TEST 5

DIRECTIONS: For questions 1 through 11, the item referred to is shown to the right of the question.

1. The bolt shown should be used
   A. in foundations
   B. in cement curbs
   C. to connect rails
   D. to connect girders

1._____

2. The screw shown is called a
   A. set screw
   B. anchor screw
   C. lag screw
   D. toggle screw

2._____

3. The anchor shown should be used in a
   A. wood post
   B. concrete wall
   C. plaster wall
   D. gypsum block wall

3._____

4. The wrench shown is called a(n)
   A. monkey wrench
   B. Allen wrench
   C. "L" wrench
   D. socket wrench

4._____

5. The anchor shown should be used in a
   A. concrete wall
   B. veneer wall
   C. plaster wall
   D. brick wall

5._____

6. The cutter shown should be used on
   A. pipes
   B. cables
   C. re-bars
   D. bolts

6._____

7. The saw shown is called a
   A. coping saw
   B. cross-cut saw
   C. hack saw
   D. back saw

7._____

8. The tool shown is a
   A. "D" clamp
   B. "C" clamp
   C. pipe vise
   D. metal vise

8._____

9. The tool shown is a
    A. hawk
    B. trowel
    C. screed
    D. joiner

9.____

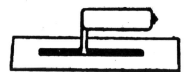

10. The tool shown is called a
    A. try square
    B. T-bevel
    C. miter box
    D. miter square

10.____

11. The tool shown should be used to
    A. make grooves in side walks
    B. turn lead bends
    C. make copper bends
    D. finish brick joints

11.____

KEYS (CORRECT ANSWERS)

1.	A	6.	A
2.	C	7.	D
3.	B	8.	B
4.	B	9.	B
5.	C	10.	C
		11.	A

EXAMINATION SECTION
TEST 1

DIRECTIONS: Each question or incomplete statement is followed by several suggested answers or completions. Select the one that BEST answers the question or completes the statement. *PRINT THE LETTER OF THE CORRECT ANSWER IN THE SPACE AT THE RIGHT.*

1. To frame out a stair well, you need headers,   1.____

   A. trimmers, tail beams, and bridal irons
   B. trimmers, tail beams, and jacks
   C. trimmers, jacks, and bridal irons
   D. jacks, tail beams, and bridal irons

2. If it takes about 30 1bs. of 8-penny nails to nail 1000 board feet of finish flooring, the   2.____
   number of pounds of nails needed for the flooring in a 12' x 14' room is MOST NEARLY

   A. 4   B. 4½   C. 5   D. 5½

3. In construction drawings, the arrangement of members in a door frame is MOST fre-   3.____
   quently shown in a(n)

   A. plan view   B. section
   C. elevation   D. front view

4. A hollow ground blade would USUALLY be used on a circular saw for   4.____

   A. smooth cutting   B. rough cross cutting
   C. cutting dados   D. cutting old flooring

5. When erecting a 2" x 4" stud partition, the size of nail that should be used to toe-nail the   5.____
   stud to the sole plate is a _____ -penny.

   A. six   B. eight   C. ten   D. twelve

6. A blade for use with a diamond-shaped arbor is MOST frequently found on a _____   6.____
   saw.

   A. jig   B. portable circular
   C. band   D. sabre

7. The one of the following that is NOT a common type of wood joint is a   7.____

   A. chamfer   B. rabbet   C. dado   D. butt

8. To determine whether the edge of a board has been planed square, it is BEST to use a   8.____
   _____ square.

   A. parallel   B. try   C. rafter   D. *T*

9. To prevent splintering of wood when planing end grain, it is BEST to plane from   9.____

   A. one edge of the wood to the opposite edge, parallel to the longer edge
   B. one edge of the wood to the opposite edge, parallel to the shorter edge
   C. opposite edges of the wood to the center
   D. the center of the wood to opposite edges

10. The number of teeth per inch on a backsaw is MOST frequently   10.____

    A. 6   B. 10   C. 14   D. 18

11. The number stamped on the shank of an auger bit refers to the size of the bit in _____   11.____
of an inch.

    A. 64ths   B. 32nds   C. 16ths   D. 8ths

12. A line level is MOST frequently used with a   12.____

    A. plumb bob   B. piece of string
    C. transit   D. tape

13. A gouge differs from a wood chisel PRINCIPALLY in that the blade on the gouge is   13.____

    A. curved
    B. longer
    C. shorter
    D. set at an angle to the handle

14. The FIRST operation in properly sharpening a hand saw is   14.____

    A. shaping   B. jointing   C. filing   D. setting

15. A compass saw MOST closely resembles, in appearance, a _____ saw.   15.____

    A. dovetail   B. coping   C. turning   D. keyhole

16. The size of a claw hammer refers to the _____ of the _____.   16.____

    A. length; head   B. diameter; face
    C. length; handle   D. weight; head

17. The one of the following power tools that has two tables, one lower than the other, is a   17.____

    A. radial saw   B. jointer
    C. shaper   D. router

18. The one of the following types of nails that is MOST frequently used to anchor wood to   18.____
masonry is a

    A. cut-nail   B. brad   C. wire nail   D. spike

19. One of the distinguishing features of a carriage bolt is that   19.____

    A. the head has a slot so that it can be driven with a screwdriver
    B. part of the body of the bolt, next to the head, is of square cross-section
    C. the entire body of the bolt from tip to head is threaded
    D. the head is square so that it can be turned with a wrench

20. A dog on a woodworking vise is used in conjunction with a   20.____

    A. bar clamp   B. brace
    C. bench stop   D. back bar

21. The type of wood used for finish flooring in apartments is MOST frequently   21.____

    A. pine   B. fir   C. walnut   D. oak

22. Interior trim is MOST frequently made of   22.____

    A. cedar   B. pine   C. hemlock   D. cypress

23. A *check* in lumber is caused by   23.____

    A. improper drying   B. exposure to rain
    C. too great a stress   D. a fungus

24. A *kerf* is made by a   24.____

    A. hammer   B. saw   C. chisel   D. plane

25. The term *dressed and matched* means the same as   25.____

    A. mortise and tenon   B. miter and spline
    C. dado and rabbet   D. tongue and groove

26. When framing a door opening, the wedging allowance between the trimmer stud and the   26.____
    side jamb is MOST frequently

    A. 1/8"   B. 1/2"   C. 1"   D. 1¼"

27. The purpose of bridging is to distribute the load   27.____

    A. over a window   B. to adjoining rafters
    C. over a door   D. to adjoining joists

28. A bird's mouth cut is USUALLY found on a   28.____

    A. joist   B. stud   C. lintel   D. rafter

29. The BEST tool to use in laying out the cuts on a rafter is a _____ square.   29.____

    A. T   B. try
    C. combination   D. framing

30. The MAIN purpose of flashing is to   30.____

    A. reflect the sun's rays   B. prevent leakage
    C. insulate walls   D. strengthen sheathing

31. The type of glue that MUST be heated before using is _____ glue.   31.____

    A. animal   B. casein   C. resin   D. contact

32. A *parting stop* is usually found   32.____

    A. between the ceiling of one story and the floor directly above
    B. between sash in a double hung window
    C. as part of a door jamb in a swinging door
    D. along the ridge in a hip roof

33. As applied to stair construction, a *carriage* is the same as a   33.____

    A. riser   B. tread   C. stringer   D. cleat

34. When laying out stairs, the product of the number of inches in the tread, exclusive of nos-
    ing, and the number of inches in the riser should be less than

    A. 60   B. 65   C. 70   D. 75

34.____

35. Both doors and windows have

    A. lock rails   B. mullions
    C. stiles   D. meeting rails

35.____

36. The chiseled out portion of a door to which the butt of a hinge is fitted is called a

    A. rabbet   B. gain   C. mortise   D. set-back

36.____

37. The one of the following tools that should be used to cut a rabbet on a curved piece of
    wood is a

    A. shaper   B. jointer
    C. circular saw   D. lathe

37.____

38. Assume that the rise between two floor levels is 9'0". It is required to construct a stair
    between these two floors with risers that have a maximum height of 7½".
    The SMALLEST number of risers that will satisfy this requirement is

    A. 12   B. 13   C. 14   D. 15

38.____

39. Zinc coated nails are often used in preference to ordinary nails MAINLY because they
    are

    A. easier to drive   B. harder to pull out
    C. stronger   D. more weather resistant

39.____

40. Of the following, the quality of white ash that is MOST important is its

    A. light weight
    B. high resistance to shock
    C. curly grain
    D. strength when wet

40.____

41. The thickness of finished maple flooring is MOST frequently

    A. 3/8"   B. 1/2"   C. 25/32"   D. 15/16"

41.____

42. Nails driven into 3/4" plywood, as compared to similar nails driven into 3/4" solid lumber
    made of the same grade of wood, are

    A. harder to pull out
    B. easier to pull out
    C. just as difficult to pull out
    D. harder or easier to pull out, depending on the number of plies in the plywood

42.____

43. The term *plain sawed* refers to the _____ board.   43.____

    A.   direction of the grain with respect to the face of a
    B.   machine that is used to cut the
    C.   shape of the edge of a
    D.   thickness of a

44. The one of the following that is a standard grade for a douglas fir plywood panel is   44.____

    A.   #1 common   B.   select
    C.   A & C   D.   construction

45. A gutter on a frame house is MOST frequently attached to a   45.____

    A.   fascia   B.   drip   C.   flashing   D.   header

46. When it is necessary to match the cut in a plywood or sheetrock wall panel to an existing   46.____
irregular wall, the method that is MOST commonly used is called

    A.   matching   B.   equalling
    C.   lining   D.   scribing

47. The one of the following that is part of a door casing is a   47.____

    A.   head frame   B.   back band
    C.   sill plate   D.   stud

48. A ground   48.____

    A.   is used as a guide for plastering
    B.   supports the studs in a partition
    C.   is the lowest piece of trim on a wall
    D.   prevents the lowest riser in a stair from moving out

49. The one of the following wood screws that is MOST frequently countersunk is a _____   49.____
head.

    A.   flat   B.   round   C.   binding   D.   pan

50. Commercial standards distinguish a softwood from a hardwood according to   50.____

    A.   the ease with which the wood can be carved
    B.   the weight of the wood
    C.   whether the wood can be bent in a short arc
    D.   the type of tree from which the wood comes

KEY (CORRECT ANSWERS)

1.	A	11.	C	21.	D	31.	A	41.	C
2.	C	12.	B	22.	B	32.	B	42.	B
3.	B	13.	A	23.	A	33.	C	43.	A
4.	A	14.	B	24.	B	34.	D	44.	C
5.	C	15.	D	25.	D	35.	C	45.	A
6.	B	16.	D	26.	B	36.	B	46.	D
7.	A	17.	B	27.	D	37.	A	47.	B
8.	B	18.	A	28.	D	38.	D	48.	A
9.	C	19.	B	29.	D	39.	D	49.	A
10.	C	20.	C	30.	B	40.	B	50.	D

TEST 2

DIRECTIONS: Each question or incomplete statement is followed by several suggested answers or completions. Select the one that BEST answers the question or completes the statement. *PRINT THE LETTER OF THE CORRECT ANSWER IN THE SPACE AT THE RIGHT.*

1. Where floor joists rest on a masonry wall, they should have a minimum bearing of _____ inches.

   A. 3   B. 4   C. 5   D. 6

   1.____

2. Expansion shields would be used to

   A. protect exterior corners of walls
   B. provide a base for plaster
   C. protect a ceiling over a boiler
   D. anchor an object to a brick wall

   2.____

3. When framing a window for use with a spring balance such as a *unique balance*, the allowance for pulley pockets is USUALLY

   A. smaller than when a sash weight is used
   B. the same as when a sash weight is used
   C. greater than when a sash weight is used
   D. completely eliminated

   3.____

4. Plywood used for sheathing is MOST frequently _____ thick.

   A. 1/4"   B. 5/16"   C. 3/8"   D. 1/2"

   4.____

5. The BEST size hinge to use for an exterior door measuring 1 3/8" thick and 36" wide is

   A. 3' x 3"   B. 3" x 3½"   C. 3½" x 4"   D. 4" x 4"

   5.____

6. The MOST frequent method of framing a 2" x 4" partition over a small window is to _____ over the window.

   A. add a steel lintel   B. truss the wall
   C. double the headers   D. use hangers

   6.____

7. Batter boards are MOST frequently used to

   A. establish corners for new construction
   B. determine the pitch of rafters
   C. support concrete forms
   D. brace stud partitions

   7.____

8. A steel square would MOST frequently be used to lay out

   A. stud lengths in a partition
   B. casings for a door
   C. treads and risers for a staircase
   D. cuts for a mortise and tenon joint

   8.____

9. Pumice stone is VERY often used in   9._____

    A. finishing furniture   B. honing tools
    C. setting bolts   D. smoothing concrete

10. Hand screws are USUALLY used when   10._____

    A. hanging shelves from a hollow partition
    B. glueing two pieces of wood together
    C. connecting sheet metal to wood
    D. erecting plywood walls

11. The MAIN reason for *setting* the teeth on a saw is to   11._____

    A. prevent the saw from binding
    B. permit the saw to make an even cut
    C. allow the saw to cut across the grain as well as with the grain
    D. eliminate the possibility of the *saw jumping* out of the cut

12. Assume that a peaked roof, with a 1/4 pitch, has a run of 12 ft.   12._____
    The rise is

    A. 3'   B. 4'   C. 5'   D. 6'

13. A dovetail saw MOST closely resembles a _____ saw.   13._____

    A. keyhole   B. compass   C. back   D. rip

14. The one of the following that is part of a window trim is a(n)   14._____

    A. astragal   B. apron   C. panel   D. butt

15. Ship lap boards are USUALLY used as   15._____

    A. sills   B. plates   C. fascia   D. shingles

16. A plow MOST NEARLY resembles a   16._____

    A. mortise   B. dado   C. miter   D. spline

17. The one of the following types of wood that has the MOST open grain is   17._____

    A. pine   B. maple   C. oak   D. birch

18. Wood is usually treated in a kiln for the purpose of   18._____

    A. fireproofing it
    B. seasoning it
    C. preserving the wood against dampness
    D. termite-proofing it

19. The wood MOST commonly used for shingles in the East is   19._____

    A. cypress   B. birch   C. cedar   D. spruce

20. Lag screws are USUALLY driven by using a   20._____

    A. wrench   B. screwdriver
    C. hammer   D. brace

21. The one of the following that should be used for the final smoothing of wood before applying lacquer is 21.____

    A. #1/2 garnet paper   B. a fine wood rasp
    C. 000 steel wool   D. 80 grit emery cloth

22. The total number of board feet in 18 2x4's, each measuring 8 ft. long, is MOST NEARLY 22.____

    A. 90   B. 92   C. 96   D. 100

23. A *fire cut* is NORMALLY made on 23.____

    A. studs   B. joists   C. rafters   D. plates

24. A *nail set* is a 24.____

    A. group of the same type of nails in different sizes
    B. group of different types of nails in the same size
    C. tool used to pull nails
    D. tool used to countersink nails

25. Auger bits are BEST sharpened by using a 25.____

    A. grinding wheel   B. file
    C. slip stone   D. whetstone

26. Casing nails are MOST similar in appearance to _____ nails. 26.____

    A. roofing   B. common
    C. finishing   D. cut

27. A water level can be made by using 27.____

    A. two glass tubes and a rubber hose
    B. a mason's level and two eye sights
    C. a pitch board and a mason's level
    D. a pitch board and a rubber hose

28. The purpose of a vapor barrier is to 28.____

    A. prevent rain from entering a building through the wall
    B. protect the exterior wall of a building from moisture already inside the building
    C. prevent condensation of water in a cellar
    D. protect a building from ground water

29. Narrow boards are better for floor boards than wide boards of the same grade of lumber PRINCIPALLY because the narrow boards 29.____

    A. cost less
    B. are easier to lay
    C. are stronger
    D. have less tendency to warp

30. 1" x 6" subflooring is USUALLY applied diagonally to the joists rather than perpendicular to the joists PRINCIPALLY because subflooring applied diagonally 30.____

    A. costs less   B. is easier to lay
    C. is stronger   D. warps less

31. A purlin USUALLY supports   31.____

    A. rafters   B. sheathing   C. joists   D. studs

32. Insulation board is MOST frequently used as   32.____

    A. sheathing   B. subflooring
    C. siding   D. scantling

33. The one of the following that is NOT a type of rafter is a   33.____

    A. hip   B. valley   C. jack   D. tail

34. Lath is USUALLY used as a base for   34.____

    A. roofing   B. plaster
    C. waterproofing   D. insulation

35. A cricket is USUALLY located   35.____

    A. at the base of a parapet wall
    B. over an exterior door
    C. between the sill and the foundation
    D. in a non-bearing partition

36. The term *gambrel* refers to a type of   36.____

    A. window   B. roof   C. door   D. floor

37. Wainscoting is part of the finish of   37.____

    A. floors   B. ceiling   C. walls   D. doors

38. *Construction Grade* lumber is LEAST frequently used for   38.____

    A. joists   B. rafters   C. studs   D. girders

39. A strip of board that is used to fasten several pieces of lumber together is called a   39.____

    A. band   B. bracket   C. girt   D. cleat

40. Building paper is MOST often used to   40.____

    A. waterproof foundations
    B. insulate walls
    C. deaden sound
    D. protect floors during painting

41. One of the MAIN reasons for using furring strips is to   41.____

    A. fire retard a stairwell
    B. support floor joists
    C. provide clearance around a chimney
    D. permit building a straight ceiling

42. A *built up* girder USUALLY refers to a girder that is   42.____

     A. supported on posts
     B. cut to size at the building
     C. braced in position to prevent twisting
     D. made up of several pieces of wood fastened together

Questions 43-45.

DIRECTIONS: Questions 43 through 45, inclusive, are to be answered in accordance with the
                 following paragraph.

    Wherever a soil pipe has to be provided for in a partition, special care must be taken that
the hubs do not project beyond the finish face of the plaster. Before framing a building, it is
desirable to ascertain where the stacks are and to provide for them. Building regulations
require the stacks to be of 4-inch cast-iron even in small dwellings. With a 4-inch stack, the
hub is 6 1/8 inches in diameter and, therefore, 2 by 6 studs must be used. Special care
should be taken that no plaster comes in contact with a soil pipe, for subsequent settlement
may cause cracking.

43. As used in the paragraph above, *subsequent* means MOST NEARLY   43.____

     A. heavy   B. sudden   C. later   D. soon

44. According to the above paragraph, 4" cast-iron soil pipes are used because   44.____

     A. they will not project beyond the face of the plaster
     B. it is easier to plaster over 4" pipe
     C. they can be located easier
     D. they are required by law

45. According to the above paragraph, the reason plaster should NOT be in direct contact   45.____
     with soil pipe is because

     A. the plaster will be damaged by moisture
     B. rust will bleed through the plaster
     C. of the possibility of cracks due to settlement
     D. it is harder to plaster over 4" pipe

Questions 46-50.

DIRECTIONS: Questions 46 through 50, inclusive, refer to the floor plan of the building shown
                 on the following page.

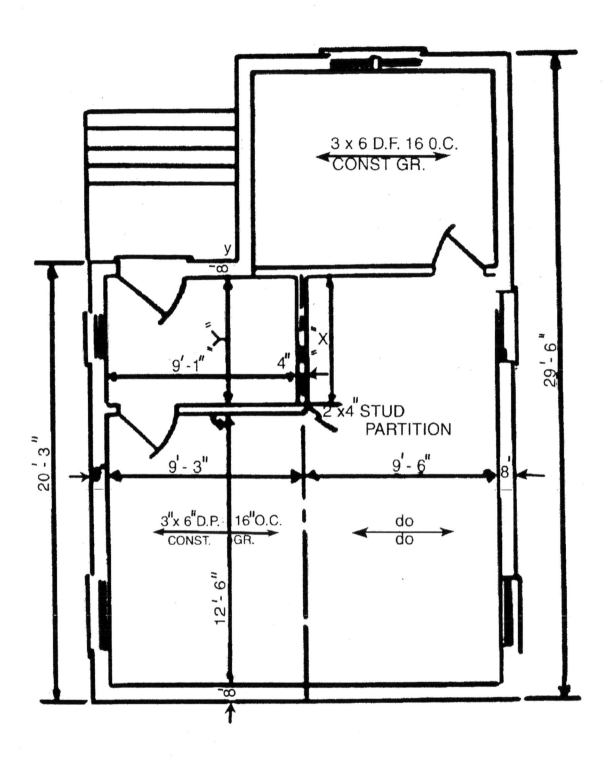

46. The dimension of the vestibule indicated by y is

    A. 6'0"   B. 6'1"   C. 6'2"   D. 6'3"

46.____

47. The number of risers indicated in the steps is

    A. 2   B. 3   C. 4   D. 5

47.____

48. The area of the large room, in square feet, is MOST NEARLY   48.____

   A. 292   B. 294   C. 296   D. 298

49. The letters D.F. over the arrow mean   49.____

   A. Douglas fir   B. diagonal subflooring
   C. doubled joists   D. deafening finish

50. If studs are placed a maximum of 16" on centers, the minimum number of studs required   50.____
in the section of wall marked *X* is

   A. 4   B. 5   C. 6   D. 7

KEY (CORRECT ANSWERS)

1. B	11. A	21. C	31. B	41. D
2. D	12. D	22. C	32. A	42. D
3. D	13. C	23. B	33. D	43. C
4. B	14. B	24. D	34. B	44. D
5. D	15. D	25. B	35. A	45. C
6. C	16. B	26. C	36. B	46. B
7. A	17. C	27. A	37. C	47. D
8. C	18. B	28. B	38. C	48. B
9. A	19. C	29. D	39. D	49. A
10. B	20. A	30. C	40. B	50. C

EXAMINATION SECTION
TEST 1

DIRECTIONS: Each question or incomplete statement is followed by several suggested answers or completions. Select the one that BEST answers the question or completes the statement. *PRINT THE LETTER OF THE CORRECT ANSWER IN THE SPACE AT THE RIGHT.*

1. The tool MOST frequently used to lay out a 45° angle on a piece of lumber is a   1.____

    A. combination square   B. try square
    C. marking gauge   D. divider

2. Beeswax would be MOST FREQUENTLY used on a(n)   2.____

    A. auger bit   B. scraper   C. hand saw   D. draw knife

3. A tool used to plane concave edges of furniture is a   3.____

    A. rabbet plane   B. wood scraper
    C. utility knife   D. spoke saw

4. A cap is found on a   4.____

    A. hammer   B. plane   C. power saw   D. lathe

5. The one of the following types of saw blades that is NOT commonly used on a circular saw is a   5.____

    A. dado   B. ply-tooth   C. novelty   D. tyler

6. The diameter of the arbor of a 12" circular saw is MOST LIKELY to be   6.____

    A. 3/8"   B. 1/2"   C. 5/8"   D. 3/4"

7. The one of the following woodworking operations that is NOT easily done on a drill press is   7.____

    A. routing   B. turning   C. shaping   D. mortising

8. A jointer may ALSO be used for   8.____

    A. mortising   B. routing   C. planing   D. shaping

9. The one of the following power tools that is NOT frequently built with a slot for a miter guage is a   9.____

    A. shaper   B. band saw   C. disc sander   D. radial saw

10. The abrasive grit on *sandpaper* is USUALLY   10.____

    A. pumice   B. boron   C. flint   D. talc

11. The abrasive grit on *open coat* paper for use on a power sander for woodwork is USU-ALLY   11.____

    A. tripoli   B. emery   C. aluminum oxide   D. carborundum

12. The one of the following used in finishing furniture that has the FINEST grit is   12.____

    A. garnet   B. carborundum
    C. pumice   D. rottenstone

13. An expansive bit should be sharpened with a(n)   13.____

    A. auger bit file   B. mill file
    C. half round file   D. grinding wheel

14. The one of the following planes that is USUALLY used with one hand is the   14.____

    A. smoothing   B. block   C. jack   D. fore

15. When sharpening a hand saw, the FIRST operation is to file the teeth so that they are all   15.____
the same height.
This is known as

    A. shaping   B. setting   C. jointing   D. leveling

16. The tool that would be used to cut out a circular disc is a   16.____

    A. circular saw   B. shaper
    C. planer   D. band saw

17. A scale on which the inch graduations are divided into 12 subdivisions, each 1/12 of an   17.____
inch in length, is USUALLY found on a _____ square.

    A. try   B. combination
    C. rafter   D. T

18. The one of the following oils that is COMMONLY used for oilstones is   18.____

    A. penetrating   B. SAE #5
    C. vinsol   D. pike

19. A tool used in hanging doors is a   19.____

    A. butt gauge   B. reamer   C. C-clamp   D. trammel

20. A spur center is used on a   20.____

    A. jigsaw   B. drill press
    C. lathe   D. disc sander

21. The length of a certain screw is measured from the top of the head to the point.   21.____
The type of screw that this is MOST LIKELY to be is a

    A. round head   B. flat head   C. oval head   D. lag

22. The size of the drill that would be used to drill a body hole for a #7 wood screw is   22.____

    A. 3/32"   B. 5/32"   C. 7/32"   D. 9/32"

23. The one of the following types of bolts that would be used to anchor a shelf bracket to a   23.____
plywood partition is a

    A. carriage   B. expansion   C. drift   D. toggle

24. For ease in driving, screws are FREQUENTLY coated with   24.____

    A. casco   B. oil   C. soap   D. urea resins

25. The length of a 10-penny nail is   25.____

    A. 3"   B. 3 1/4"   C. 3 1/2"   D. 3 3/4"

26. To increase the holding power of nails, the nails are FREQUENTLY coated with   26.____

    A. alundum   B. aluminum   C. zinc   D. cement

27. Galvanized nails would MOST PROBABLY be used in nailing   27.____

    A. shingles   B. finished flooring
    C. joists   D. interior trim

28. Splitting of wood can be reduced by using nails with points that are   28.____

    A. long and sharp   B. blunt
    C. spirally grooved   D. common

29. The standard size of a 2" X 6" S4S is   29.____

    A. 1 5/8" X 5 5/8"   B. 1 5/8" X 5 3/4"
    C. 1 1/2" X 5 1/2"   D. 1 1/2" X 5 5/8"

30. The West Coast Lumber Inspection Bureau has recently changed the names of the   30.____
grades of lumber for Douglas Fir and Hemlock.
The grade that was PREVIOUSLY called No. 1 common is NOW called

    A. construction   B. utility
    C. select   D. structural

31. The strength of lumber is affected by   31.____

    A. whether it is cut from a live tree or a dead tree
    B. the time of the year in which the lumber is cut
    C. whether the tree is virgin growth or second growth
    D. the moisture content of the lumber

32. The one of the following woods that is classed as *open grained* is   32.____

    A. douglas fir   B. long leaf yellow pine
    C. spruce   D. oak

33. The one of the following woods that is classed as a hardwood is   33.____

    A. cedar   B. poplar
    C. douglas fir   D. hemlock

34. The one of the following woods that is MOST difficult to work with hand tools is   34.____

    A. cedar, northern white   B. pine, southern yellow
    C. hemlock, western   D. cypress, southern

35. The one of the following heartwoods that has the GREATEST resistance to decay is   35.____

    A. douglas fir   B. spruce   C. oak   D. birch

36. The one of the following woods that is EASIEST to glue is   36.____

    A. beech   B. birch   C. cedar   D. walnut

37. Flooring, for surfaces that will have very heavy wear, such as gymnasiums, is USUALLY   37.____
made of

    A. oak   B. maple
    C. long leaf yellow pine   D. larch

38. The BEST grades of finished flooring are _____ sawed.   38.____

    A. quarter   B. flat   C. end   D. plain

39. Lumber used for floor joists in the East is USUALLY   39.____

    A. oak   B. gum   C. hemlock   D. pine

40. The wood MOST COMMONLY used for shingles is   40.____

    A. alder   B. larch   C. cedar   D. spruce

41. Millwork is USUALLY made of   41.____

    A. ash   B. chestnut   C. hemlock   D. pine

42. The wood MOST FREQUENTLY used for the rungs of the BEST quality ladders is   42.____

    A. locust   B. hickory   C. oak   D. balsam

43. Dressed and matched lumber would MOST LIKELY be   43.____

    A. dove-tailed   B. bevel siding
    C. crown molding   D. tongue and groove

44. Creosote is used to   44.____

    A. intensify the grain of wood prior to finishing
    B. preserve wood from rot
    C. glue wood in laminated girders
    D. prevent checking

45. The one of the following that is COMMONLY used as a vapor barrier is   45.____

    A. asphalt roll roofing   B. Kraft paper
    C. plywood   D. gypsum board

46. Corners of a building are USUALLY located by means of   46.____

    A. batter boards   B. framing squares
    C. line levels   D. base plates

47. Horizontal beams used to reinforce concrete forms and sheet piling are known as   47.____

    A. stirrups   B. walers   C. sheathing   D. braces

48. When using a post to shore a form for a reinforced concrete girder, the BEST practice is to cut the post   48.____

    A. to exact length, so that no driving will be required
    B. slightly larger than required, so that the post must be driven into place
    C. with a slight bevel, so that the post can be wedged into place
    D. several inches too short, so that wedges will be needed

49. Corner posts of a frame building in the East MUST be at least the equivalent of three _____ inch timbers.   49.____

    A. 2X4   B. 2X6   C. 3X6   D. 4X4

50. The size of cross bridging between joists is MOST FREQUENTLY   50.____

    A. 1" X 2"   B. 1" X 3"   C. 2" X 4"   D. 2" X 6"

KEY (CORRECT ANSWERS)

1.	A	11.	C	21.	B	31.	D	41.	D
2.	C	12.	D	22.	B	32.	D	42.	B
3.	D	13.	A	23.	D	33.	B	43.	D
4.	B	14.	B	24.	C	34.	B	44.	B
5.	D	15.	C	25.	A	35.	A	45.	A
6.	D	16.	D	26.	D	36.	C	46.	A
7.	B	17.	C	27.	A	37.	B	47.	B
8.	C	18.	D	28.	B	38.	A	48.	D
9.	D	19.	A	29.	A	39.	C	49.	A
10.	C	20.	C	30.	A	40.	C	50.	B

TEST 2

DIRECTIONS: Each question or incomplete statement is followed by several suggested answers or completions. Select the one that BEST answers the question or completes the statement. *PRINT THE LETTER OF THE CORRECT ANSWER IN THE SPACE AT THE RIGHT.*

1. The MAXIMUM spacing between bridging should be

    A. 6 ft.   B. 8 ft.   C. 10 ft.   D. 12 ft.

    1.____

2. The one of the following methods of nailing cross bridging that is the MOST ACCEPT-ABLE is

    A. the tops and bottoms should be nailed before the subflooring is in place
    B. the tops and bottoms should be nailed after the subflooring is in place
    C. *only* the bottoms should be nailed. The tops should be nailed after the subflooring is in place
    D. *only* the tops should be nailed. The bottoms should be nailed after the subflooring is in place

    2.____

3. The one of the following that may be used as a shim to raise the end of a joist resting on a concrete wall is

    A. gypsum block   B. wood
    C. sheet rock   D. slate

    3.____

4. When framing joists around a chimney, the MINIMUM clear distance from wood to the chimney permitted in the East is

    A. 4"   B. 6"   C. 8"   D. 10"

    4.____

5. The ends of joists are FREQUENTLY supported on

    A. hanger bolts   B. tie plates
    C. bridle irons   D. gusset plates

    5.____

6. When there is a tight knot in a joist, the joist should

    A. be placed with the knot up
    B. be placed with the knot down
    C. be reinforced
    D. not be used

    6.____

7.

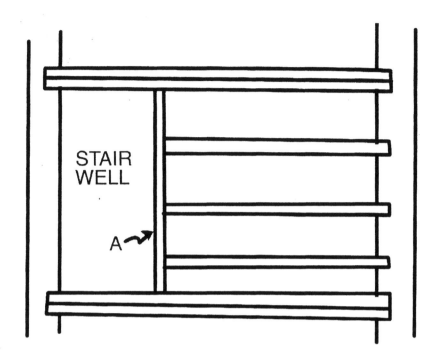

The short joist indicated by the letter *A* above is known as

A. trimmer   B. tail beam   C. header   D. lattice

8.

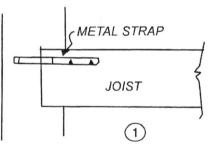

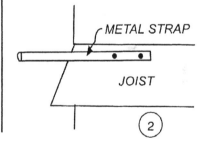

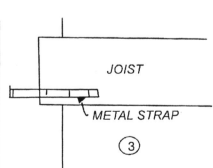

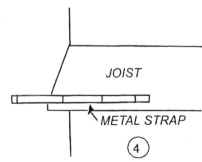

The diagram above that shows the BEST method of anchoring a wood joist to a brick is numbered

A. *1*   B. *2*   C. *3*   D. *4*

7.____

8.____

9. Where a non bearing partition runs over and is parallel to the joists, standard practice requires that 9.____

    A. a post be placed midway under the joist supporting the partition
    B. sag rods be used to transfer the load to the adjoining joists
    C. the joist directly under the partition be increased in depth
    D. the joist directly under the partition be doubled

10. 10.____

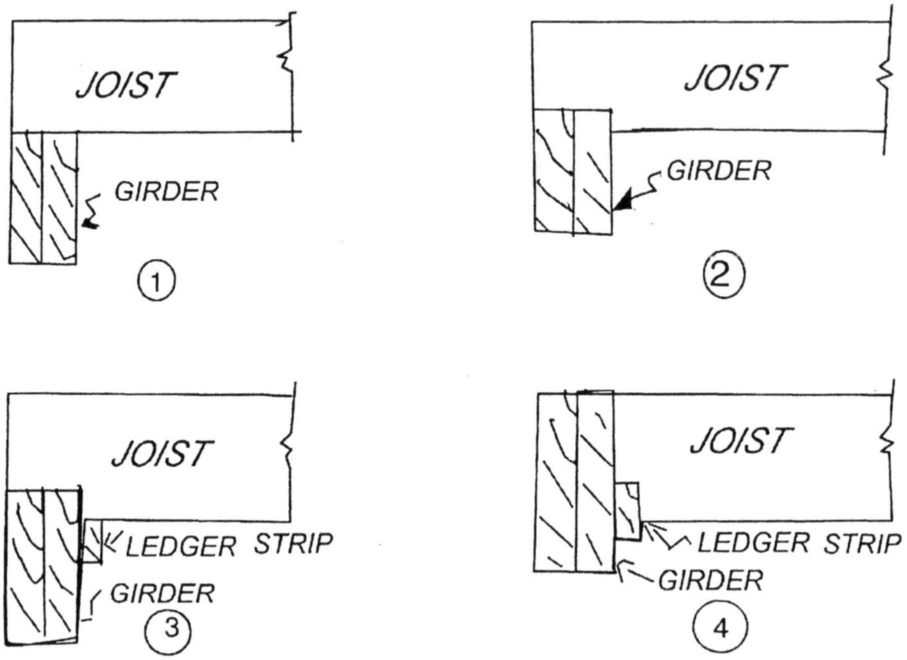

The diagram above that shows the BEST method of supporting a joist on a girder is numbered

    A. 1   B. 2   C. 3   D. 4

11. The one of the following statements that is CORRECT when *roofers* are used for subflooring is diagonal subflooring 11.____

    A. requires less lumber than subflooring applied at right angles to the joists
    B. requires approximately the same amount of lumber as subflooring applied at right angles to the joists
    C. requires more lumber than subflooring applied at right angles to the joists
    D. may require more or less lumber than subflooring applied at right angles to the joists, depending on the dimensions of the building

12. A timber laid directly on the ground or on a concrete base to support a floor is called a 12.____

    A. sleeper   B. sizing   C. rail   D. ledger board

13. Diagonal subflooring is preferred to subflooring laid square across the joists because the   13.____
    diagonal subflooring

    A. stiffens the building
    B. is easier to lay
    C. is more economical to lay
    D. does not require as much nailing

14. A meeting rail is usually found on a   14.____

    A. stair   B. door   C. roof   D. window

15. The size of a sill plate, for a frame building, laid on a continuous concrete wall in the East   15.____
    is USUALLY

    A. 4" X 6"   B. 4" X 10"   C. 2" X 10"   D. 2" X 8"

16. A valley is made watertight by means of a   16.____

    A. cornice   B. flashing   C. drip sill   D. furring

17. A strip of wood whose purpose is to assist the plasterers to make a straight wall is called   17.____
    a

    A. casing   B. ground
    C. belt course   D. gauge

18. A hip rafter is framed between   18.____

    A. plate and ridge   B. plate and valley
    C. valley and ridge   D. valley and overhang

19. 2" X 8" rafters are being used on a roof with a pitch of one quarter.   19.____
    The size of ridge board that would MOST PROBABLY be used is

    A. 2" X 8"   B. 3" X 8"   C. 2" X 10"   D. 2" X 12"

20. When planks intended to be used for roof rafters are not straight, the one of the following   20.____
    statements that is CORRECT is

    A. all rafters should be erected with the cambers (crown) up
    B. all rafters should be erected with the cambers (crown) down
    C. the rafters should be erected with the cambers (crown) alternately up and down
    D. the plank should not be used for rafters

21.   21.____

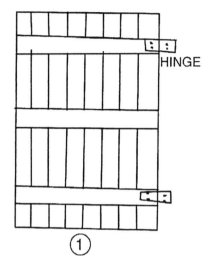
①

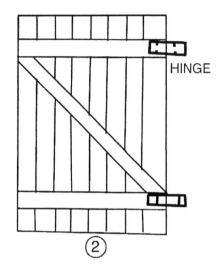
③

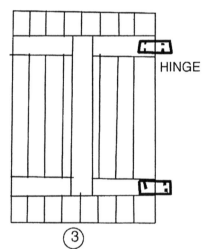
②

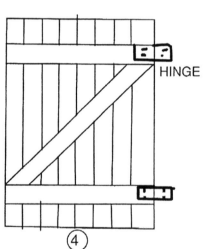
④

The diagram above that shows the BEST method of building a door for a shed is numbered

    A. *1*   *B.* *2*   C. *3*   D. *4*

22. A vertical member separating two windows is called a   22.____

    A. muntin   B. mullion   C. stile   D. casing

23. Wood girders framing on a masonry wall in the East should have a MINIMUM bearing of 23.____

    A. 2"   B. 4"   C. 6"   D. 8"

24. A collar beam is used to tie   24.____

    A. floor joists   B. laminated girders
    C. roof rafters   D. columns

25. Nosing would MOST probably be found in   25.____

    A. window frames   B. stairs
    C. saddles   D. scarfs

26. To help prevent plaster cracks when a 2" X 4" stud partition is cut for a doorway, it is USUAL to   26._____

    A. provide a steel lintel B. use joint   B. hangers
    C. double the header   D. corbel the studs

27. The side support for steps or stairs is called a   27._____

    A. ledger board   B. pitch board
    C. riser   D. stringer

28. The type of joint MOST FREQUENTLY used where baseboards meet at the corner of a room is a   28._____

    A. miter   B. mortise and tenon
    C. spline   D. butt

29. The purpose of a water table is to   29._____

    A. prevent water from entering at the top of a foundation wall
    B. distribute water from a downspout directly on the ground
    C. prevent water from entering a cellar through the cellar floor
    D. prevent water from leaking through a roof at the chimney

30. The one of the following materials that will produce the MOST rigid wall is _____ sheathing.   30._____

    A. 1" X 8" horizontal
    B. 1" X 8" diagonal
    C. 29/32" fiberboard
    D. 1/4" plywood

31. Split ring connectors are COMMONLY used to   31._____

    A. anchor joists to girders
    B. join members of a truss
    C. anchor veneer to framework
    D. connect wood girder to steel column

32. A strike plate would be attached to a   32._____

    A. sill   B. fascia   C. jamb   D. saddle

33. Blanket insulation is USUALLY placed between   33._____

    A. siding and sheathing
    B. sheathing and vapor barrier
    C. vapor barrier and rock lath
    D. rock lath and finished plaster

34. A pipe column filled with concrete is called a   34._____

    A. pintle   B. buttress   C. pilaster   D. lally

35. If you were required to build forms for spandrels, the location of these forms would be at   35._____

    A. footing level between piers
    B. roof level between girders
    C. floor level between columns
    D. footing level over the grillage

36. Where a 2-inch horizontal hole must be made in a 3" X 12" floor joist supporting a uni-   36._____
form live load, the BEST place to make this hole is in the _____ of the joist at the
_____ of the span.

    A. center; end
    C. center; center
                B. bottom; end
                D. bottom; center

37. To strengthen box corners in new furniture, common practice is to use   37._____

    A. tie rods
    C. glue blocks
                 B. molly bolts
                 D. webbing

38. The joint MOST frequently used for attaching the sides of drawers to the fronts is   38._____

    A. mortise and tenon
    C. dovetailed
                 B. doweled
                 D. splined

39. The pitch of a roof is one-sixth. If the run is 10 ft., the rise is   39._____

    A. 1'-8"   B. 3'-4"   C. 5'-0"   D. 6'-8"

40. The number of board feet in a 3" X 8", 16 ft. long, is   40._____

    A. 26   B. 28   C. 30   D. 32

41. A right triangle has sides of 5, 12, and 13 inches respectively.   41._____
The area of the triangle, is, in square inches,

    A. 30   B. 32 1/2   C. 60   D. 78

42. The one of the following that would be the dimension used to lay out a right angle is   42._____
_____ feet.

    A. 3, 4, 6   B. 4, 5, 9   C. 6, 8, 10   D. 7, 9, 13

43. A partition wall, with no openings in it, is to be 46 ft. long.   43._____
If studs are spaced 16" o.c. maximum, the number of studs that should be used in this
wall is

    A. 33   B. 34   C. 35   D. 36

44. A flight of stairs has 8 risers. The number of treads it has is   44._____

    A. 7   B. 8   C. 9   D. 10

45. A round post 4 inches in diameter and 4 feet high can carry 12,000 pounds.   45._____
A 6-inch post of the same height, and the same grade and species of wood, can carry
_____ pounds.

    A. 18,000   B. 21,000   C. 24,000   D. 27,000

46. The sum of the following dimensions,
    4'-3 1/4", 3'-2 15/16", 2'-3 1/2", 3'-4 3/4", 4'-7 3/16" is

    A. 17'-9 7/16"   B. 17'-9 1/2"
    C. 17'-9 9/16"   D. 17'-9 5/8"

46._____

Questions 47 - 50.

    Questions 47 to 50 refer to the sketch below representing the 1st floor plan of a small tool shed.

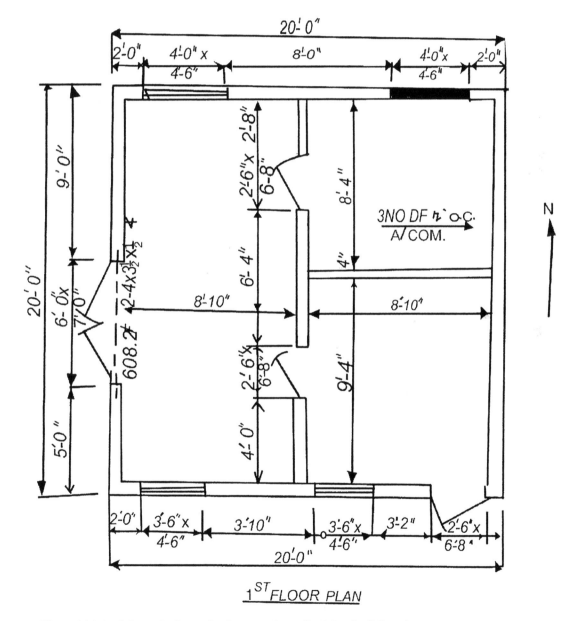

1ST FLOOR PLAN

47. The width* of the windows in the south wall of the building is

    A. 2'-6"   B. 3'-6"   C. 3'-10"   D. 4'-6"

47._____

48. The lintel over the large doorway is a

    A. single wood girder   B. built up wood girder
    C. steel beam and plates   D. steel channel and angles

48._____

49. The size of the LARGEST room is

    A. 8'-10" X 16'-0"   B. 8'-10" X 17'-0"
    C. 8'-10" X 18'-0"   D. 8'-10" X 19'-0"

49._____

50. The floor area of the SMALLEST room is, in square feet, MOST NEARLY

    A. 72   B. 74   C. 76   D. 78

50._____

KEY (CORRECT ANSWERS)

1.	B	11.	C	21.	B	31.	B	41.	A
2.	D	12.	A	22.	B	32.	C	42.	C
3.	D	13.	A	23.	B	33.	B	43.	D
4.	A	14.	D	24.	C	34.	D	44.	A
5.	C	15.	A	25.	B	35.	C	45.	D
6.	A	16.	B	26.	C	36.	C	46.	D
7.	C	17.	B	27.	D	37.	C	47.	B
8.	D	18.	A	28.	D	38.	C	48.	D
9.	D	19.	C	29.	A	39.	B	49.	C
10.	A	20.	A	30.	D	40.	D	50.	B

EXAMINATION SECTION
TEST 1

DIRECTIONS: Each question or incomplete statement is followed by several suggested answers or completions. Select the one that BEST answers the question or completes the statement. *PRINT THE LETTER OF THE CORRECT ANSWER IN THE SPACE AT THE RIGHT.*

1. *Dimension lumber* is used MAINLY for   1.____

    A. door and sash cuttings   B. exterior trim
    C. interior trim   D. studding

2. *Blind nailing* is the term used to describe nailing   2.____

    A. when it is not known into what material the nails are driven
    B. done with finishing nails
    C. done with assorted size nails
    D. done in such a way that the heads are not visible on the face of the work

3. If two 2 x 4's are to be securely nailed to make one 4x4 (approximately) and the nail points are not to come through, of the following, the BEST size nails to use is _____ penny.   3.____

    A. 20   B. 10   C. 8   D. 6

4. Lumber used in building construction should be well-seasoned because this   4.____

    A. makes it more fire-resistant
    B. helps prevent shakes
    C. prevents damage by termites
    D. prevents shrinkage and warping

5. Timber that has been pressure creosoted is MOST likely to be used as   5.____

    A. beams in buildings to support heavy loads
    B. columns in buildings to support heavy loads
    C. rafters in a roof truss
    D. piles in wet ground

6. Toe nailing is illustrated in the sketch marked   6.____

A   B   C   D

7. A ribband or ribbon is a horizontal strip of wood notched into the studs.   7.____
   It is used ONLY in _____ -frame construction.

      A. balloon   B. braced   C. platform   D. western

8. The bracing between wood floor beams is called   8.____

      A. internal bracing   B. bridging
      C. reinforcing   D. cross-bracing

9. The MAXIMUM allowable spacing for the bracing described in the preceding question,   9.____
   according to the Building Code, is _____ feet.

      A. 6   B. 8   C. 10   D. 12

10. In wooden floor construction, the bracing described above is used PRIMARILY to   10.____

       A. prevent the joists from turning over before the flooring is placed
       B. transfer load from the joist directly under a load on the floor to adjacent joists
       C. keep a uniform spacing of the joists
       D. eliminate the need for header and trimmer beams at floor openings

11. In floor construction, the bracing described in the same question should   11.____

       A. be nailed at the top and the lower ends left loose until the sub-flooring is nailed in
          position
       B. be nailed at both ends before the sub-flooring is placed in position
       C. not be nailed at all until after the sub-flooring is nailed in position
       D. not be nailed until after the sub-flooring is nailed and the finished flooring placed

12. Of the following, the wood that is MOST commonly used today for floor joists is   12.____

       A. long leaf yellow pine   B. douglas fir
       C. oak   D. birch

13. Quarter-sawed lumber is preferred for the best finished flooring PRINCIPALLY because it   13.____

       A. has the greatest strength
       B. shrinks the least
       C. is the easiest to nail
       D. is the easiest to handle

14. A tool used in hanging doors is a   14.____

       A. miter gauge   B. line level
       C. try square   D. butt gauge

15. Of the following, the MAXIMUM height that would be considered acceptable for a stair   15.____
    riser is _____ inches.

       A. 6½   B. 7½   C. 8½   D. 9½

16. The PRINCIPAL reason for *cross banding* the layers of wood in a plywood panel is to _____ of the panel.   16._____

    A. reduce warping   B. increase the strength
    C. reduce the cost   D. increase the beauty

17. The part of a tree that will produce the DENSEST wood is the _____ wood.   17._____

    A. spring   B. summer   C. sap   D. heart

18. Casing nails MOST NEARLY resemble _____ nails.   18._____

    A. common   B. roofing   C. form   D. finishing

19. In woodwork, countersinking is MOST often done for   19._____

    A. lag screws   B. carriage bolts
    C. hanger bolts   D. flat head screws

20. Bridging is MOST often used in connection with   20._____

    A. door frames   B. window openings
    C. floor joists   D. stud walls

21. A saddle is part of a   21._____

    A. doorway   B. window
    C. stairwell   D. bulkhead

22. To make it easier to drive screws into hard wood, it is BEST to   22._____

    A. use a screwdriver that is longer than that used for soft wood
    B. rub the threads of the screw on a bar of soap
    C. oil the screw threads
    D. use a square shank screwdriver assisted by a wrench

23. In using a doweled joint to make a repair of a wooden door, it is IMPORTANT to remember that   23._____

    A. the dowel hole must be smaller in diameter than the dowel so that there is a tight fit
    B. the dowel hole must be longer than the dowel to provide a room for excess glue
    C. the dowel must be of the same type of wood as the door frame
    D. the dowel must be held in place by a small screw while waiting for the glue to set

24. The edges of MOST finished wood flooring are   24._____

    A. tongue and groove   B. mortise and tenon
    C. bevel and miter   D. lap and scarf

25. For the SMOOTHEST finish, sanding of wood should be done   25._____

    A. in a circular direction
    B. diagonally against the grain
    C. across the grain
    D. parallel with the grain

KEY (CORRECT ANSWERS)

1.	D		11.	A
2.	D		12.	B
3.	B		13.	B
4.	D		14.	D
5.	D		15.	B
6.	A		16.	A
7.	A		17.	D
8.	B		18.	D
9.	B		19.	D
10.	B		20.	C

21.	A
22.	B
23.	B
24.	A
25.	D

TEST 2

DIRECTIONS: Each question or incomplete statement is followed by several suggested answers or completions. Select the one that BEST answers the question or completes the statement. *PRINT THE LETTER OF THE CORRECT ANSWER IN THE SPACE AT THE RIGHT.*

Questions 1-5.

DIRECTIONS: Questions 1 through 5 refer to the following specification for wood flooring. In answering these questions, refer to this specification.

2" x 4" wood sleepers laid flat @ 16" o.c.
1" x 6" sub-flooring, laid diagonally; cut at butt joints with parallel cuts; joints at center of sleepers, well staggered, no two joints side by side. Not less than 1/8" space between boards.
One layer of 15# asphalt felt on top of sub-floor.
Finish floor – North Rock Maple, T & G, laid perpendicular to sleepers; 8d nails not more than 12" apart; end joints well scattered with at least 2 flooring strips between joints.
Flooring 25/32" x 2 1/4" face - 1st quality.

1.   It is MOST likely that the floor referred to in the specification is to be laid   1.____

    A.   directly on the ground   B.   on a concrete base
    C.   on wood joists   D.   on steel beams

2.   The BEST reason for specifying that the sub-flooring be parallel cut at butt joints is that   2.____
      this

    A.   requires less material
    B.   provides staggered joints
    C.   provides more nailing surface
    D.   allows the joint to fall between sleepers

3.   The BEST reason for specifying a minimum space between the sub-floor boards is that it   3.____

    A.   saves on material   B.   reduces creaking
    C.   allows for expansion   D.   prevents dry rot

4.   The BEST reason for specifying at least 2 flooring strips between joints in the finish floor-   4.____
      ing is that

    A.   it looks better
    B.   it is more economical
    C.   each board is supported by two adjoining boards
    D.   each finish board is supported by at least two sub-floor boards

5.   The BEST reason for placing asphalt felt on top of the sub-floor is to   5.____

    A.   deaden noise   B.   preserve the wood
    C.   reduce dampness   D.   permit movement

6. The number of board feet in a piece of lumber is equal to the cross-sectional area in square inches divided by 12 and multiplied by the length of the piece in feet. Therefore, among four different pieces of lumber of equal length, the GREATEST number of board feet would be in the piece whose other two dimensions are

    A. 1" x 12"   B. 2" x 10"   C. 3" x 8"   D. 4" x 4"

6._____

7. When sandpapering wood by hand, the sanding should be done

    A. with the grain   B. across the grain
    C. diagonally to the grain   D. with a circular motion

7._____

8. A drift pin is used to

    A. line up holes   B. set nails
    C. enlarge holes   D. keep a nut from turning

8._____

Questions 9-13.

DIRECTIONS: In Questions 9 through 13, for each figure in Column I, representing a cross-section of a piece of lumber, select the letter preceding the term in Column II which is MOST closely associated with figure.
                 NOTE: These figures are not to scale.

<u>COLUMN I</u>

9.

<u>COLUMN II</u>

A. Flooring
B. Siding
C. Baseboard
D. Window steel
E. Threshold
F. Shingle

9._____

10.

10._____

11.

11._____

12.

12._____

13.

13._____

14. Lumber in quantity is ordered by   14.____

    A. cubic feet   B. foot board measure
    C. lineal feet   D. weight and length

15. The ends of a joist in a brick building are cut to a bevel.   15.____
This is done PRINCIPALLY to prevent damage to a

    A. joist   B. floor   C. sill   D. wall

16. Of the following terms, all of which refer to tools, the one which is LEAST related to the   16.____
others is

    A. back   B. box-end   C. cross-cut   D. rip

17. Of the following tools, the one which is LEAST like the others is   17.____

    A. brace and bit   B. draw-knife
    C. plane   D. spoke-shave

18. When wood splits easily, it is advisable to drill a hole for each nail.   18.____
The hole for the nail should be _____ the nail.

    A. larger in diameter than
    B. smaller in diameter than
    C. exactly the same diameter as
    D. less than one-quarter the length of

19. The length of a 10-penny nail is, in inches,   19.____

    A. $2\frac{1}{2}$ B. 3   C. $3\frac{1}{2}$ D. 4

20. The decimal equivalent of 31/64 of an inch is MOST NEARLY   20.____

    A. 0.45   B. 0.46   C. 0.47   D. 0.48

21. Of the following, the one which is BEST classified as an abrasive is   21.____

    A. a saw   B. a chisel   C. graphite   D. sandpaper

22. A claw hammer is PROPERLY used for   22.____

    A. driving a cold chisel   B. driving brads
    C. setting rivets   D. flattening a ¼" metal bar

23. It is POOR practice to hold a piece of wood in the hands or lap when tightening a screw   23.____
in the wood because

    A. sufficient leverage cannot be obtained
    B. the screwdriver may bend
    C. the wood will probably split
    D. personal injury is likely to result

24. Open-end wrenches are made with the sides of the jaws at about a 15° angle to the line   24.____
    of the handle.
    This angle

    A. is useful when working the wrench in close quarters
    B. increases the strength of the jaws
    C. prevents extending the handle with a piece of pipe
    D. serves only to improve the appearance of the wrench

25. When laying tongue and groove flooring, each piece is laid with the tongue to the front   25.____
    and the groove fitted to the tongue of the previously laid piece.
    In order to make this a tight fit before nailing into place, it is good practice when lay-
    ing each piece to

    A. temporarily toe-nail through its tongue to draw it up tight
    B. fit a small piece of scrap flooring to it and strike the scrap piece
    C. strike it only on the middle of the tongue
    D. pull it into place using a chisel as a pry bar

———————

KEY (CORRECT ANSWERS)

1.	B	11.	E
2.	C	12.	A
3.	C	13.	B
4.	C	14.	B
5.	C	15.	D
6.	C	16.	B
7.	A	17.	A
8.	A	18.	B
9.	C	19.	B
10.	D	20.	D

21.	D
22.	B
23.	D
24.	A
25.	B

TEST 3

DIRECTIONS: Each question or incomplete statement is followed by several suggested answers or completions. Select the one that BEST answers the question or completes the statement. *PRINT THE LETTER OF THE CORRECT ANSWER IN THE SPACE AT THE RIGHT.*

1. The MAIN purpose of bridging in building floor construction is to   1._____

   A. spread floor loads evenly to joists
   B. reduce the number of joists required
   C. permit use of thinner subflooring
   D. reduce noise passage through floors

2. Of the following, the material MOST commonly used for subflooring is   2._____

   A. rock lath   B. insulation board
   C. plywood   D. transite

3. In connection with stair construction, the one of the following that is LEAST related to the others is   3._____

   A. tread   B. cap   C. nosing   D. riser

4. The type of nail MOST commonly used in flooring is   4._____

   A. common   B. cut   C. brad   D. casing

5. The edge joint of flooring boards is COMMONLY   5._____

   A. mortise and tenon   B. shiplap
   C. half lap   D. tongue and groove

6. The purpose of a ridge board in building construction is to   6._____

   A. locate corners of a building
   B. keep plaster work smooth
   C. support the ends of roof rafters
   D. conceal openings at the eaves

7. Holes are USUALLY countersunk when installing   7._____

   A. carriage bolts   B. lag screws
   C. flathead screws   D. square nuts

8. Of the following, the tool that is LEAST easily broken is a   8._____

   A. file   B. pry bar
   C. folding rule   D. hacksaw blade

9. The wood joint which is a mortise and tenon is   9._____

55

10. Of the following, the saw MOST frequently employed by a carpenter is a _____ saw.   10._____

    A. keyhole   B. jig   C. crosscut   D. miter

11. Of the following, a chain saw would MOST likely be used to cut   11._____

    A. bevelled edges   B. tongue and groove joints
    C. heavy timbers   D. long thin wood members

12. Wire for other than electrical work is USUALLY specified by   12._____

    A. number of mils   B. gauge number
    C. number of circular mils   D. weight per foot

13. Lumber that has NOT been seasoned properly   13._____

    A. is brittle   B. has a tendency to rot
    C. will have pitch pockets   D. will tend to warp

14. The specifications state that an 8-penny common nail is required as a fastener.   14._____
Such nail should measure, in inches, MOST NEARLY

    A. 2 B. $2\frac{1}{2}$ C. 3 D. $3\frac{1}{2}$

15. To drill a hole 1 1/2 inches in diameter, a carpenter would MOST likely use a(n)   15._____

    A. 1 1/2" diameter drill   B. keyhole saw
    C. expansion bit   D. doall saw

16. A newel is part of a   16._____

    A. stairway   B. door   C. window   D. skylight

17. The area occupied by the building in the   17._____
sketch at the right, in square feet, is
MOST NEARLY
    A. 3300
    B. 4200
    C. 15,000
    D. 4050

building →

18. When timbers are bolted together, a flat washer is GENERALLY used under the head of   18._____
the bolt to

    A. prevent the bolt from turning
    B. increase the strength of the bolt
    C. reduce crushing of the wood when the bolt is tightened
    D. make it easier to turn the bolt

19. The sketch at the right shows a gauge used to
    A. measure the depth of a hole
    B. determine if a board has been smoothly planed
    C. check the width of a brick
    D. scribe a line on a board parallel to its edge

19.____

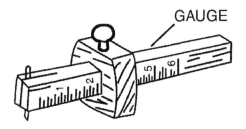

GAUGE

20. The joints in long vertical supporting timbers of wooden scaffolds are made with the timbers butted, rather than lapped, PRINCIPALLY because this results in

20.____

    A. better appearance
    B. more resistance to the weather
    C. lighter timbers
    D. less strain on the nails

———

KEY (CORRECT ANSWERS)

1.	A		11.	C
2.	C		12.	B
3.	B		13.	D
4.	B		14.	B
5.	D		15.	C
6.	C		16.	A
7.	C		17.	A
8.	B		18.	C
9.	B		19.	D
10.	C		20.	D

———

EXAMINATION SECTION
TEST 1

DIRECTIONS: Each question or incomplete statement is followed by several suggested answers or completions. Select the one that BEST answers the question or completes the statement. *PRINT THE LETTER OF THE CORRECT ANSWER IN THE SPACE AT THE RIGHT.*

1. A requisition for nails was worded as follows: *100 lbs., 10d, 3 inch, common wire nails, galvanized.*
    The UNNECESSARY information in this requisition is

    A. 100 lbs.   B. common   C. galvanized   D. 3 inch

    1._____

2. Of the following, the MOST important advantage of a ratchet wrench as compared to an open-end wrench is that the ratchet wrench

    A. is adjustable
    B. cannot strip the threads of a nut
    C. can be used in a limited space
    D. measures the force applied

    2._____

3. One advantage of plywood is that it

    A. is cheaper than soft pine
    B. does not contain any glue
    C. never splinters
    D. resists warping

    3._____

4. When floor beams are to be supported by nailing to vertical supports, then the STRONGEST arrangement would be provided by the method shown in

    4._____

5. Wood is LEAST likely to split when a nail is driven through it if the wood

    A. is very thin
    B. is very hard
    C. has been bleached white by the sun
    D. is soft

    5._____

6. The side support for steps or stairs is called a

    A. ledger board   B. runner
    C. stringer   D. riser

    6._____

7. A gouge is a tool used for

    A. planing wood smooth   B. grinding metal
    C. drilling steel   D. chiseling wood

    7._____

8. A router is used PRINCIPALLY to   8._____

    A. clean pipe   B. cut grooves in wood
    C. bend electric conduit   D. sharpen tools

9. The principle of operation of a sabre saw is MOST similar to that of a _____ saw.   9._____

    A. circular   B. radial   C. swing   D. jig

10. A staircase has twelve risers, each 6 3/4" high. The TOTAL rise of the staircase is   10._____

    A. 6'2¼"   B. 6'9"   C. 7'0"   D. 7'3¾"

11. A twenty-foot straight ladder placed at an angle against a wall should be at a distance   11._____
from the wall equal to _____ feet.

    A. 3   B. 5   C. 7   D. 9

12. The leverage that can be obtained with a wrench is determined MAINLY by the   12._____

    A. material of which the wrench is made
    B. gripping surface of the jaw
    C. length of the handle
    D. thickness of the wrench

13. Of the following, the MAIN reason why flashing is used in the building trade is to make an   13._____
area

    A. decorative   B. watertight
    C. level   D. heat-resistant

14. A spandrel beam will USUALLY be found   14._____

    A. at the wall   B. around stairs
    C. at the peak of a roof   D. underneath a column

15. The MAIN reason for using oil on an oilstone is to   15._____

    A. make the surface of the stone smoother
    B. prevent clogging of the pores of the stone
    C. reduce the number of times the stone has to be *dressed*
    D. prevent gouging of the stone's surface

16. End grain of a post can be MOST easily planed by use of a _____ plane.   16._____

    A. rafter   B. jack   C. fore   D. block

17. A butt gauge is used when   17._____

    A. hanging doors   B. laying out stairs
    C. making rafter cuts   D. framing studs

18. Assume that you have been asked to remove a door knob. You inspect the door and find   18._____
that it has a mortise lock, and that the door knob is fastened with a set screw. Which of
the following is the FIRST step that you should take in removing the door knob?

A. Unscrew the set screw on the slimmest part of the knob
B. Saw off the knob at its thinnest point
C. Turn the knob repeatedly to the right and to the left until it finally falls off
D. Use a pinchbar to spring the lock

19. To *shim a hinge* means to   19._____

A. swing the hinge from side to side
B. paint the hinge
C. polish the hinge
D. raise up the hinge

20. To hold work that is being planed, sawed, drilled, shaped, sharpened, or riveted, you   20._____
should use a

A. punch   B. rasp   C. reamer   D. vise

21. In the wood frame shown at the right,   21._____
whose corners are all square, the TOTAL
length of one-inch boards is _____
inches.
A. 42
B. 43
C. 44
D. 45

22. Clutch-head, offset, Phillips, and spiral-ratchet are all different types of   22._____

A. drills   B. files
C. wrenches   D. screwdrivers

23. Of the following, the MOST important reason for keeping tools in perfect working order is   23._____
to make sure

A. the proper tool is being used for the required work
B. the tools can be operated safely
C. each employee can repair a variety of building defects
D. no employee uses a tool for his private use

24. In order to properly hang a door, shims are frequently inserted under the hinges.   24._____
These shims are MOST often made of

A. cardboard
B. sheet steel
C. bakelite
D. the same materials as the hinges

25. Flooring nails are USUALLY _____ nails.   25._____

    A. casing   B. common   C. cut   D. clinch

———

KEY (CORRECT ANSWERS)

1.	D		11.	B
2.	C		12.	C
3.	D		13.	B
4.	B		14.	A
5.	D		15.	B
6.	C		16.	D
7.	D		17.	A
8.	B		18.	A
9.	D		19.	D
10.	B		20.	D

21. C
22. D
23. B
24. A
25. C

———

TEST 2

DIRECTIONS: Each question or incomplete statement is followed by several suggested answers or completions. Select the one that BEST answers the question or completes the statement. *PRINT THE LETTER OF THE CORRECT ANSWER IN THE SPACE AT THE RIGHT.*

1. A non-bearing wall unit between columns enclosing a structure is known as a _____ wall.

      A. panel   B. curtain   C. apron   D. spandrel

   1.____

2. *Drywall* is installed by

      A. carpenters   B. lathers
      C. plasterers   D. masons

   2.____

3. A cantilever beam would MOST likely be used in connection with a

      A. floor opening   B. balcony
      C. warehouse floor   D. roof opening

   3.____

4. A floor is designed as a reinforced concrete floor with a hardwood surface. A section through the floor would MOST likely be

5. With respect to flooring, shrinkage in a wood joist is MOST serious in

      A. length   B. width
      C. depth   D. all of the above

   5.____

6. A *screw pitch gauge* measures only the

      A. looseness of threads
      B. tightness of threads
      C. number of threads per inch
      D. gauge number

   6.____

7. An offset screwdriver is MOST useful for turning a wood screw when

      A. a strong force needs to be applied
      B. the screw head is marred
      C. space is limited
      D. speed is desired

   7.____

8. Specifications which contain the term *kiln dried* would MOST likely refer to   8.____

    A. asphalt shingles   B. brick veneer
    C. paint lacquer   D. lumber

9. Headers and stretchers are used in the construction of   9.____

    A. floors   B. walls   C. ceilings   D. roofs

10. Construction of a dormer window does NOT usually involve   10.____

    A. cut rafters   B. rafter headers
    C. trimmer rafters   D. hip rafters

11. A frame building with 2x4 studding has an interior partition with 2x6 studding.   11.____
    The MOST probable reason for the heavier studding is to provide

    A. heat insulation   B. sound insulation
    C. room for a soil stack   D. room for steam pipes

12. The length of a 20 penny nail is MOST NEARLY _____ inches.   12.____

    A. 2½   B. 3   C. 3½   D. 4

13. Of the following, which is the HIGHEST grade of lumber?   13.____

    A. Construction   B. Utility
    C. Standard   D. Run of the mill

14. In a stairway, the number of   14.____

    A. treads and risers is the same
    B. treads is one more than the number of risers
    C. risers is one more than the number of treads
    D. treads is two more than the number of risers

15. Lumber is usually sold by the board foot, and a board foot is defined as a board one foot   15.____
    square and one inch thick.
    If the price of one board foot of lumber is $1.80 and you need 20 feet of lumber 6
    inches wide and 1 inch thick, the cost of the 20 feet of lumber is

    A. $18.00   B. $24.00   C. $36.00   D. $48.00

16. When an unusually high degree of accuracy is required with woodwork, lines should be   16.____
    marked with a

    A. pencil ground to a chisel point
    B. pencil line over a crayon line
    C. sharp knife point
    D. scriber

17. The two planes which make up the MOST useful combination for general carpentry work   17.____
are the _____ plane and the _____ plane.

    A. jack; jointer   B. jack; block
    C. smooth; block   D. fore; jointer

18. The terms *plank, scantling, heavy joists,* when used in connection with lumber, refer to   18.____

    A. dimensions   B. use
    C. grade   D. finish

19. Of the following woods, the one that is the HARDEST is   19.____

    A. douglas fir   B. sitka spruce
    C. southern pine   D. hickory

20. A specification on finished hardware refers to roses and escutcheon plates.   20.____
These are MOST likely to be installed on

    A. desks   B. blackboards
    C. windows   D. doors

21. Wall sheathing can be installed either diagonally or horizontally on the studs.   21.____
When installed diagonally, the wall is

    A. cheaper   B. smoother
    C. more weatherproof   D. more rigid

22. A wall of a building which supports any load other than its own weight is called a   22.____
_____ wall.

    A. curtain   B. retaining   C. parapet   D. bearing

23. Soffits are USUALLY located in   23.____

    A. the roofing   B. bathrooms
    C. stairways   D. the flooring

24. A specification on carpentry for a housing project calls for the use of a nail set.   24.____
Of the following, the BEST reason for this requirement is that

    A. certain nails are to be removed
    B. the points of certain nails are to be bent over for better anchorage
    C. the heads of certain nails are to be sunk
    D. certain nails are to be spaced at a specified interval

25. Of the following grades of lumber, the one that is MOST likely to be specified for interior   25.____
finish which is to be painted is Grade

    A. No. 1 Common   B. No. 2 Common
    C. No. 1 Clear   D. D, Select

―――――

KEY (CORRECT ANSWERS)

1.	B	11.	C
2.	A	12.	D
3.	B	13.	A
4.	A	14.	C
5.	C	15.	A
6.	C	16.	C
7.	C	17.	B
8.	D	18.	A
9.	B	19.	D
10.	D	20.	D

21.	D
22.	D
23.	C
24.	C
25.	C

TEST 3

DIRECTIONS: Each question or incomplete statement is followed by several suggested answers or completions. Select the one that BEST answers the question or completes the statement. *PRINT THE LETTER OF THE CORRECT ANSWER IN THE SPACE AT THE RIGHT.*

1. A four-foot mason's level is USUALLY used to determine whether the top of a wall is level and whether it is

   A. square   B. plumb   C. rigid   D. in line

   1._____

2. To match a tongue in a board, the matching board MUST have a

   A. rabbet   B. chamfer   C. bead   D. groove

   2._____

3. When driving screws in close quarters, the BEST type of screwdriver to use is a(n)

   A. Phillips   B. offset   C. butt   D. angled

   3._____

4. Panel doors may have horns which must be cut off before the door is hung. In the sketch at the right, the arrow which indicates a horn is labeled number

   A. 1
   B. 2
   C. 3
   D. 4

   4._____

5. In carpentry work, the MOST commonly used hand saw is the _____ saw.

   A. hack   B. rip   C. buck   D. cross-cut

   5._____

6. The device which USUALLY keeps a doorknob from rotating on the spindle is a

   A. cotter pin   B. tapered key
   C. set screw   D. stop screw

   6._____

7. The one of the following types of nails that USUALLY requires the use of a tool known as a nail set is the _____ nail.

   A. finishing   B. sheetrock   C. 6-penny   D. cut

   7._____

8. To locate a point on a floor directly under a point on the ceiling, the PROPER tool to use is a

   A. square   B. line level
   C. height gauge   D. plumb bob

   8._____

9. A *fire cut* is *made* on   9.____

   A. timber posts   B. rafters
   C. floor joists   D. lathing

10. The one of the following items that is LEAST related to the others is   10.____

   A. joist hanger   B. pintle
   C. bridle iron   D. stirrup

11. The PROPER order of nailing subflooring and bridging is   11.____

   A. top of bridging, bottom of bridging, subflooring
   B. bottom of bridging, subflooring, top of bridging
   C. top of bridging, subflooring, bottom of bridging
   D. bottom of bridging, top of bridging, subflooring

12. Sleepers would be found in   12.____

   A. walls   B. doors   C. footings   D. floors

13. The one of the following woods that is MOST commonly used for finish flooring is   13.____

   A. hemlock   B. cypress   C. larch   D. oak

14. Spacing of studs in a stud partition is MOST frequently _____ " o.c.   14.____

   A. 12   B. 14   C. 16   D. 18

15. A wood screw which can be tightened by a wrench is known as a _____ screw.   15.____

   A. lag   B. Phillips   C. carriage   D. monkey

16. Of the following kinds of lumber, the one that is MOST likely to be specified for finish   16.____
    flooring for a gymnasium is

   A. spruce   B. hemlock   C. pine   D. maple

17. Ninety 2" x 4"s, 16' long, S4S are needed.   17.____
    The number of board feet required is MOST NEARLY

   A. 840   B. 960   C. 1080   D. 1200

18. Of the following, the wood section that is NOT commonly used for siding is   18.____

   A. tongue and groove   B. shiplap
   C. splined plank   D. clapboard

19. If the allowable load on a wooden scaffold is 60 pounds per square foot and the scaffold   19.____
    surface area is 3 feet by 12 feet, then the MAXIMUM total distributed load that is permit-
    ted on the scaffold is _____ pounds.

   A. 720   B. 1800   C. 2160   D. 2400

20. A piece of lumber with a cross-section as shown at the right is used in connection with

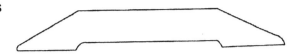

20._____

    A. stairs
    B. baseboards
    C. doors
    D. windows

Questions 21-25.

DIRECTIONS: For each item in the sketch shown below, labelled 21 to 25, select that letter that MOST NEARLY identifies the item and print that letter in the space next to the number of the item.

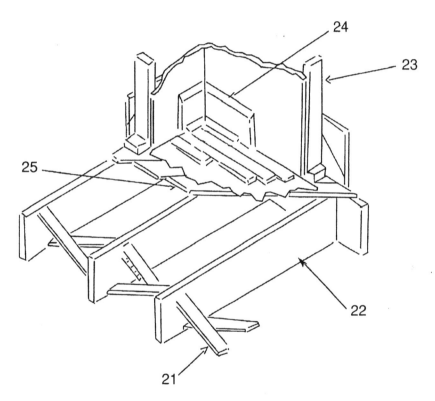

A. Sheathing	H. Header	21._____
B. Finish flooring	I. Sole	22._____
C. Paper	J. Cap	23._____
D. Subflooring	K. Bridging	24._____
E. Baseboard	L. Wainscoting	25._____
F. Shoe	M. Stud	
G. Joist	N. Ledger	

KEY (CORRECT ANSWERS)

1.	B		11.	C
2.	D		12.	D
3.	B		13.	D
4.	D		14.	C
5.	D		15.	A
6.	C		16.	D
7.	A		17.	B
8.	D		18.	C
9.	C		19.	C
10.	B		20.	C

21.	K
22.	G
23.	M
24.	E
25.	D

EXAMINATION SECTION
TEST 1

DIRECTIONS: Each question consists of a statement. You are to indicate whether the statement is TRUE (T) or FALSE (F). *PRINT THE LETTER OF THE CORRECT ANSWER IN THE SPACE AT THE RIGHT.*

1. Finished, three inch flooring measures $2\frac{1}{2}$" on the face.

1._____

2. A cripple jack is a rafter whose ends are framed in between a hip and the ridge.

2._____

3. Scribing is a method of planing a board straight.

3._____

4. A novelty saw blade is used on a circular saw for smooth cutting.

4._____

5. A hanger bolt is used in furniture construction.

5._____

6. The brace table can be found on the framing square.

6._____

7. A roof of strips is better than a solid sheathed roof on which to lay wood shingles.

7._____

8. A dowel sharpener is a tool used to measure the diameter of a dowel.

8._____

9. A butt gauge is a tool used in hanging interior or exterior doors.

9._____

10. A back band is part of a door casing.

10._____

11. An arch center is a form used in concrete form construction.

11._____

12. Braced framing is structurally stronger than balloon framing.

12._____

13. Hip rafters extend from ridge to plate.

13._____

14. Valley rafters extend from ridge to plate.

14._____

15. A lolly column is a wooden post.

15._____

16. Tail joists are set between trimmers.

16._____

17. Floor beams are sized to even widths.

17._____

18. Floor beams are set with hollow edges up.

18._____

19. Beam tops, in places where deafening occurs, should be chamfered.

19._____

20. Grounds are used at rough openings as a guide for plastering.

20._____

21. The first layer of wood over the rough frame is known as sheathing.

21._____

22. Sheathing boards are usually made from white pine lumber.

22._____

23. N.C. pine is commonly used for exterior siding.

23._____

24. Insulation materials are usually put between the sheathing and the siding.

24._____

25. Sub-flooring should be tightly drawn together at the joints by toe nailing.   25.____

26. A spoke shave has a curved blade.   26.____

27. Trees are classified into two groups.   27.____

28. A shake is caused by improper seasoning.   28.____

29. Lagging strips are parts of a jack arch form.   29.____

30. White pine comes from a broad leaf tree.   30.____

31. Wood screws range in length from $\frac{1}{4}$" to 6".   31.____

32. A round-head screw requires no countersinking.   32.____

33. A drive screw requires the use of a screwdriver.   33.____

34. Wood screws are ordered by wire gauge as well as by the lengths.   34.____

35. Counterboring is a term used when screws or nails are hidden below the surface.   35.____

36. Carriage bolts are bolts with square heads.   36.____

37. Expansion shields are used when fastening wood to brick or concrete walls.   37.____

38. A semi-elliptical arch has only one radius.   38.____

39. A skillsaw is commonly used in the construction of frame buildings.   39.____

40. A mould consisting of a cove and an ogee is called a crown moulding.   40.____

41. A bastard file is as effective as sandpaper to smooth a curved surface.   41.____

42. A T sill used in balloon frame construction needs no fire stops.   42.____

43. Flush girder construction requires the use of a ledger board.   43.____

44. Balloon frame studding requires the studs to run from sill to roof plate.   44.____

45. Crown is a term used in setting floor joists.   45.____

46. A jack stud may consist of one or more pieces.   46.____

47. In balloon framing, the wall studs rest on a shoe nailed to the sill.   47.____

48. The plates at the corner of a frame building meet in a half lap joint.   48.____

49. The rough opening for a window frame using unique balances need not be made as wide as the opening for a sash weight balanced window.   49.____

50. The location of the stud should be marked on the plate and shoe at the same time.   50.____

KEY (CORRECT ANSWERS)

1. F	11. T	21. T	31. T	41. F
2. F	12. T	22. F	32. T	42. T
3. F	13. T	23. F	33. T	43. T
4. T	14. T	24. F	34. F	44. T
5. T	15. F	25. F	35. T	45. T
6. T	16. T	26. T	36. F	46. T
7. T	17. T	27. T	37. T	47. T
8. F	18. F	28. F	38. F	48. F
9. T	19. T	29. T	39. T	49. T
10. T	20. T	30. F	40. T	50. T

TEST 2

DIRECTIONS: Each question consists of a statement. You are to indicate whether the statement is TRUE (T) or FALSE (F). *PRINT THE LETTER OF THE CORRECT ANSWER IN THE SPACE AT THE RIGHT.*

1. Truss roof construction is usually found in prefabricated homes.   1._____

2. A lintel is the head member of a double hung window frame.   2._____

3. A story pole is used to support a girder.   3._____

4. An astragal is used on a double window frame.   4._____

5. A battened door has no panels.   5._____

6. Floor joists should have at least four inches of bearing on a supporting wall.   6._____

7. Floor joists embedded in brick walls should be cut on a bevel.   7._____

8. Hot glue sets slower than cold glue.   8._____

9. A ridge board is generally 2" wider than the rafters resting against it.   9._____

10. The combined thickness of two 2" x 4" measures 3 3/4" when dressed.   10._____

11. A waler is a member usually found in brace frame construction.   11._____

12. A row of wood shingles for a starting row on an asphalt shingle roof is considered good construction.   12._____

13. Good practice calls for making the risers in ordinary stair construction from 9 to 10 inches high.   13._____

14. Butts generally used on a 1 3/8" thick inside door measure $3\frac{1}{2}$" x $3\frac{1}{2}$".   14._____

15. Herringbone is a design in flooring.   15._____

16. At the heel of a standard framing square, there is generally an inch divided into 100 parts.   16._____

17. A pilaster and a column are the same.   17._____

18. Sheathing grade plywood is usually 5/8 inch thick.   18._____

19. Sheathing is always nailed diagonally on a frame building.   19._____

20. Solid bridging is usually nailed in between floor joists at the ends of the joists.   20._____

21. Dowels are usually made of maple wood.   21._____

22. A ribbon board is a board notched in and nailed to the studs to carry floor joists.   22._____

23. End grain holds nails better than edge grain.   23._____

24. Interior doors in dwellings are usually hung so as to swing into the hall rather than into the room.   24._____

25. The standard length of wood lath is usually 4 feet.   25._____

26. Gross-bridging is always nailed securely at both ends before sub-flooring is laid.   26._____

27. A muntin divides the glass panes in colonial type window sash.   27._____

28. The horizontal division between a double hung window is a mullion.   28._____

29. Mitering is generally considered the best method to fit base moulding at corners.   29._____

30. The upright members of an ordinary wood scaffold are usually of 2" x 4" lumber.   30._____

31. Matched T and G flooring is always milled to standard lengths.   31._____

32. The table of a band saw is in two parts.   32._____

33. The motion of a band saw is continuous in one direction.   33._____

34. The moulding on top of a base board is called a bed mould.   34._____

35. A cleat is a strip of wood used to hold two or more pieces of wood together.   35._____

36. Rafters running from hip to plate are known as jack rafters.   36._____

37. Holes drilled for lag screws should be drilled 1/16" larger than the diameter of the lag screw.   37._____

38. Window and door openings of three or more feet should have header constructed from 2" x 6" beams doubled up.   38._____

39. The upper and lower hinges on an interior door are always placed the same distance from top and bottom of the door respectively.   39._____

40. It is not necessary to drill holes to receive nails in hard wood flooring before nailing.   40._____

41. Using the figures 7-10, 11-13, or 5-8 on a framing square would make square miter joints.   41._____

42. Batter boards are supports in a truss roof.   42._____

43. An *octagon* is a seven-sided figure.   43._____

44. White pine is a soft wood with close grain.   44._____

45. Broken hack saw blades may be effectively repaired by welding.   45._____

46. A bull nose plane is used for planing close to projecting parts.   46._____

47. A corona is a member of a cornice.   47._____

48. A take-apart framing square has three parts.   48._____

49. A queen truss has four sides. 49.____

50. A king post directly supports the rafters of a gable roof. 50.____

KEY (CORRECT ANSWERS)

1. T	11. F	21. F	31. F	41. F
2. F	12. T	22. T	32. T	42. F
3. F	13. F	23. F	33. T	43. F
4. F	14. T	24. F	34. F	44. T
5. T	15. T	25. T	35. T	45. F
6. T	16. T	26. F	36. T	46. T
7. T	17. F	27. T	37. F	47. T
8. F	18. F	28. F	38. T	48. F
9. T	19. F	29. T	39. F	49. T
10. F	20. F	30. T	40. F	50. F

TEST 3

DIRECTIONS: Each question consists of a statement. You are to indicate whether the statement is TRUE (T) or FALSE (F). *PRINT THE LETTER OF THE CORRECT ANSWER IN THE SPACE AT THE RIGHT.*

1. Drop siding and bevel siding are the same.   1._____

2. A cross band is a layer of wood in a three-ply panel.   2._____

3. A ribbon board and a ledger board mean the same.   3._____

4. All corner posts should consist of three members.   4._____

5. A twelve penny common nail is $3\frac{1}{2}$" long.   5._____

6. A water table and a belt course may be found in the same building.   6._____

7. Bridging can be made from wood or metal.   7._____

8. Box sill construction is usually found in balloon frame construction.   8._____

9. Headers run parallel to floor joists.   9._____

10. Collar beams are the main support in a gambrel roof.   10._____

11. A snug gable is part of a gambrel roof.   11._____

12. A soffit is part of a roof cornice.   12._____

13. Hard woods are generally sawed into standard widths and lengths.   13._____

14. Logs should be thoroughly dried before they are sawed into boards.   14._____

15. The heartwood of a tree usually is lighter in color than the sapwood.   15._____

16. The pith of a tree has no structural value.   16._____

17. Pine wood is a suitable wood for making shingles.   17._____

18. Chestnut wood and locust wood make good fence posts.   18._____

19. Red cedar is mostly used for the structural members of a frame building.   19._____

20. The framing square and the combination square have the same graduations of measurements.   20._____

21. The scale of inches on one part of the framing square is divided into twelfths.   21._____

22. The T bevel is used to test $90°$ angles.   22._____

23. The spur of a marking gauge can be used for making chamfers and bevels.   23._____

24. The hand cross-cut saw usually ranges from 20 to 26 inches in length.   24._____

25. The points of the teeth of a cross-cut saw are chisel-shaped.   25.____

26. A working drawing usually shows three views at all times.   26.____

27. The lever cap of a jack plane curls the shavings and prevents the plane from splitting the   27.____
    wood.

28. The bed of a jack plane is 16 inches long.   28.____

29. The lateral adjustment of a jack plane is usually controlled by a thumbscrew adjustment.   29.____

30. Round shank drills are made for use in a hand drill.   30.____

31. Auger bits are sharpened on a grinding wheel.   31.____

32. The nibs of an auger bit are always sharpened on the outside.   32.____

33. The teeth of a back saw are sharpened in the same manner as those of a cross-cut saw.   33.____

34. A socket chisel is better than a tang chisel when it is to be driven with a mallet.   34.____

35. Dowels are used in edge joints to strengthen them.   35.____

36. A butt joint is not more difficult to make than a rabbet joint.   36.____

37. Laminated stock is stock which has been glued edge to edge.   37.____

38. The stile is the horizontal member of a door frame.   38.____

39. The bottom rail of a door is usually made wider than the upper.   39.____

40. The teeth of a wood file are coarser than those of a wood rasp.   40.____

41. The flat mill file is suitable for filing a scraper blade.   41.____

42. Bar clamps and hand screws are usually made of like material.   42.____

43. A turning saw and coping saw can be used for the same type of work.   43.____

44. The framing square has four tables which can be used by the carpenter for laying out and   44.____
    figuring his work.

45. Maple and beech have similar texture of grain.   45.____

46. A mending plate is a flat piece of metal with holes for wood screws.   46.____

47. Metal corner brace and corner plates are the same.   47.____

48. A shaper is the proper machine to use for moulding an edge on a board.   48.____

49. A circular saw can have two arbors.   49.____

50. A band saw is always used to cut inside scroll work.   50.____

KEY (CORRECT ANSWERS)

1.	F	11.	F	21.	T	31.	F	41.	T
2.	F	12.	T	22.	F	32.	F	42.	F
3.	T	13.	F	23.	F	33.	T	43.	T
4.	F	14.	F	24.	T	34.	T	44.	T
5.	F	15.	F	25.	F	35.	T	45.	T
6.	T	16.	T	26.	F	36.	T	46.	T
7.	T	17.	T	27.	F	37.	F	47.	F
8.	F	18.	T	28.	F	38.	F	48.	T
9.	F	19.	F	29.	F	39.	T	49.	T
10.	F	20.	F	30.	T	40.	F	50.	F

TEST 4

DIRECTIONS: Each question consists of a statement. You are to indicate whether the statement is TRUE (T) or FALSE (F). *PRINT THE LETTER OF THE CORRECT ANSWER IN THE SPACE AT THE RIGHT.*

1. A jig saw and a band saw have similar rotary action.   1._____

2. A mortise machine will cut the tenon as well as the mortise.   2._____

3. The teeth of band saw blades have a standard number of teeth to the inch.   3._____

4. A number 13 auger bit will drill a 3/4 inch hole.   4._____

5. Staging is a method of setting up a balloon frame type of building.   5._____

6. A swing saw is usually used to cut lumber to a finish length.   6._____

7. A window stool is a part of the exterior trim of a window.   7._____

8. Diagonal sheathing strengthens the building more than horizontal sheathing does.   8._____

9. Window frame for brick or for frame houses are constructed in the same manner.   9._____

10. A bed moulding is also known as a crown moulding.   10._____

11. A drip cap is part of a window frame in a brick house.   11._____

12. A transom is a sash over a door or window.   12._____

13. A hinged transom and pivoted transom are the same.   13._____

14. A bay window is a window projection on a roof top.   14._____

15. Bay windows always have casement type sash.   15._____

16. Sub-flooring and the rough floor are the same.   16._____

17. A gable dormer has two valleys.   17._____

18. A saddle board is part of a roof.   18._____

19. Crown moulding, base moulding, and back bands are all parts of interior trim.   19._____

20. Entrance doors are usually glazed with putty.   20._____

21. A nosing is a term used in stairbuilding.   21._____

22. Open and closed stringers are laid out the same way.   22._____

23. Casing nails and finishing nails are the same.   23._____

24. A strap hinge and a T hinge are the same.   24._____

25. Unique balances are used on casement windows.   25._____

26. A water level is sometimes used by carpenters.   26._____

27. A flexible anchor bolt is threaded for nuts on both ends. 27._____

28. A segmental arch form has two radii of unequal length. 28._____

29. A rabbet joint can be cut on a jointer machine. 29._____

30. A pitch block is used in concrete form construction. 30._____

31. Corner braces are usually found in both western and balloon types of frame construction. 31._____

32. A combination square and a T bevel can be always used for the same purpose. 32._____

33. A miter box is used to cut curves of different radii. 33._____

34. An open mortise and tenon joint is considered to be the best method of constructing screens and storm sash. 34._____

35. Some circular saw blades have inserted teeth. 35._____

36. A face plate is part of a lathe. 36._____

37. The underslung belt sander has a sliding work table. 37._____

38. Gumming a circular saw blade is filing the teeth so that they are all the same height. 38._____

39. Sash lifts help to balance a double hung window sash. 39._____

40. A thumb latch is applied to the face of a door. 40._____

41. Sheathing applied horizontally shrinks mostly in a horizontal direction. 41._____

42. Flat sawing consists in cutting the timber tangential to the annual rings and along the grain. 42._____

43. Spruce wood is non-resinous. 43._____

44. When setting a cross-cut saw, the whole tooth should be bent. 44._____

45. Wet or green lumber requires less amount of set in a saw than lumber that is thoroughly dry. 45._____

46. Built-up posts, columns, and beams are safer from the standpoint of fires than solid ones. 46._____

47. The length of a screwdriver is determined from the points to the top of the handle. 47._____

48. Oil should be removed from an oil stove before putting it away. 48._____

49. The holes of a dowel joint should be the same depth as the length of the dowels. 49._____

50. Through nailing of a finished floor is inferior to toe-nailing. 50._____

KEY (CORRECT ANSWERS)

1.	F	11.	F	21.	T	31.	T	41.	F
2.	F	12.	T	22.	T	32.	F	42.	T
3.	F	13.	F	23.	F	33.	F	43.	F
4.	F	14.	F	24.	F	34.	F	44.	F
5.	F	15.	F	25.	F	35.	T	45.	F
6.	T	16.	T	26.	T	36.	T	46.	F
7.	F	17.	T	27.	T	37.	T	47.	F
8.	T	18.	T	28.	F	38.	F	48.	T
9.	F	19.	T	29.	T	39.	F	49.	F
10.	F	20.	F	30.	T	40.	T	50.	T

EXAMINATION SECTION
TEST 1

DIRECTIONS: Each question consists of a statement. You are to indicate whether the statement is TRUE (T) or FALSE (F). *PRINT THE LETTER OF THE CORRECT ANSWER IN THE SPACE AT THE RIGHT.*

1. Quarter sawn lumber is less expensive to buy than common sawn lumber. 1.____

2. Window sashes are usually held together by dowel joints. 2.____

3. Usually there is a yoke or head jamb in a casement window frame. 3.____

4. A muntin bar is the center rail of a double hung window. 4.____

5. The weight of pulley sash weights is determined by the size of the sash. 5.____

6. Casement windows are hinged at the top. 6.____

7. Pulley stiles are parts of a window frame. 7.____

8. A built-up girder consists of two or more members. 8.____

9. Box sill construction is generally found in balloon-type frame dwellings. 9.____

10. Footings are usually 12 inches thicker than the foundation wall. 10.____

11. Anchor bolts are used to hold together the plate of a frame dwelling. 11.____

12. Trimmer joists usually run at right angles to the regular joists. 12.____

13. Bridging can be laid out with a framing square. 13.____

14. No. 1 grade lumber is free from all knots and sap. 14.____

15. Maple flooring stands up better than oak flooring under heavy traffic. 15.____

16. Hardwoods split more readily than soft woods. 16.____

17. Oak is a closer grained wood than maple. 17.____

18. Cypress is a close grained soft wood. 18.____

19. Most deciduous woods are soft. 19.____

20. The teeth of a band saw are of the rip saw type. 20.____

21. Most soft woods are flexible. 21.____

22. A 2d nail measures one inch in length. 22.____

23. When boards are to be surfaced, the symbol *B.M.* is used to denote the fact. 23.____

24. A stop chamfer extends the full length of the piece on which it is formed. 24.____

25. Lumber is graded according to area of its cross-section. 25.____

26. Carpenters' rules are usually graduated to sixteenths of an inch on one side and to thirty-seconds on the other side. 26.____

27. The outside of the nibs of an auger bit should be sharpened when sharpening the bit. 27.____

28. To draw a circle on a board, a pair of calipers is the best tool to use. 28.____

29. Auger bits are sharpened with a special file for that purpose. 29.____

30. In rough carpentry work, thumb gauging with a pencil is suitable for marking cutting lines. 30.____

31. A crown mold is the molding on top of a base board. 31.____

32. A framing chisel is smaller than a firming chisel. 32.____

33. Round holes can be cut with a compass saw. 33.____

34. The tongue is the short arm of a framing square. 34.____

35. The treads and risers for a flight of stairs can be laid off with a steel square. 35.____

36. Sandpapering of wood should be done across the grain. 36.____

37. Narrow boards are less likely to warp than wide ones in construction work. 37.____

38. *Batter boards* are used to locate the corners of a building about to be constructed. 38.____

39. A piece of timber framed between two trimmers and supporting the ends of the tail pieces is called a header. 39.____

40. Wood framing at floors should be set firmly against the brickwork of the chimney. 40.____

41. Cross bridging in a floor is only to keep the joists in place. 41.____

42. A gable roof has three plane surfaces. 42.____

43. There are two different pitches or slopes on each side of a gambrel roof. 43.____

44. To use a driftpin, a hole slightly larger than the pin should be bored in the wood. 44.____

45. Plane irons and wood chisels are sharpened in a similar way. 45.____

46. In all frame buildings, the ceiling joists should rest on a 1" x 4" ribband. 46.____

47. Rafters which are square with the plate and intersect hip rafters are called jack rafters. 47.____

48. When laying double floors, the baseboard should not extend to the rough floor but only to the face of the finished floor. 48.____

49. 1000 ft. B.M. of 1" x 4" T & G are sufficient to cover a floor area of 50' x 20'. 49.____

50. The end of the rafter which rests against the ridge piece is called the *heel.* 50.____

———

KEY (CORRECT ANSWERS)

1.	F	11.	F	21.	F	31.	F	41.	F
2.	F	12.	F	22.	T	32.	F	42.	F
3.	T	13.	T	23.	F	33.	T	43.	T
4.	F	14.	F	24.	F	34.	T	44.	F
5.	F	15.	T	25.	F	35.	T	45.	T
6.	F	16.	F	26.	F	36.	F	46.	F
7.	T	17.	F	27.	F	37.	T	47.	T
8.	T	18.	T	28.	F	38.	T	48.	T
9.	F	19.	F	29.	T	39.	T	49.	F
10.	T	20.	T	30.	T	40.	F	50.	F

TEST 2

DIRECTIONS: Each question consists of a statement. You are to indicate whether the state-ment is TRUE (T) or FALSE (F). *PRINT THE LETTER OF THE CORRECT ANSWER IN THE SPACE AT THE RIGHT.*

1. The seat cut of a rafter is the part which rests on the plate. 1._____

2. If the rise of a rafter and the run of a rafter are of equal length, the roof will have a half pitch. 2._____

3. Sheathing applied diagonally to a building requires more material for an equal area than if applied horizontally. 3._____

4. Boards of 10 feet or more in length ordinarily come in multiples of 2 feet. 4._____

5. For inside trim, common nails are preferred. 5._____

6. A hammer is the proper tool to use to drive in lag screws. 6._____

7. Windshake in lumber is a separation of the annual rings. 7._____

8. 6d finish nails are usually used to lay 1" x 4" T & G flooring. 8._____

9. Moist lumber is more flexible than dry lumber. 9._____

10. Hickory is one of the most brittle woods. 10._____

11. Ledger boards are supports for the second floor joists of a balloon frame house. 11._____

12. When placing joists, the crowned edge should be upwards. 12._____

13. Galvanized nails should be used to attach shingles. 13._____

14. Finished flooring should be laid with its lengths extending in the same direction as those of the rough floor. 14._____

15. Lag screws and coach screws mean the same. 15._____

16. Wire nails are more rust resisting than cut nails. 16._____

17. The total rise of rafters is the vertical distance from the level of the plate to the top of the ridge. 17._____

18. Spiking is the only method of fastening tail beams to the headers. 18._____

19. Seasoning or controlled drying of lumber lessens its strength. 19._____

20. A jack rafter whose ends are framed in between a hip and valley is called a cripple jack. 20._____

21. Iron stirrups are sometimes used to join headers to floor joists. 21._____

22. Nails, spikes, and driftpins hold well in green lumber. 22._____

23. The number of a saw is determined by the number of teeth points per inch. 23._____

24. When using a hand saw, a carpenter should pull up rather than push down when starting the first stroke.   24._____

25. Nails when driven across the grain hold better than when driven with the grain.   25._____

26. Timber which is alternately wet and dry will rot sooner than timber which is continually wet.   26._____

27. Cedar is not a suitable wood for shingles.   27._____

28. Lack of ventilation is a cause of dry rot in lumber.   28._____

29. The number of risers in a flight of stairs is one more than the number of treads.   29._____

30. 25 pieces of lumber 2" x 6" and 12 feet long contain 300 board feet.   30._____

31. A nosing is the rounded and projecting edge of a stair tread.   31._____

32. An angle of 45 degrees is a right angle.   32._____

33. S.2.E. means dressed on two sides and one edge.   33._____

34. There are approximately 200 6d nails to the pound.   34._____

35. A finishing nail is a wire nail with a small inconspicuous head.   35._____

36. A 2d nail is half as long as a 6d nail.   36._____

37. A 10d nail is twice as long as a 4d nail.   37._____

38. Scantling is lumber with a cross-section from 2" x 4" to and including 2" x 6".   38._____

39. Lag screws are driven into place with a screwdriver.   39._____

40. A drift pin is a threaded bolt used to hold heavy pieces of timber together.   40._____

41. When ordering surfaced lumber, the quantity in board feet is calculated on the basis of the dimensions after surfacing.   41._____

42. Larch is commercially known as a soft wood.   42._____

43. Basswood is commercially known as a hard wood.   43._____

44. Wood is seasoned naturally by keeping it in the open exposed to air and rain.   44._____

45. Torn grain results from digging out a part of the wood when dressing it.   45._____

46. The term *matched* in flooring signifies that all pieces must be cut to the same length.   46._____

47. Spruce is not suitable lumber for scaffold planks.   47._____

48. A jointer plane is the most suitable plane to cut across the grain on the end of a piece of lumber.   48._____

49. When sawing wood to measurements, the saw should follow through the center of the pencil line marked on the wood.   49.____

50. In dwellings, the interior doors should be hung so as to open into the rooms rather than into the halls.   50.____

KEY (CORRECT ANSWERS)

1. T	11. T	21. T	31. T	41. F
2. T	12. T	22. F	32. F	42. T
3. T	13. T	23. T	33. F	43. T
4. T	14. F	24. T	34. T	44. F
5. F	15. F	25. T	35. T	45. T
6. F	16. T	26. T	36. T	46. F
7. T	17. T	27. F	37. T	47. F
8. F	18. F	28. T	38. F	48. F
9. T	19. F	29. T	39. F	49. F
10. F	20. T	30. T	40. F	50. T

TEST 3

DIRECTIONS: Each question consists of a statement. You are to indicate whether the statement is TRUE (T) or FALSE (F). *PRINT THE LETTER OF THE CORRECT ANSWER IN THE SPACE AT THE RIGHT.*

1. 6'8" is the standard height for ordinary doors.   1._____

2. A dotted line on a drawing usually represents a hidden edge or surface.   2._____

3. Siding is generally laid with a one inch lap and nailed at each stud.   3._____

4. A half surface butt has one face at right angles to the other when the butt is closed.   4._____

5. In good construction, exterior doors are usually 1¼" thick.   5._____

6. A right angle mitre joint can be made by cutting two pieces of wood at an angle of 45°   6._____

7. A stair baluster and stair hand rail mean the same thing.   7._____

8. A 16d nail is 4 inches long.   8._____

9. When stating the size of a window or door, the width should always be given first.   9._____

10. To provide for waste and loss in matching a 4" matched flooring, approximately one-third 10._____
    more than the area to be covered should be ordered.

11. Figures given on drawings should be accepted in preference to scaled measurements.   11._____

12. Forty studs, 16" O.C., will be required for a partition wall 50 feet long.   12._____

13. There are 12 board feet contained in a cubic foot of timber.   13._____

14. A good grade of lumber for framing is known as #1 Grade.   14._____

15. *Story by story* type of framing is represented by a frame building with a double plate   15._____
    under the second floor joists.

16. When the ends of joists are to be laid in a brick wall, they should be fire cut.   16._____

17. 1000 feet B.M. of 1" & 4" T & G flooring will cover an area of 1000 square feet.   17._____

18. When grinding a tool, the stone should revolve towards the bevel edge of the tool that is 18._____
    pressed against it.

19. A steel stirrup is one type of joist hanger.   19._____

20. A purlin is a timber upon which roof rafters rest.   20._____

21. 2" x 4" lumber is generally used for uprights to erect ordinary scaffolding.   21._____

22. The pitch of a gable roof can be determined by dividing the total rise by the length of 22._____
    span.

23. The upright members of a door are called stiles.   23.____

24. The horizontal distance from the first riser to the last riser of a stairway is the run.   24.____

25. The expression *to the weather* is used in reference to putting on sheathing.   25.____

26. Veneer and plywood mean the same thing.   26.____

27. A plinth block is part of a door casing.   27.____

28. One of the purposes of bridging is to distribute the bearing strength over the whole floor area.   28.____

29. Flush type doors usually have laminated cores.   29.____

30. White pine and fir are used extensively for stock doors.   30.____

31. A glass bead is the molding around the panels of a door.   31.____

32. A joist hanger is usually made of sheet metal.   32.____

33. The block plane is larger than the jack plane.   33.____

34. A hack saw is for the purpose of cutting thin wood.   34.____

35. A wood chisel is sharpened on both sides.   35.____

36. A hand saw is set to give clearance for the blade.   36.____

37. A nail is set below the surface with a countersink.   37.____

38. In woodwork, rabbeting is a term used to denote the recessing of the edge of stock.   38.____

39. The spokeshave and circular plane can be used for the same purposes.   39.____

40. A brass or iron ring called the ferrule is placed on the lower end of a plane handle.   40.____

41. To bore a hole through a piece of wood, the auger bit should be driven all the way through the piece in one operation.   41.____

42. It is good practice to examine the grain of the wood before commencing to plane it.   42.____

43. A seven-point saw is one that is 7 inches wide at the heel.   43.____

44. A narrow board that is to be planed on the end will not usually split if a piece of wood is placed behind the edge while planing.   44.____

45. The cap iron of a smooth plane is fastened to the flat side of the blade to act as a chip breaker.   45.____

46. A run of 18 feet and a rise of 9 feet will make a 1/3 pitch roof.   46.____

47. Dowels are generally made of soft wood.   47.____

48. The best way by which to test the setting of the cutter of a plane is to run the fingers over the sole of the plane.   48.____

49. If a building is to be sheathed horizontally, more material will be required than the actual   49.____
    measured area to be covered.

50. Horizontally placed sheathing boards nailed to studs make a wall as rigid as if placed   50.____
    diagonally.

KEY (CORRECT ANSWERS)

1.	T	11.	T	21.	T	31.	F	41.	F
2.	T	12.	F	22.	T	32.	F	42.	T
3.	T	13.	T	23.	T	33.	F	43.	F
4.	T	14.	T	24.	T	34.	F	44.	T
5.	F	15.	T	25.	F	35.	F	45.	T
6.	T	16.	T	26.	F	36.	T	46.	F
7.	F	17.	F	27.	T	37.	F	47.	F
8.	F	18.	T	28.	T	38.	T	48.	F
9.	T	19.	T	29.	T	39.	T	49.	T
10.	T	20.	T	30.	T	40.	F	50.	F

TEST 4

DIRECTIONS: Each question consists of a statement. You are to indicate whether the statement is TRUE (T) or FALSE (F). *PRINT THE LETTER OF THE CORRECT ANSWER IN THE SPACE AT THE RIGHT.*

1. Casement windows are balanced with weights. 1.____

2. Measurements and cuts of valley rafters are determined in the same manner as for hip rafters. 2.____

3. Loose pin butts are generally used on inside doors. 3.____

4. A valley jack is a rafter, the top end of which is framed against a hip. 4.____

5. A 1/3-pitch roof is steeper than a 1/2-pitch roof. 5.____

6. Twelve pieces of lumber, each ½" x 6 x 12' would be billed as 72 board feet. 6.____

7. An auger bit and a chisel would be two of the proper tools to use in making a mortise for a mortise lock on a door. 7.____

8. Stringers or carriages are frames on which stairs are carried. 8.____

9. A mullion is a horizontal division between windows. 9.____

10. An inside lock set is mortised into the door. 10.____

11. A meeting rail is found on a double hung sash window. 11.____

12. A pocket can be found in a D.H. window frame. 12.____

13. The grain in oak is more noticeable when the piece is quarter-sawn. 13.____

14. A lintel iron is a part in a frame building. 14.____

15. A screwdriver is used to drive a nail below the surface of the wood. 15.____

KEY (CORRECT ANSWERS)

1.	F	6.	T	11.	T
2.	T	7.	T	12.	T
3.	T	8.	T	13.	T
4.	F	9.	F	14.	F
5.	F	10.	T	15.	F

READING COMPREHENSION
UNDERSTANDING AND INTERPRETING WRITTEN MATERIAL

EXAMINATION SECTION
TEST 1

DIRECTIONS: Each question or incomplete statement is followed by several suggested answers or completions. Select the one that BEST answers the question or completes the statement. *PRINT THE LETTER OF THE CORRECT ANSWER IN THE SPACE AT THE RIGHT.*

Questions 1-4.

DIRECTIONS: Questions 1 through 4 refer to the following paragraph.

Hot hide glue is an excellent adhesive, but it is generally not used by the home handyman. You can buy hide glue in cake, flake, or ground forms. Soak the glue in lukewarm water overnight, following the manufacturer's instructions. Use glass ovenware or metal containers, double-boiler fashion, to keep it below 150° F. and apply hot. Heat only the quantity needed; frequent reheating weakens the glue. It sets fast, but requires tight clamping and matched joints for proper bonding.

1. According to the paragraph, the number of forms in which hide glue can be bought is   1.____

   A. 2   B. 3   C. 4   D. 5

2. According to the above paragraph, hide glue should   2.____

   A. be used only by the home handyman
   B. be boiled twice
   C. never be used by the home handyman
   D. be prepared according to manufacturer's instructions

3. According to the above paragraph, frequent reheating of hide glue   3.____

   A. makes it set fast   B. weakens it
   C. keeps it below 150° F   D. is desirable

4. The one of the following which is the MOST appropriate title for the above paragraph is   4.____

   A. TIPS FOR THE HOME HANDYMAN
   B. PREPARATION AND USE OF HIDE GLUE
   C. WHAT IS HIDE GLUE?
   D. REPAIR OF GLASS OVENWARE AND METAL CONTAINERS

Questions 5-9.

DIRECTIONS: Questions 5 through 9 are based on the paragraph below. Use only the information contained in this paragraph in answering these questions.

Common nails and brads are designated by the letter *d*, indicating *penny;* thus 8d = 8 penny. In order to determine the length required of a nail in pennies, the thickness of the board to be penetrated, for example, 25/32 of an inch, is multiplied by 8. Then, 11/2 is added to the result, which in this instance indicates an 8d nail: (25/32 x 8 = 61/4 + 11/2=73/4= 8).

To reverse the computation, when only the penny size is known, to determine the length in inches (up to 10d), the penny size is divided by 4 then 1/2 is added. For example, an 8d nail measures 2 1/2 inches because 8 ÷ 4 = 2 + 1/2=2 1/2.

5. The letter used to designate common nails and brads is

   A. a   B. b   C. c   D. d

5._____

6. To penetrate a board 15/16" thick, the length of nail required, in pennies, is

   A. 8   B. 9   C. 10   D. 11

6._____

7. The length of a 6 penny nail, in inches, is

   A. 2   B. 3   C. 4   D. 5

7._____

8. The word *penetrated,* as used in the above paragraph, means MOST NEARLY

   A. congealed   B. dulled
   C. hanged   D. pierced

8._____

9. The word *designated,* as used in the above paragraph, means MOST NEARLY

   A. considered   B. driven
   C. named   D. probed

9._____

Questions 10-17.

DIRECTIONS: Questions 10 through 17 are based on the paragraph below. Use only the information contained in this paragraph in answering these questions.

Lumber is measured according to a system known as board measure (bm). The unit is a board foot, which is equal in volume to a board 1 foot wide, 1 foot long, and 1 inch thick, or 144 cubic inches. To compute board measure, if the board is less than 1 inch thick, consider the fraction as a full inch. If it is thicker than 1 inch, however, figure the inches and fractions of an inch exactly. Thus, a 1/2 inch board is considered as 1 inch thick bm, but a 1 1/2 inch board as 1 1/2 inches. To compute board feet, multiply the length of the board, in feet, by the width, in feet, and multiply this product by the thickness in inches.

10. The unit of measuring lumber is a

   A. ampere   B. board foot
   C. milligram   D. pound per square inch

10._____

11. Lumber is measured according to a system known as

   A. board measure   B. cubic capacity
   C. linear feet   D. logarithms

11._____

12. A board foot is equal to   12.____

    A. 144 cubic inches   B. 3 linear feet
    C. 4 by 8 feet   D. 72 cubic inches

13. If a piece of lumber is 3/4" thick, in computing board measure, its thickness will be con-   13.____
sidered as

    A. 4"   B. 3/4"   C. 1"   D. 1 1/2"

14. If a piece of lumber is 1 3/4" thick, in computing board measure, its thickness will be con-   14.____
sidered as

    A. 1/2"   B. 1"   C. 1 1/2"   D. 1 3/4"

15. The number of board feet in a board 12 feet long by 18 inches wide by 1/2 inch thick is   15.____

    A. 9   B. 18   C. 108   D. 216

16. The number of board feet in a board 12 feet long by 18 inches wide by 1 3/4 inches thick   16.____
is

    A. 18   B. 31.5   C. 216   D. 270

17. The word *compute,* as used in the above paragraph, means MOST NEARLY   17.____

    A. add   B. calculate   C. divide   D. subtract

Questions 18-24.

DIRECTIONS: Questions 18 through 24 are based on the paragraph below. Use only the
information contained in this paragraph in answering these questions.

    Screws can be purchased in lengths varying fro1/4" to 6". Lengths from 1/4" to 1"
increase by 1/8" units; those from 1" to 3" by 1/4" units; and from 3" to 5" by 1/2" units. They
come with flat, round, or oval heads, the flat head type being used for countersinking. Soap-
ing the screw first will facilitate driving it in, especially when working with hardwood.

18. Of the following, the kind of head with which screws do NOT come is   18.____

    A. flat   B. round   C. oval   D. square

19. The one of the following lengths of screws which can be purchased is   19.____

    A. 1/8"   B. 3/16"   C. 5/16"   D. 3/8"

20. The one of the following lengths of screws which CANNOT be purchased is   20.____

    A. 1 1/8"   B. 1 1/2"   C. 1 1/2"   D. 13/4"

21. The one of the following lengths of screws which can be purchased is   21.____

    A. 3 3/4"   B. 4 1/2"   C. 4 2/4"   D. 4 3/4"

22. The type of screw used for countersinking is the one whose head is   22.____

    A. flat   B. round   C. oval   D. square

23. To facilitate driving a screw in, it should FIRST be   23._____

    A. countersunk   B. sanded
    C. soaped   D. varnished

24. The word *facilitate,* as used in the above paragraph, means MOST NEARLY to make   24._____

    A. angular   B. artificial   C. difficult   D. easy

Questions 25.

DIRECTIONS: Question 25 is based on the following statement.

Interior painting may be done at any time, provided that temperature can be kept above 50° F for ordinary paints and above 65° F for enamels and varnishes.

25. According to this statement, the temperature for enameling and varnishing should be   25._____

    A. above 50° F   B. between 50° F and 65° F
    C. below 65° F   D. above 65° F

KEY (CORRECT ANSWERS)

1. B		11. A	
2. D		12. A	
3. B		13. C	
4. B		14. D	
5. D		15. B	
6. B		16. B	
7. A		17. B	
8. D		18. D	
9. C		19. D	
10. B		20. A	

21. C
22. A
23. C
24. D
25. D

TEST 2

DIRECTIONS: Each question or incomplete statement is followed by several suggested answers or completions. Select the one that BEST answers the question or completes the statement. *PRINT THE LETTER OF THE CORRECT ANSWER IN THE SPACE AT THE RIGHT.* Questions 1 through 8 are based on the paragraphs below. Use only the information contained in these paragraphs in answering these questions.

Glue may be either hot or cold. Hot glue, an animal product, is purchased in dry flakes or sheets which must be soaked in water, then heated in a glue pot which is similar to a double boiler. Its main advantage is that it sets quickly, in fact so quickly that one must work fast to complete the joint before the glue sets.

There are numerous kinds of cold glue. One of the best is casein glue, which is manufactured from skimmed milk. It comes as a powder, which must be freshly mixed with water for each job, as the mixture will lose its valuable adhesive properties if stored. Cold glue is just as strong as hot glue, and casein glue resists moisture more effectively, but it needs considerable time to set.

1. The MAIN advantage of hot glue is that it 1.____

   A. is easily prepared
   B. is inexpensive
   C. resists moisture more effectively than cold glue
   D. sets quickly

2. Hot glue is purchased as 2.____

   A. dry flakes or sheets   B. a liquid
   C. a powder   D. wet film

3. Casein glue 3.____

   A. does not need to be mixed with water before application
   B. is purchased as a powder dissolved in water
   C. must be freshly mixed with water for each job
   D. should be mixed with water before storing away

4. The strength of cold glue in relation to that of hot glue is 4.____

   A. less
   B. the same
   C. greater
   D. variable, depending on type of glue

5. The time in which hot glue sets in relation to the time in which cold glue sets is 5.____

   A. shorter
   B. the same
   C. longer
   D. variable, depending on type of glue

6. If casein glue is mixed with water before storing, its adhesive strength will   6.____

    A. be lost
    B. remain the same
    C. increase
    D. increase or diminish, depending on amount of water used

7. Casein glue in relation to hot glue resists moisture   7.____

    A. less effectively
    B. about the same
    C. more effectively
    D. in varying degrees, depending on type of glue

8. The word *adhesive,* as used in the above paragraph, means MOST NEARLY   8.____

    A. costly   B. economical
    C. glowing brightly   D. sticking together

Questions 9-25.

DIRECTIONS: Each question consists of a statement. You are to indicate whether the statement is TRUE (T) or FALSE (F). *PRINT THE LETTER OF THE CORRECT ANSWER IN THE SPACE AT THE RIGHT.*

Questions 9-13.

DIRECTIONS: Questions 9 through 13, inclusive, are to be answered in accordance with the paragraph below.

    Wood kept constantly dry or continuously submerged in water does not decay, regardless of species or the presence of sapwood. A large *proportion* of wood in use is kept so dry at all times that it lasts indefinitely. Moisture and temperature are the principal factors affecting the rate of decay. When exposed to conditions that favor decay, wood in warm humid areas of the United States deteriorates more rapidly than in cool or dry areas. High altitudes, as a rule, are less favorable to decay than are low altitudes because the *average* temperatures are lower and the growing season for fungi, which cause decay, are shorter.

9. A wooden beam is supporting a pier and is constantly under water. According to the   9.____
    above paragraph, the beam will have a high rate of decay.

10. According to the above paragraph, the cause of decay in wood is fungi.   10.____

11. According to the above paragraph, the LOWEST rate of decay in wood is found in cli-   11.____
    mates that are warm and humid.

12. As used in the above paragraph, *proportion* means MOST NEARLY *percent.*   12.____

13. As used in the above paragraph, *average* means MOST NEARLY *lowest.*   13.____

Questions 14-18.

DIRECTIONS: Questions 14 through 18, inclusive, are to be answered in accordance with the paragraph below.

HOW WOOD IS SEASONED

There are two common methods of drying lumber after it has been sawed. These two methods are air seasoning and kiln drying. Some woods may be air dried *satisfactorily* while others must be put through the kiln drying process before the wood can be successfully used for furniture-making. Most soft, non-porous woods are more easily air-dried than the harder woods. In the air drying process, the lumber is stacked carefully in large piles in the open air. Thin strips are laid between each layer of boards to prevent them from *warping* and to allow the air to circulate between them.

14. According to the above paragraph, all wood can be dried by stacking the lumber in the open air.   14.____

15. According to the above paragraph, if the wood in non-porous, it is better to air dry it.   15.____

16. According to the above paragraph, drying of lumber is done after it is cut to size.   16.____

17. As used in the above paragraph, the word *satisfactorily* means *quickly.*   17.____

18. As used in the above paragraph, the word *warping* means *twisting.*   18.____

Questions 19-25.

DIRECTIONS: Questions 19 through 25, inclusive, are to be answered in accordance with the paragraph below.

CARE OF FURNITURE

Furniture, like floors, interior *trim,* and automobiles, requires frequent care to keep its finish in good condition. The finish of new furniture can be kept in good condition for many years if a coat of wax is *applied* to it regularly at least once each year. The coat of wax maintains the luster of the finish, protects the finishing coat from dampness, and aids in preventing the surface from being *marred* easily.

Excessive use of oil polishes should be avoided since they have a tendency to eventually produce a dull, lifeless surface and cause dust to collect on the finish.

If water has been allowed to remain on a finished surface for some time, it often causes the finish to turn white. The natural color of the finish may usually be restored by rubbing the spots lightly with a cloth moistened with alcohol, followed by the application of a small amount of sweet oil or linseed oil. Excessive moisture often collects on the furniture during the winter season as a result of improper ventilation and the use of open-flame gas stoves. This condition effects the joints and finish and causes the furniture to deteriorate rapidly.

A touch-up pencil may be obtained for the purpose of filling and removing deep scratches and other blemishes from a finished surface.

19. According to the above paragraph, one function of a coat of wax on furniture is to prevent penetration of moisture.   19.____

20. According to the above paragraph, water stains can be removed by FIRST applying a small amount of linseed oil.   20.____

21. According to the above paragraph, it is good practice to apply frequent coats of oil polish.   21.____

22. According to the above paragraph, one reason for the excess moisture that collects on furniture in the winter time is poor ventilation.   22.____

23. As used in the above paragraph, the word *trim* means *walls*.   23.____

24. As used in the above paragraph, the word *marred* means *damaged*.   24.____

25. As used in the above paragraph, the word *applied* means *rubbed*.   25.____

KEY (CORRECT ANSWERS)

1.	D		11.	F
2.	A		12.	T
3.	C		13.	F
4.	B		14.	F
5.	A		15.	F
6.	A		16.	T
7.	C		17.	F
8.	D		18.	T
9.	F		19.	T
10.	T		20.	F

21.	F
22.	T
23.	F
24.	T
25.	F

TEST 3

DIRECTIONS: Each question consists of a statement. You are to indicate whether the statement is TRUE (T) or FALSE (F). *PRINT THE LETTER OF THE CORRECT ANSWER IN THE SPACE AT THE RIGHT.*

Questions 1 -7.

DIRECTIONS: Questions 1 through 7, inclusive, are to be answered in accordance with the paragraph below.

There are several types of lines in a blueprint. The solid line that represents edges of surfaces are somewhat heavier than the other lines on the drawing and are known as working lines. These lines may be straight or curved, depending upon the shape and view of the object. Dotted lines are the same as working lines, except that the surface which is represented by dotted lines is hidden from sight when the object is viewed. To show the size of any structure, or part of it, dimension lines are used. These lines are light lines drawn between two working lines to show the dimensions between two points. If the dimension lines cannot readily be placed on view, the working lines are lengthened or extended in order that the dimension lines may be drawn. These lines are known as extension lines. A shaded area of a drawing made by a series of parallel lines drawn close together at any angle to the working lines of the view is sometimes found on a blueprint. These are known as section lines. They represent what would be seen if that part of the view covered by such lines were cut through and a portion removed.

1. The number of different types of blueprint lines described in the above paragraph is 4. 1.____

2. According to the above paragraph, the HEAVIEST lines on a blueprint are usually the working lines. 2.____

3. According to the above paragraph, extension lines are continuations of working lines 3.____

4. The following line appears on a blueprint 6'4". According to the above paragraph, this line is BEST described as a dimension line. 4.____

5. According to the above paragraph, the shaded area of a blueprint represents what would be seen if that part of the view were cut through and a portion removed. 5.____

6. According to the above paragraph, dimension lines may appear between two section lines. 6.____

7. According to the above paragraph, a series of parallel lines drawn close together at an angle to the working lines are the dotted lines. 7.____

Questions 8-14.

DIRECTIONS: Questions 8 through 14, inclusive, are to be answered in accordance with the paragraph below.

Native species of trees are divided into two *classes*-hardwoods, which have broad leaves, and softwoods, which have scalelike leaves, as the cedars, or needlelike leaves, as the pines. Hardwoods, except in the warmest regions, shed their leaves at the end of each growing season. Native softwoods, except cypress, tamarack and larch, are evergreen. The terms *hardwood* and *softwood* have no direct application to the hardness or softness of the wood. In fact, such hardwood trees as cottonwood and aspen have softer wood than the white pines and true firs, and *certain* softwoods, such as longleaf pine and Douglas-fir, produce wood that is as hard as that of basswood and yellow-poplar.

8. According to the above paragraph, softwoods are differentiated from hardwoods by the types of leaves.

8._____

9. According to the above paragraph, if a tree sheds its leaves in the winter, you can be sure it is a hardwood.

9._____

10. According to the above paragraph, an example of a tree that stays green throughout the year is cypress.

10._____

11. According to the above paragraph, hardwoods are NOT necessarily *harder* than softwoods.

11._____

12. According to the above paragraph, one of the *harder* softwoods is basswood.

12._____

13. As used in the above paragraph, *classes* means *groups*.

13._____

14. As used in the above paragraph, *certain* means *sure*.

14.

Questions 15-20.

DIRECTIONS: Questions 15 through 20, inclusive, are to be answered in accordance with the paragraph below.

Sometimes it is impossible to scrape and sand out all blemishes and defects in the wood surfaces. Nail holes left where nailheads have been set below the surface, dents, checks, and pits caused by faulty grain, especially in cedar, usually cannot be removed from the surface. It, therefore, is necessary to fill these defects with a special filler. Some of the better types of fillers used for this purpose include colored stick shellac, plastic wood, and various *types* of crack fillers. It is especially important to use a filler that will match the color of the wood when it is finished. It is *usually* best to stain a scrap piece of wood with the stain that is to be used on the finished project and match the color of the filler to it. Stick shellac and plastic wood may be obtained in various colors, but these colors cannot be changed satisfactorily. Crack fillers may be obtained in various colors and may also be colored to match the color of the stain being used.

15. According to the above paragraph, one of the defects often found in wood is knots.

15._____

16. According to the above paragraph, the BEST method of insuring good color match is to first test the color on a piece of scrap wood.

16._____

17. According to the above paragraph, the one of the types of fillers whose color can be changed is *crack filler*.

17._____

18. According to the above paragraph, it is fairly easy to remove defects from the surface of the wood.

18._____

19. As used in the above paragraph, the word *usually* means *frequently*.

19._____

20. As used in the above paragraph, the word *types* means *kinds.*   20.____

Questions 21-25.

DIRECTIONS: Questions 21 through 25, inclusive, are to be answered in accordance with the paragraph below.

By *squaring stock* is meant the process of working all the surfaces of the stock until they have been made smooth and true, until they are at right angles to the adjoining surfaces, and until opposite surfaces are *parallel* to each other. The quality of your finished project will be determined largely by your ability to square stock quickly and accurately. The *process* of squaring stock is the fundamental basis of all woodworking. Each part of the piece should be accurately squared to *dimensions* in order to insure a proper fit when joined with the other parts of the project.

21. According to the above paragraph, one of the reasons for squaring stock is so that the pieces will fit properly when joined.   21.____

22. According to the above paragraph, the quality of the work will depend upon how accurately you can square.   22.____

23. As used in the above paragraph, the word *parallel* means *at right angles.*   23.____

24. As used in the above paragraph, the word *process* means *ability.*   24.____

25. As used in the above paragraph, the word *dimensions* means *sizes*   25.____

KEY (CORRECT ANSWERS)

1.	F		11.	T
2.	T		12.	F
3.	T		13.	T
4.	T		14.	F
5.	T		15.	F
6.	F		16.	T
7.	F		17.	T
8.	T		18.	F
9.	F		19.	F
10.	F		20.	T

21.	T
22.	T
23.	F
24.	F
25.	T

FRAME CONSTRUCTION

Section I. FLOOR FRAMES AND FLOOR COVERINGS

1. Framing

After the foundation is built and the batterboards placed, the carpenter builds the framework. The framework includes the beams, trusses, foundation walls, outside walls, flooring, partitions, roofing, and ceiling.

a. Light Framing. Light framing is used in barracks, bathhouses, administration buildings, light shop buildings, hospitals, and similar buildings. Figure 1 shows some details for a 20-foot-wide building; the ground level; window openings, braces, and splices; and names the framing parts.

b. Light Frame Construction. Much of the framing can be done while staking out and squaring is being completed. When the skeleton is far enough along, boards can be nailed on without need for cutting if they are standard 8-, 10-, 12-, 16-, or 18-foot lengths. The better skilled men should construct the frame. With good organization, a large force of men can be kept busy during framing.

c. Expedient Framing. Expedient framing depends on the conditions. The ideas below may suggest other expedients.

(1) *Light siding.* Chicken wire and water resistant bituminous paper can be sandwiched to provide adequate temporary framing in temperate climates.

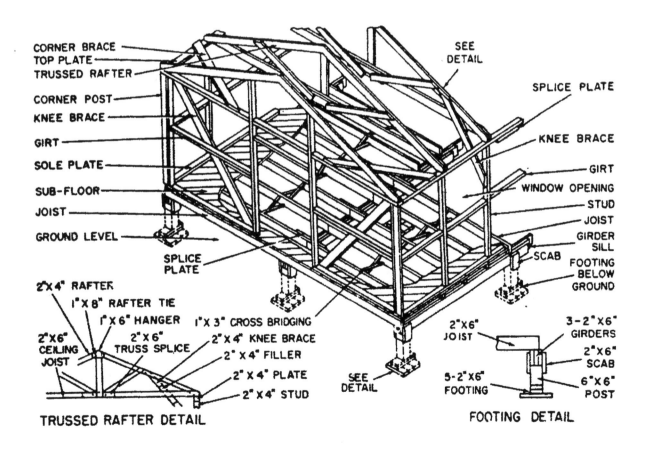

Figure 1. View of a light frame building substructure.

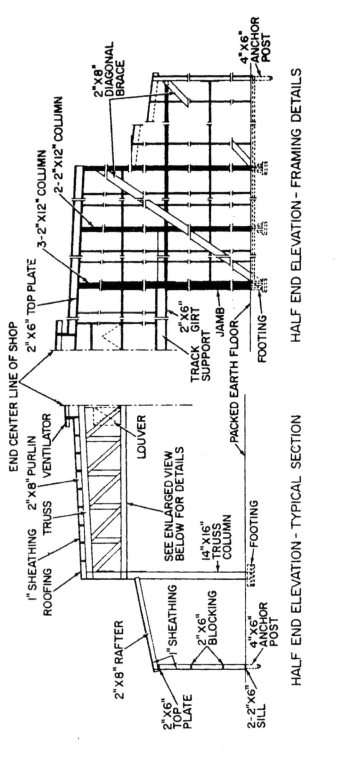

2"x8" DIAGONAL BRACE

2-2"x12" COLUMN

3-2"x12" COLUMN

2"x6" TOP PLATE

END CENTER LINE OF SHOP

2"x8" PURLIN

TRUSS VENTILATOR

I" SHEATHING

ROOFING

TRUSS

2"x8" RAFTER

2"x6" TOP PLATE

I" SHEATHING

2"x6" BLOCKING

2-2"x6" SILL

4"x6" ANCHOR POST

LOUVER

SEE ENLARGED VIEW BELOW FOR DETAILS

14"x16" TRUSS COLUMN

FOOTING

4"x6" ANCHOR POST

2"x6" GIRT

JAMB

TRACK SUPPORT

PACKED EARTH FLOOR

FOOTING

HALF END ELEVATION - FRAMING DETAILS

HALF END ELEVATION - TYPICAL SECTION

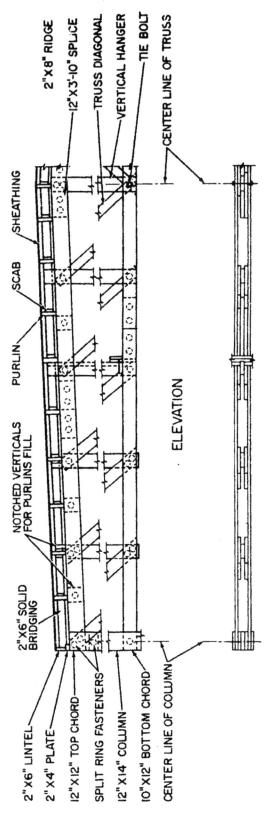

2"x8" RIDGE

12"x3'-10" SPLICE

TRUSS DIAGONAL

VERTICAL HANGER

TIE BOLT

CENTER LINE OF TRUSS

SHEATHING

SCAB

PURLIN

NOTCHED VERTICALS FOR PURLINS FILL

2"x6" SOLID BRIDGING

2"x6" LINTEL

2"x4" PLATE

12"x12" TOP CHORD

SPLIT RING FASTENERS

12"x14" COLUMN

10"x12" BOTTOM CHORD

CENTER LINE OF COLUMN

ELEVATION

TOP VIEW OF BOTTOM CHORD

Figure 2. Sectional view of a heavy frame building.

(2) *Salvaged framing.* Salvaged sheet metal such as corrugated material or gasoline cans can be used as siding in the construction of emergency housing.

(3) *Local timber.* Poles trimmed from saplings or bamboo can be constructed into reasonably sound framing. Such materials may be secured with native vines as a further expedient.

(4) *Wood substitute framing.* Adobe soil, straw, and water puddled to proper consistency can be used for form walls, floors, and foundations. A similar mixture may be used to form sun-dried bricks for construction use.

(5) *Excavations.* Proper excavation and simple log cribbing may be covered with sod and carefully drained to provide adequate shelter.

d. Heavy Framing. Heavy frame buildings are more permanent, generally warehouses, depots, and shops. Figure   2 shows the details of heavy frame construction.

2. Sills

a. Types. The sill (fig.   1) is the foundation that supports all the building above it. It is the first part of the building to be set in place. It rests directly on the foundation piers or on the ground; it is joined at the corners and spliced when necessary. Figure   3 shows the most common sills. The type used depends on the type of construction used in the frame.

(1) *Box sills.* Box sills are used often with the very common style of platform framing, either with or without the sill plate. In this type of sill (1 and 2, fig.   3), the part that lies on the foundation wall or ground is called the sill plate. The sill is laid edgewise on the outside edge of the sill plate.

(2) *T-sills.* There are two types of T-sill construction; one commonly used in dry, warm climates (3, fig.   3), and one commonly used in less warm climates (4, fig.   3). Their construction is similar except that in the latter case the joists are nailed directly to the studs, as well as to the sills, and headers are used between the floor joists.

(3) *Braced framing sill.* The sill shown in 5, figure   3, is generally used in braced-framing construction. The floor joists are notched out and nailed directly to the sill and studs.

(4) *Built-up sills.* Where built-up sills are used, the joints are staggered (1, fig.   4). The corner joints are made as shown in 2, figure 4.

b. Sill Requirement for Piers. If piers are used in the foundation, heavier sills are used. They

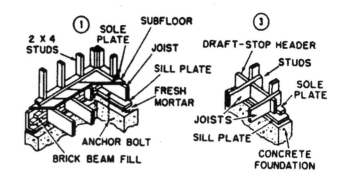

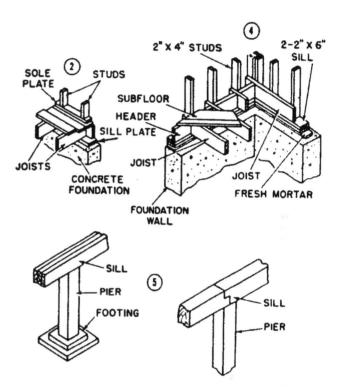

Figure   3. Types of sills.

are single heavy timbers or built up of two or more pieces of timber. Where heavy timber or built-up sills are used, the joints should occur over piers. The size of the sill depends upon the load to be carried and upon the spacing of the piers. The sill plates are laid directly on graded earth or on piers. Where earth floors are used, the studs are nailed directly to the sill plate.

3. Girders

The distance between two outside walls is often too great to be spanned by a single joist. When two or more joists are needed to cover the span, intermediate support for inboard joist-ends is provided by one or more girders. A girder is a large beam that supports other smaller beams or joists.

a. Construction. A girder may be made up of

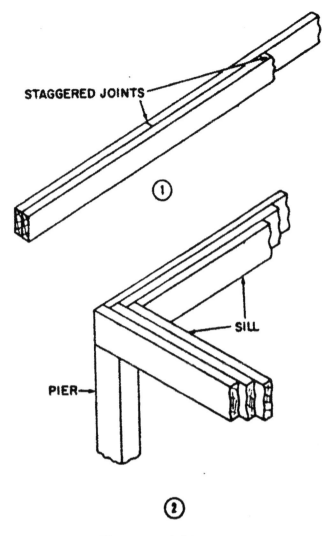

STAGGERED JOINTS

①

SILL

PIER

②

Figure 4. Sill fabrication.

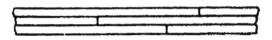

PLAN VIEW OF GIRDER SHOWING
METHOD OF STAGGERING JOINTS

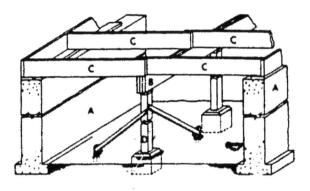

Figure 5. Built-up girder.

d. Use of Ledger Board. A girder with a ledge board upon which the joists rest is used where vertical space is limited. This arrangement is useful in providing more headroom in basements.

several beams nailed together with 16d common nails; or it may be solid wood, steel, reinforced concrete, or a combination of these materials.

b. Design Requirements. Girders carry a very large proportion of the weight of a building. They must be well designed, rigid, and properly supported at the foundation walls and on the columns. Precautions must be taken to avoid or counteract any future settling or shrinking that might cause distortion of the building. The girders must also be installed so that they will properly support joists.

c. Illustration. Figure 5 shows a built-up girder. A shows the two outside masonry walls, B the built-up girder, C the joists, and D the support columns which support the girder B. Notice that the joists rest on top of the girder. This type of girder is commonly used in house construction. It is generally made of three planks spiked together (fig. 5) with 16d common nails.

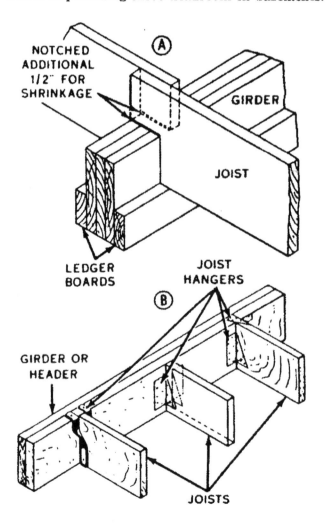

NOTCHED
ADDITIONAL
1/2" FOR
SHRINKAGE

Ⓐ

GIRDER

JOIST

LEDGER
BOARDS

JOIST
HANGERS

Ⓑ

GIRDER OR
HEADER

JOISTS

Figure 6. Joist-to-girder attachment.

e. Joist Hangers. A girder over which joist hangers have been placed to carry the joists is also used where there is little headroom or where the joists carry an extremely heavy load and nailing cannot be relied on. These girders are illustrated in figure 6.

f. Size Requirements. The principles which govern the size of a girder are—

(1) The distance between girder posts.

(2) The girder load area.

(3) The total floor load per square foot on the girder.

(4) The load per linear foot on the girder.

(5) The total load on the girder.

(6) The material to be used.

g. Size Determination. A girder should be large enough to support any ordinary load placed upon it; any size larger than that is wasted material. The carpenter should understand the effect of length, width, and depth on the strength of a wood girder before attempting to determine its size.

h. Depth. When the depth of a girder is doubled, the safe load is increased four times. In other words, a girder that is 3 inches wide and 12 inches de·p will carry four times as much wight as a girder 3 inches wide and 6 inches deep. In order to obtain greater carrying capacity through the efficient use of material, it is better to increase the depth within limits than it is to increase the width of the girder. The sizes of built-up wood girders for various loads and spans may be determined by using table 1. (LOCATED IN BACK OF CHAPTER)

i. Load Area. The load area of a building is carried by both foundation walls and the girder. Because the ends of each joist rest on the girder, there is more weight on the girder than there is on either of the walls. Before considering the load on the girder, it may be well to consider a single joist. Suppose that a 10-foot plank weighing 5 pounds per foot is lifted by two men. If the men were at opposite ends of the plank, they would each be supporting 25 pounds.

(1) Now assume that one of these men lifts the end of another 10-foot plank with the same weight as the first one, and a third man lifts the opposite end. The two men on the outside are each supporting one-half of the weight of one plank, or 25 pounds apiece, but the man in the center is supporting one-half of each of the two planks, or a total of 50 pounds.

(2) The two men on the outside represent the foundation walls, and the center man represents the girder; therefore, the girder carries one-half of the weight, while the other half is equally divided between the outside walls. However, the girder may not always be located halfway between the outer walls. To explain this, the same three men will lift two planks which weigh 5 pounds per foot. One of the planks is 8 feet long and the other is 12 feet long. Since the total length of these two planks is the same as before and the weight per foot is the same, the total weight in both cases is 100 pounds.

(3) One of the outside men is supporting one-half of the 8-foot plank, or 20 pounds. The man on the opposite outside end is supporting one-half of the 12-foot plank, or 30 pounds. The man in the center is supporting one-half of each plank, or a total of 50 pounds. This is the same total weight he was lifting before. A general rule that can be applied when determining the girder load area is that a girder will carry the weight of the floor on each side to the midpoint of joists which rest upon it.

j. Floor Load. After the girder load area is known, the total floor load per square foot must be determined in order to select a safe girder size. Both dead and live loads must be considered in finding the total floor load.

(1) The first type of load consists of all weight of the building structure. This is called the dead load. The dead load per square foot of floor area, which is carried to the girder either directly or indirectly by way of bearing partitions, will vary according to the method of construction and building height. The structural parts included in the dead load are—

Floor joists for all floor levels.

Flooring materials, including attic if it is floored.

Bearing partitions.

Attic partitions.

Attic joists for top floor.

Ceiling lath and plaster, including basement ceiling if it is plastered.

(2) For a building of light-frame construction similar to an ordinary frame house, the dead load allowance per square foot of all the structural parts must be added together to determine the total dead load. The allowance for average subfloor, finish floor, and joists without basement plaster should be 10 pounds per square foot. If the basement ceiling is plastered, an additional 10 pounds should be allowed. When girders (or bearing partitions) support the first floor partition, a load allowance of 20 pounds must be

allowed for ceiling plaster and joists when the attic is unfloored. If the attic is floored and used for storage, an additional 10 pounds (per sq ft) should be allowed.

(3) The second type of load to be considered is the weight of furniture, persons, and other movable loads which are not actually a part of the building but are still carried by the girder. This is called the live load. Snow on the roof is considered a part of the live load. The live load per square foot will vary according to the use of the building and local weather conditions. The allowance for the live load on floors used for living purposes is usually 30 pounds per square foot. If the attic is floored and used for light storage, an additional 20 pounds per square foot should be allowed. The allowance per square foot for live loads is usually governed by specifications and regulations.

(4) When the total load per square foot of floor area is known, the load per linear foot on the girder is easily figured. Assume that the girder load area of the building shown in figure 7 is sliced into 1-foot lengths across the girder. Each slice represents the weight supported by 1 foot of the girder. If the slice is divided into 1-foot units, each unit will represent 1 square foot of the total floor area. The load per linear foot of girder is determined by multiplying the number of units by the total load per square foot. Note in figure 7 that the girder is off center. Therefore, the joist length on one side of the girder is 7 feet (one-half of 14 feet) and the other side is 5 feet (one-half of 10 feet), for a total distance of 12 feet across the load area. Since each slice is 1 foot wide, it has a total floor area of 12 square feet. Now, if we assume that the total floor load for each square foot is 70 pounds, multiply the length times the width (7' x 12') to get the total square feet supported by the girder (7' x 12' = 84 sq ft).

```
     84 sq ft
x   70 lb per sq ft (live and dead load)
 5,880 lb total load on girder
```

k. Material. Wooden girders are more common than steel in small frame-type buildings. Solid timber may be used or they may be built up by using two or more 2-inch planks. Built-up girders have the advantage of not warping as easily as solid wooden girders and are less likely to have decayed wood in the center.

(1) When built-up girders are used, the pieces should be securely spiked together to prevent them from buckling individually. A two-

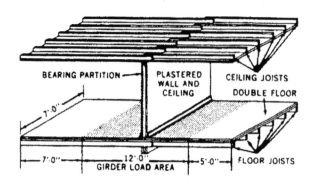

Figure 7. Girder load area.

piece girder of 2-inch planks should be spiked on both sides with 16d common nails. The nails should be located near the bottom, spaced approximately 2 feet apart near the ends and 1 foot apart in the center. A three-piece girder should be nailed in the same way as a two-piece girder.

(2) Regardless of whether the girder is built-up or solid, it should be of well-seasoned material. For a specific total girder load and span, the size of the girder will vary according to the kinds of wood used. The reason for this variation is that some kinds are stronger than others.

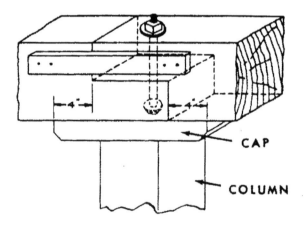

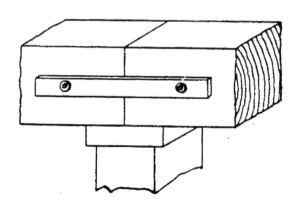

Figure 8. Half-lap and butt joints.

l. Splicing. To make a built-up girder, select straight lumber free from knots and other defects. The stock should be long enough so that no more than one joint will occur over the span between footings. The joints in the beam should be staggered, with care taken to insure that the planks are squared at each joint and butted tightly together. Sometimes a half-lap joint is used to join solid beams. In order to do this correctly, the beam should be placed on one edge so that the annual rings run from top to bottom. The lines for the half-lap joint are then laid out as illustrated in figure 8, and the cuts are made along these lines. The cuts are then checked with a steel square to assure a matching joint. To make the matching joint on the other beam, proceed in the same way and repeat the process.

(1) The next step is to tack a temporary strap across the joint to hold it tightly together. Now drill a hole through the joist with a bit about 1/16 inch larger than the bolt to be used. Fasten together with a bolt, washer, and nut.

(2) Another type of joint is called the strapped butt joint. The ends of the beam should be cut square, and the straps, which generally are 18 inches long, are bolted to each side of the beams.

m. Supports. When building small houses where the services of an architect are not available, it is important that the carpenter have some knowledge of the principles that determine the proper size of girder supports.

(1) A column or post is a vertical member designed to carry the live and dead loads imposed upon it. It may be made of wood, metal, or masonry. The wooden columns may be solid timbers or may be made up of several wooden members spiked together with 16d or 20d common nails. Metal columns are made of heavy pipe, large steel angles, or I-beams.

(2) Regardless of the material used in a column, it must have some form of bearing plate at the top and bottom. These plates distribute the load evenly over the cross sectional area of the column. Basement posts that support girders should be set on masonry footings. Columns should be securely fastened to the load-bearing member at the top and to the footing on which they rest at the bottom. Figure 9 shows a solid wooden column with a metal bearing cap drilled to provide a means of fastening it to the column and to the girder. The bottom of this type of column may be fastened to the masonry footing by a metal dowel inserted in a hole drilled in the bottom of the column and in the

masonry footing. The base at this point is coated with asphalt to prevent rust or rot.

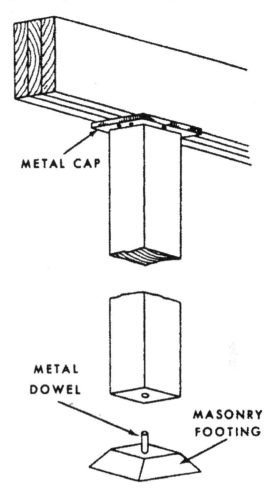

Figure 9. Solid wood column with metal bearing cap.

(3) When locating columns, it is well to avoid spans of more than 10 feet between columns that are to support the girders. The farther apart the columns are spaced, the heavier the girder must be to carry the joists over the span between the columns.

(4) A good arrangement of the girder and supporting columns for a 24- x 40-foot building is shown in figure 10. Column B will support one-half of the girder load existing in the half of the building lying between the wall A and column C. Column C will support one-half of the girder load between columns B and D. Likewise, column D will share equally the girder loads with column C and the wall E.

n. Girder Forms. Girder forms for making concrete girders and beams are constructed from 2-inch-thick material (fig. 11) dressed on all sides. The bottom piece of material should be constructed in one piece to avoid the necessity of cleats. The bottom piece of the form should never

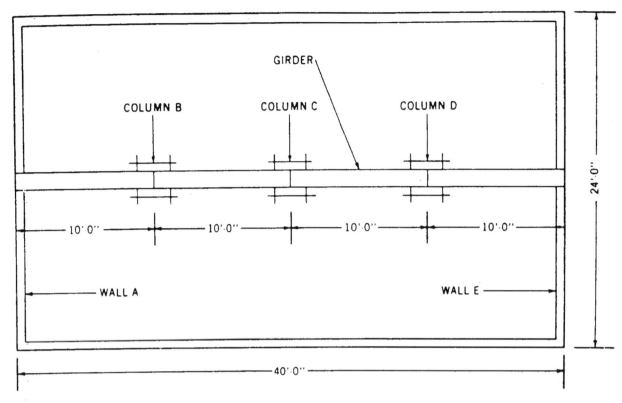

Figure 10. Column spacing.

overlap the side pieces. The side pieces must always overlap the bottom. The temporary cleats shown in figure 11 are tacked on to prevent the form from collapsing when handled.

4. Floor Joists

Joists are the wooden members that make up the body of the floor frame. The flooring or subflooring is nailed to them. They are usually 2 or 3 inches thick. Joists as small as 2 by 6 inches are sometimes used in light buildings. These are too small for floors with spans over 10 feet but are frequently used for ceiling joists. Joists usually carry a uniform load of materials and personnel. The latter loads carry a uniform

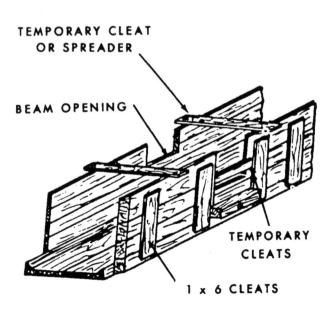

Figure 11. Girder and beam form.

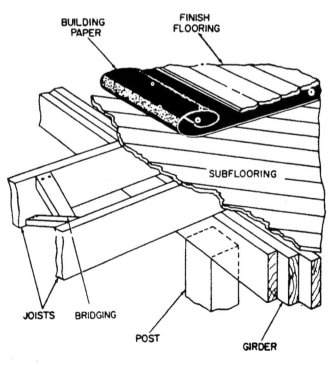

Figure 12. Floor joists.

load of materials and personnel. The latter loads are "live loads"; the weight of joists and floors is a "dead load". The joists carry the flooring directly on their upper surface and they are supported at their ends by sills, girders, bearing partitions, or bearing walls (fig. 12). They are spaced 16 or 24 inches apart, center to center; sometimes the spacing is 12 inches, but where such spacing is necessary, heavier joists should

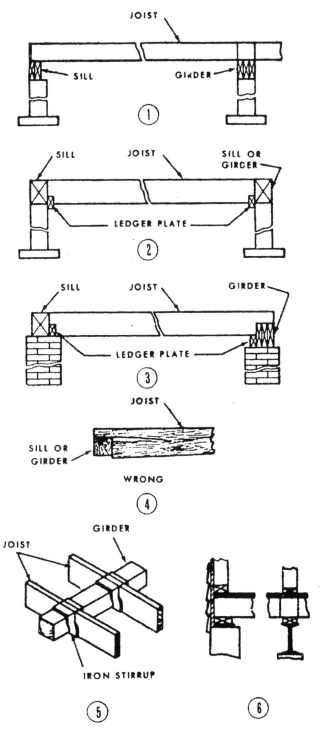

Figure 13. Sill and joist connections.

be used. Two-inch material should not be used for joists more than 12 inches apart.

5. Connecting Joists to Sills, Girders, and I-Beams

a. Joining to Sills. In joining joists to sills, be sure that the connection is able to hold the load that the joists will carry. A joist resting upon the sill is shown in 1, figure 13. This method (of several methods) is most commonly used because it provides the strongest possible joint. The methods shown in 2 and 3, figure 13, are used where it is not desirable to use joists on top of the sill. The ledger plate (*e* below) should be securely nailed and the joist should not be notched over one-third of its depth to prevent splitting (4, fig. 13).

b. Joining to Girders. In the framing of the joists to the girders, the joists must be level. Therefore, if the girder is not the same height as the sill, the joist must be notched as shown in 3, figure 13. If the girder and sill are of the same height, the joist must be connected to the sill and girder to keep the joist level. In placing joists, always have the crown up since this counteracts the weight on the joist; in most cases there will be no sag below a straight line. Overhead joists are joined to plates as shown in 1 and 2, figure 14. The inner end of the joist rests on the plates of the partition walls. When a joist is to rest on plates or girders, either the joist is cut long enough to extend the full width of the plate or girder, or it is cut so as to meet in the center of the plate or girder and is connected with a scab. Where two joist ends lie side by side on a plate, they should be nailed together. Joists may also be joined to girders by using ledger strips (3 and 4, fig. 14).

c. Iron Stirrups. One of the strongest supports for the joists is straps or hangers (iron stirrups) as shown in 5 of figure 13.

d. I-Beams. The simplest and probably the best way to carry joists on steel girders is to rest them on top, as shown in 6, figure 13, provided headroom is not too much restricted. If there is a lack of headroom, use the method shown in 5, figure 13.

e. Use of Ledger Plates (fig. 14). In connecting joists to girders and sills where piers are used, a 2 by 4 is nailed to the face of the sill or girder, flush with the bottom edge; this is called a "ledger plate" (1, fig. 14). These pieces should be nailed securely with 20-penny nails about 12 inches apart. Where 2 by 4 or 2

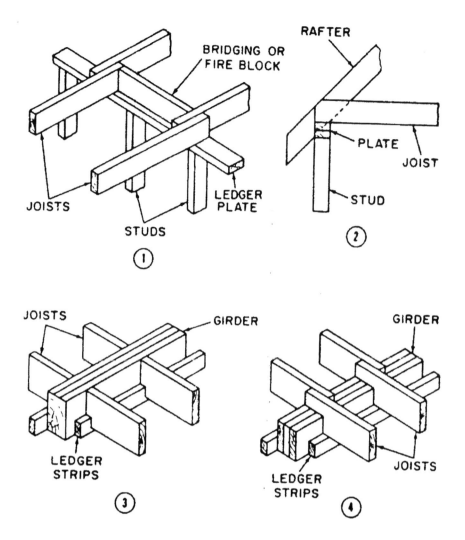

Figure 14. Ledger plates.

by 8 joists are used, it is better to use 2 by 2's to prevent the joists from splitting at the notch. When joists are 10 inches deep and deeper, 2 by 4's may be used without reducing the strength of the joists. If a notch is used, joist ties may be used to overcome this loss of strength. These ties are short 1 by 4 boards nailed across the joist; the ends of the boards are flush with the top and bottom edge of the joists.

6. Bridging

a. General. When joists are used over a long span, they have a tendency to sway from side to side. Floor frames are bridged in order to stiffen the floor frame, to prevent unequal deflection of the joists, and to enable an overload joist to receive some help from the joists on either side of it. A pattern for the bridging stock is obtained by placing a piece of material between the joists as shown in figure 15, then marking and sawing it. When sawed, the cut will form the correct

angle. Always nail the top of the bridging with 8- or 10-penny nails. Do not nail the bottom of the bridging until the rough floor has been laid, in order to keep the bridging from pushing up any joist which might cause an unevenness in the floor.

b. Construction. Bridging is of two kinds: solid (or horizontal) bridging (1, fig. 15) and cross bridging (2, fig. 15). Cross bridging is the one most generally used; it is very effective and requires less material than horizontal bridging. Cross bridging looks like a cross and consists of pieces of lumber, usually 1 by 3 or 2 by 3 inches in size, cut in diagonally between the floor joists. Each piece is nailed to the top of each joist and forms a cross (x) between the joists. These pieces between joists should be placed as near to each other as possible. Bridging should be nailed and the bottoms left until the subfloor is laid. This permits the joists to adjust themselves to their final positions. The bottom ends of bridging

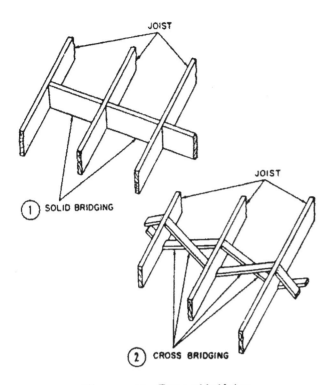

Figure 15. Types of bridging.

may then be nailed, forming a continuous truss across the whole length of the floor and preventing any overloaded joist from sagging below the others. Cutting and fitting the bridging by hand is a slow process; a power saw should be used if it is available. After joists have once been placed, a pattern may be made and used to speed up the process of cutting. On joists over 8 feet long, one line of bridging should be placed and on joists over 16 feet long, two lines.

7. Floor Openings

a. General. Floor openings for stairwells, ventilators, and chimneys are framed by a combination of headers and trimmers (fig. 16). Headers run at right angles to the direction of the joists and are doubled. Trimmers run parallel to the joists and are actually doubled joists. The joists are framed to the headers where the headers form the opening frame at right angles to the joists. These shorter joists, framed to the headers, are called tail beams, tail joists, or header joists. The number of headers and trimmers needed at any opening depends upon the shape of the opening, whether it is a simple rectangle or contains additional angles; upon the direction in which the opening runs in relation to the direction in which the joists run; and upon the position of the opening in relation to partitions or walls. Figure 16 gives examples of openings, one of which runs parallel to the

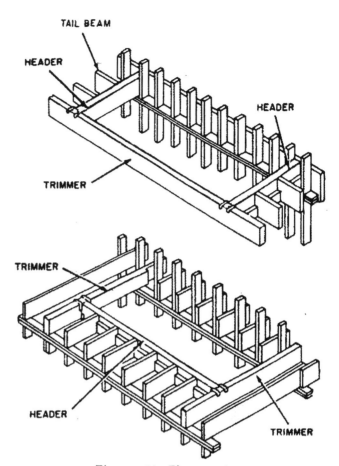

Figure 16. Floor openings.

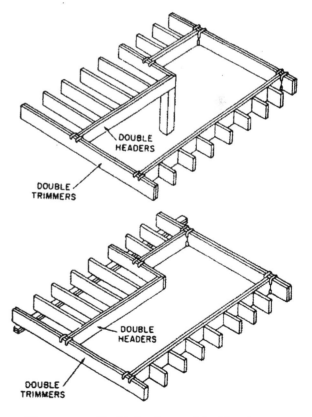

Figure 17. Double headers and double trimmers.

joist and requires two headers and one trimmer, while the other runs at right angles to the run of the joists and, therefore, requires one header and two trimmers. The openings shown in figure 17 are constructed with corner angles supported in different ways. The cantilever method requires that the angle be fairly close to a supporting partition with joists from an adjacent span that run to the header.

b. Construction. To frame openings of the type shown in figure 18, first install joists A and C, then cut four pieces of timber that are the same size as the joists with their length corresponding to the distance between the joists A and C at the outside wall. Nail two of these pieces between the joists at the desired distances from the ends of the joists; these pieces are shown as headers Nos. 1 and 2, figure 18. Install short joists X and Y, as shown. The nails should be 16- or 20-penny nails. By omitting headers Nos. 3 and 4 and joists B and D, the short joists X and Y can be nailed in place through the header and the headers can be nailed through the joists A and B into its end. After the header and short joists have been securely nailed, headers Nos. 3 and 4 are nailed beside Nos. 1 and 2. Then joist B is placed beside joists A and joist D beside C, and all are nailed securely.

8. Subfloors and Finish Floors

a. Subfloors. After the foundation and basic framework of a building are completed, the floor is constructed. The subfloor, if included in the plans, is laid diagonally on the joists and nailed with 8- to 10-penny nails. The floor joists form a framework for the subfloor. Subflooring boards 8 inches wide or over should have three or more nails per joist. Where the subfloor is over 1 inch thick, larger nails should be used. Figure 12

shows the method of laying a subfloor. Preferably it is laid before the walls are framed so that it can be used as a floor to work on while framing the walls.

b. Finish Floors.

(1) *General.* A finish floor in the theater of operations, in most cases, is of 3/4-inch material, square edged (fig. 19) or tongued and grooved (fig. 20), and varying from 3 1/4 to 7 1/4 inches wide. It is laid directly on floor joists or on a subfloor and nailed with 8-penny common nails in every joist. When laid on a subfloor, it is best to use building paper between the two floors to keep out dampness and insects. In warehouses, where heavy loads are to be carried on the floor, 2-inch material should be used. The flooring, in this case, also is face-nailed with 16- or 20-penny nails. It is not tongued and grooved and ranges in width from 4 to 12 inches. The joints are made on the center of the joist.

(2) *Wood floors.* Wood floors must be strong enough to carry the load. The type of building and the use for which it is intended determines the general arrangement of the floor system,

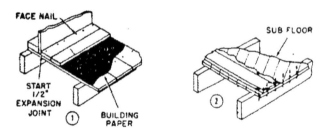

Figure 19. Methods for nailing square-edged flooring.

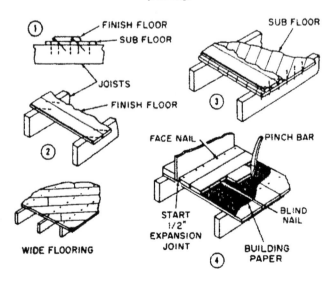

Figure 20. Methods for nailing tongued-and-grooved flooring.

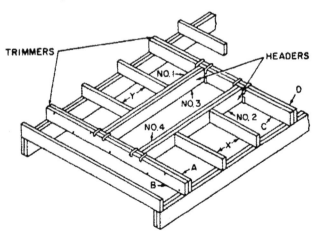

Figure 18. Floor opening construction.

thickness of the sheathing, and approximate spacing of the joists.

(3) *Concrete floors.* Concrete floors may be constructed for shops where earthen or wood floors are not suitable such as in repair and assembly shops for airplanes and heavy equipment and in certain kinds of warehouses. These floors are made by pouring concrete on the ground after the earth has been graded and tamped. This type of floor is likely to be damp unless protected. Drainage is provided, both for the floor area and for the area near the floor, to prevent flooding after heavy rains. The floor should be reinforced with steel or wire mesh. Where concrete floors are to be poured, a foundation wall may be poured first and the floor poured after the building is completed. This gives protection to the concrete floor while it sets.

(4) *Miscellaneous types of floors.* Miscellaneous floors may include earth, adobe brick, duckboard, or rushes. Use of miscellaneous flooring is usually determined by a shortage of conventional materials, the need to save time or labor, the extremely temporary nature of the facilities, or the special nature of the structure. The selection of material is usually determined by availability. Duckboard is widely used for shower flooring; earthen floors are common and conserve both materials and labor if the ground site is even without extensive grading. Rush or thatch floors are primarily an insulating measure and must be replaced frequently.

(5) *Supports.* In certain parts of the floor frame, in order to support some very heavily concentrated load or a partition wall, it may be necessary to double the joist or to place two joists together (fig. 21).

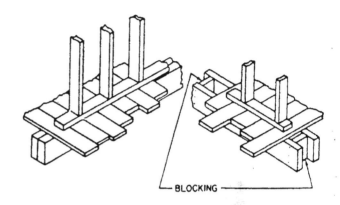

Figure 21. Reinforced joists.

Section II. WALLS AND WALL COVERINGS

9. General

Wall framing (fig. 22) is composed of regular studs, diagonal bracing, cripples, trimmers, headers, and fire blocks and is supported by the floor sole plate. The vertical members of the wall framing are the studs, which support the top plates and all of the weight of the upper part of the building or everything above the top plate line. They provide the framework to which the wall sheathing is aniled on the outside and which supports the lath, plaster, and insulation on the inside.

10. Wall Components

Walls and partitions which are classed as framed constructions (fig. 23) are composed of structural elements which are usually closely spaced, slender, vertical members called studs. These are arranged in a row with their ends bearing on a long horizontal member called a bottom plate or sole plate, and their tops capped with another plate, called a top plate. Double top plates are used in bearing walls and partitions. The bearing strength of stud walls is determined by the strength of the studs.

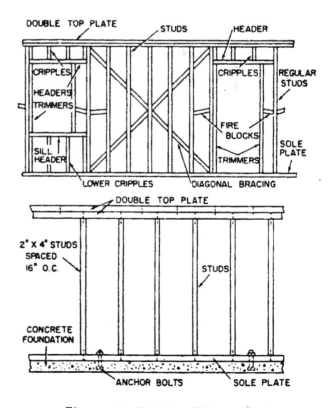

Figure 22. Typical wall frame details.

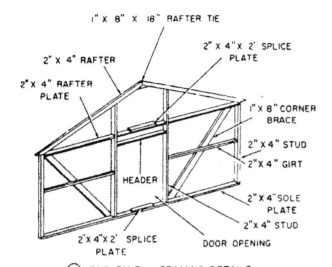

① END PANEL - FRAMING DETAILS

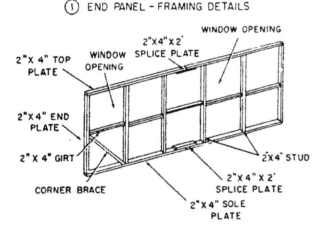

② SIDE PANEL - FRAMING DETAILS

Figure 23. Typical wall construction showing openings.

a. *Corner Posts.* The studs used at the corners of frame construction are usually built up from three or more ordinary studs to provide greater strength. These built-up assemblies are corner-partition posts. The corner posts are set up, plumbed, and temporarily braced. The corner posts (fig. 24) may be made in the following ways:

(1) A corner post may consist of a 4 by 6 with a 2 by 4 nailed on the board side, flush with one edge, as shown in figure 24. This type of corner is for a 4-inch wall. Where walls are thicker, heavier timber is used.

(2) A 4 by 4 may be used with a 2 by 4 nailed to two of the adjoining sides, shown in 2, figure 24.

(3) Two 2 by 4's may be nailed together with blocks between and a 2 by 4 flush with one edge, shown in 3, figure 24.

(4) A 2 by 4 may be nailed to the edge of another 2 by 4, the edge of one flush with the side of the other (4, fig. 24). This type is used extensively in the theater of operations where no inside finish is needed.

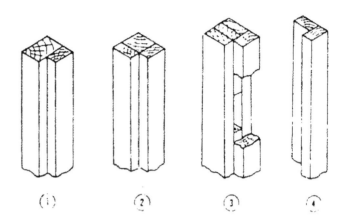

Figure 24. Corner post construction.

b. *T-Posts.* Whenever a partition meets an outside wall, a stud wide enough to extend beyond the partition on both sides is used; this provides a solid nailing base for the inside wall finish. This type of stud is called a T-post (fig. 25) and is made in the following different ways:

(1) A 2 by 4 may be nailed and centered on the face side of a 4 by 6 (1, fig. 25).

(2) A 2 by 4 may be nailed and centered on two 4 by 4's nailed together (2, fig. 25).

(3) Two 2 by 4's may be nailed together with a block between them and a 2 by 4 centered on the wide side (3, fig. 25).

(4) A 2 by 4 may be nailed and centered on the face side of a 2 by 6, with a horizontal bridging nailed behind them to give support and stiffness (4, fig. 25).

c. *Partition and Double T-Posts.* Where a partition is finished on one side only, the partition post used consists of a simple stud, set in the outside wall, in line with the side of the partition

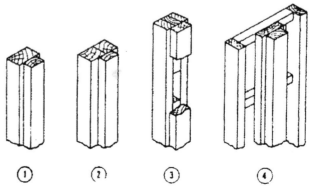

Figure 25. T-post construction.

wall, and finished as stud A in 1, figure 26. These posts are nailed in place along with the corner post. The exact position of the partition walls must be determined before the posts are placed. Where the walls are more than 4 inches thick, wider timber is used. In special cases, for example where partition walls cross, a double T-post is used. This is made by using methods in *b*(1), (2), or (3) above, and nailing another 2 by 4 to the opposite wide side, as shown in 2, 3, and 4, figure 26.

d. Studs.

(1) After the sills, plates, and braces are in place, and the window and door openings are laid out, the studs are placed and nailed with two 16- or 20-penny nails through the top plate. Then the remaining or intermediate studs are laid out on the sills or soles by measuring from one corner the distances the studs are to be set apart. Studs are normally spaced 12, 16, and 24 inches on centers, depending upon the type of outside and inside finish. Where vertical siding is used, studs are set wider apart since the horizontal girts between them provide nailing surface.

(2) When it is desirable to double the post of the door opening, first place the outside studs into position and nail them securely. Then cut short studs, or *filler studs*, the size of the opening, and nail these to the inside face of the outside studs as shown in figure 27. In making a window opening, a bottom header must be framed; this header is either single or double. When it is doubled, the bottom piece is nailed to the opening studs at the proper height and the top piece of the bottom header is nailed into place flush with the bottom section. The door header is framed as shown in figure 27. The filler stud rests on the sole at the bottom.

e. Girts. Girts are always the same width as the studs and are flush with the face of the stud, both outside and inside. Girts are used in hasty construction where the outside walls are covered with vertical siding. Studs are placed from 2 to 10 feet apart, with girts, spaced about 4 feet apart, running horizontally between them (fig. 27). The vertical siding acts in the same way as to studs and helps to carry the weight of the roof. This type of construction is used extensively in the theater of operations.

f. Top Plate and Sole Plate.

(1) *Top plate.* The top plate ties the studding together at the top and forms a finish for the walls; it furnishes a support for the lower ends of the rafters (fig. 22). The top plate serves as a connecting link between the wall and the roof, just as the sills and girders are connecting links between the floors and the walls.

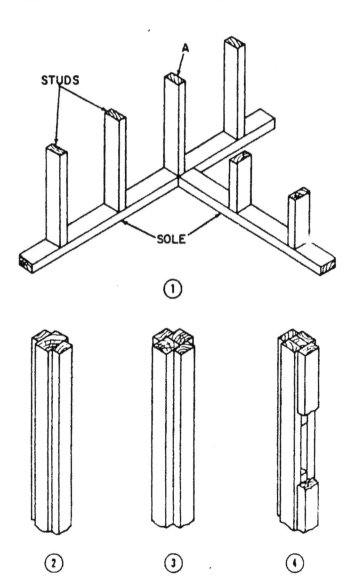

Figure 26. Partition posts.

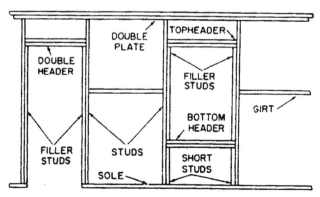

Figure 27. Door and window framing.

The plate is made up of one or two pieces of timber of the same size as the studs. In cases where the studs at the end of the building extend to the rafters, no plate is used at the end of the building. When it is used on top of partition walls, it is sometimes called the cap. Where the plate is doubled, the first plate or bottom section is nailed with 16- or 20-penny nails to the top of the corner posts and to the studs. The connection at the corner is made as shown in 1, figure 28. After the single plate is nailed securely and the corner braces are nailed into place, the top part of the plate is then nailed to the bottom section with 16- or 20-penny nails either over each stud, or spaced with two nails every 2 feet. The edges of the top section should be flush with the bottom section and the corner joints lapped as shown in 1 and 2, figure 28.

(2) *Sole plate.* All partition walls and outside walls are finished either with a 2 by 4 or with a piece of timber corresponding to the thickness of the wall; this timber is laid horizontally on the floor or joists. It carries the bottom end of the studs (fig. 22). This timber is called the "sole" or "sole plate". The sole should be nailed with two 16- or 20-penny nails at each joist that it crosses. If it is laid lengthwise on top of a girder or joist, it should be nailed with two nails every 2 feet.

g. Bridging. Frame walls are bridged, in most cases, to make them more sturdy. There are two methods of bridging:

(1) *Diagonal bridging.* Diagonal bridging is nailed between the studs at an angle (1, fig. 29). It is more effective than the horizontal type since it forms a continuous truss and tends to keep the walls from sagging. Whenever possible, both interior partitions and exterior walls should be bridged alike.

(2) *Horizontal bridging.* Horizontal bridging is nailed between the studs horizontally and halfway between the sole and the plate (2, fig. 29). This bridging is cut to lengths which correspond to the distance between the studs at the bottom. Such bridging not only stiffens the wall but also will help straighten studs.

11. Partitions

Partition walls divide the inside space of a building. These walls in most cases are framed as part of the building. Where floors are to be installed after the outside of the building is completed, the partition walls are left unframed. There are two types of partition walls: the bearing, and the non-bearing types. The bearing type supports ceiling joists. The nonbearing type supports only itself. This type may be put in at any time after

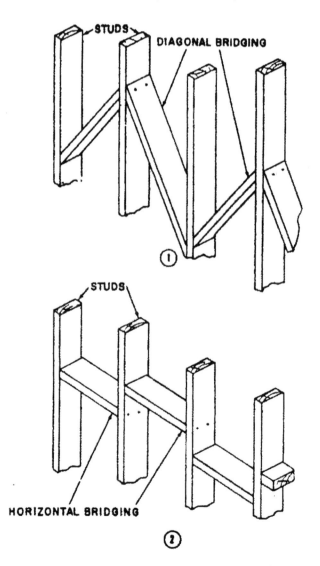

Figure 29. Types of wall bridging.

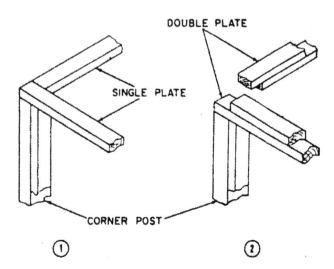

Figure 28. Plate construction.

the other framework is installed. Only one cap or plate is used. A sole plate should be used in every case, as it helps to distribute the load over a larger area. Partition walls are framed the same as outside walls, and door openings are framed as outside openings. Where there are corners or where one partition wall joins another, corner posts or T-posts are used as in the outside walls; these posts provide nailing surfaces for the inside wall finish. Partition walls in the theater of operations one-story building may or may not extend to the roof. The top of the studs has a plate when the wall does not extend to the roof; but when the wall extends to the roof, the studs are joined to the rafters.

12. Methods of Plumbing Posts and Straightening Walls

a. General. After the corner post, T-post, and intermediate wall studs have been nailed to the plates or girts, the walls must be plumbed and straightened so that the permanent braces and rafters may be installed. This is done by using a level or plumb bob and a chalkline.

b. Plumbing Posts.

(1) To plumb a corner with a plumb bob, first attach to the bob a string long enough to extend to or below the bottom of the post. Lay a rule on top of the post so that 2 inches of the rule extends over the post on the side to be plumbed; then hang the bob-line over the rule so that the line is 2 inches from the post and extends to the bottom of it, as shown in 1, figure 30. With another rule, measure the distance from the post to the center of the line at the bottom of the post; if it does not measure 2 inches, the post is not plumb. Move the post inward or outward until the distance from the post to the center of the line is exactly 2 inches. Then nail the temporary brace in place. Repeat this procedure from the other outside face of the post. The post is then plumb. This process is carried out for the remaining corner posts of the building. If a plumb bob or level is not available, a rock, a half-brick, or some small piece of metal may be used instead.

(2) An alternate method of plumbing a post is illustrated in 2, figure 30. Attach the plumb bob string securely to the top of the post to be plumbed, making sure that the string is long enough to allow the plumb bob to hang near the bottom of the post. Use two blocks of wood identical in thickness as gage blocks. Tack one block near the top of the post between the plumb bob string and the post (gage block No. 1), in-

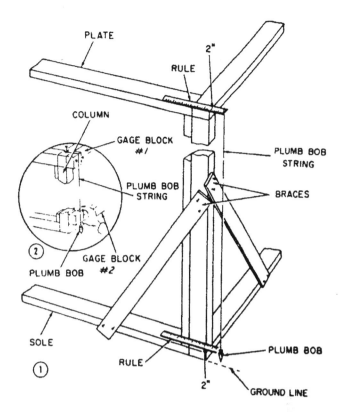

Figure 30. Plumbing a post.

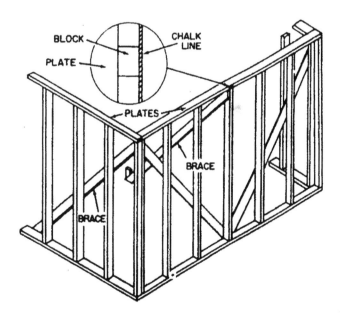

Figure 31. Straightening a wall.

serting the second block between the plumb bob string and the bottom of the post (gage block No. 2). If the entire face of the second block makes contact with the string, the post is plumb.

c. Straightening Walls (fig. 31). Plumb one corner post with the level or plumb bob and nail temporary braces to hold the post in place (*b* above). Repeat this procedure for all corner posts. Fasten a chalkline to the outside of one post at the top and stretch the line to the post the same as for the first post. Place a small 3/4-inch block under each end of the line as shown in figure 31 to give clearance. Place temporary braces at intervals small enough to hold the wall straight. When the wall is far enough away from the line to permit a 3/4-inch block to slide between the line and the plate, the brace is nailed. This procedure is carried out for the entire perimeter of the building. Inside partition walls should be straightened the same way.

13. Braces

Bracing is used to stiffen framed construction and make it rigid. The purpose of bracing may be to resist winds, storm, twist, or strain stemming from any cause. Good bracing keeps corners square and plumb and prevents warping, sagging, and shifts resulting from lateral forces that would otherwise tend to distort the frame and cause badly fitting doors and windows and the cracking of plaster. There are three commonly used methods of bracing frame structures:

a. Let-In Bracing (1, fig. 32). Let-in bracing is set into the edges of studs so as to be flush with the surface. The studs are always cut to let in the braces; the braces are never cut. Usually 1 by 4's or 1 by 6's are used, set diagonally from top plates to sole plates.

b. Cut-In Bracing (2, fig. 32). Cut-in bracing is toenailed between studs. It usually consists of 2 by 4's cut at an angle to permit toenailing, inserted in diagonal progression between studs running up and down from corner posts to sill or plates.

c. Diagonal Sheathing (3, fig. 32). The strongest type of bracing is sheathing applied diagonally. Each board acts as a brace of the wall. If plywood sheathing 5/8-inch thick or more is used, other methods of bracing may be omitted.

14. Exterior Walls

The exterior surfaces of a building usually consist of vertical, horizontal, or diagonal sheathing and composition, sheet-metal, or corrugated roofing. However, in theaters of operation the materials are not always available and substitutes must be provided. Concrete block, brick, rubble stone, metal, or earth may be substituted for wood in treeless regions. In the tropics, improvised siding and roofs can be made from bamboo and grasses. Roofing felt, sandwiched between two layers of light wire mesh, may serve for wall and roof materials where climate is suitable.

a. Sheathing. Sheathing is nailed directly onto the framework of the building. Its purpose is to strengthen the building, to provide a base wall onto which the finish siding can be nailed,

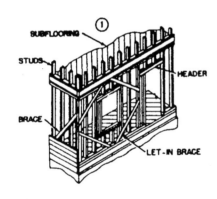

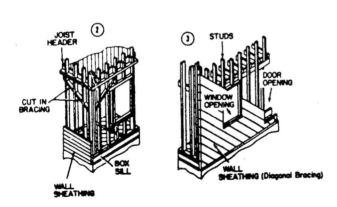

Figure 32. Common types of bracing.

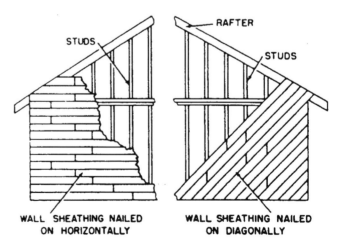

Figure 33. Diagonal and horizontal wooden sheathing.

to act as insulation, and in some cases to be a base for further insulation. Some of the common types of sheathing include—

(1) Wood, 11/16-inch thick by 6, 8, 10, or 12 inch wide of No. 1 common square or matched-edge material. It may be nailed on horizontally or diagonally (fig. 33).

(2) Gypsum board wall-sheathing, 1/2 inch thick by 24 inches wide and 8 feet long.

(3) Fiberboard, 25/32 inch thick by 24 by 48 inches wide and 8, 9, 10, and 12 feet long.

(4) Plywood, 5/16, 3/8, 1/2, 5/8 inches thick by 48 inches wide and 8, 9, 10, and 12 feet long.

b. *Application.*

(1) Wood wall sheathing comes in almost all widths, lengths, and grades. Generally, widths are from 6 to 12 inches, with lengths selected for economical use. Almost all solid wood wall sheathing used is 13/16 inches thick and either square or matched edge. This material may be nailed on horizontally or diagonally (fig. 33). Diagonal application adds much greater strength to the structure. Sheathing should be nailed on with three 8-penny common nails to each bearing if the pieces are over 6 inches wide. Wooden sheathing is laid on tight, with all joints made over the studs. If the sheathing is to be put on horizontally, it should be started at the foundation and worked toward the top. If it is to be put on diagonally, it should be started at the corners of the building and worked toward the center or middle of the building.

(2) Gypsum board sheathing (fig. 34) is made by casting a gypsum core within a heavy water-resistant fibrous envelope. The long edges of the 4- by 8-foot boards are tongued and grooved. Each board is a full 1/2 inch thick. Its

use is mostly with wood siding that can be nailed directly through the sheathing and into the studs. Gypsum sheathing is fireproof, water resistant, and windproof; does not warp nor absorb water; and does not require the use of building papers.

(3) Plywood as a wall sheathing (fig. 34) is highly recommended by its size, weight, stability, and structural properties, plus the ease and speed of application. It adds consider-

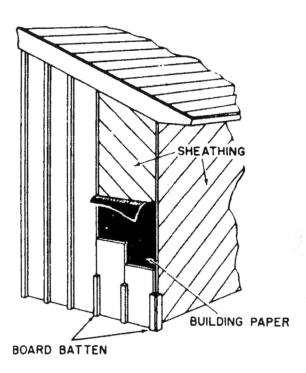

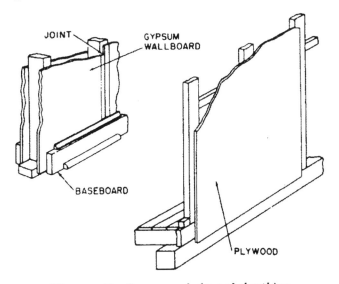

Figure 34. Gypsum and plywood sheathing.

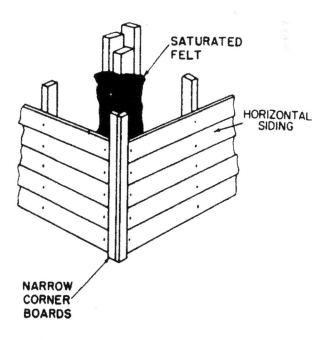

Figure 35. Vertical and horizontal wooden siding.

ably more strength to the frame than does diagonally applied wood boards. When plywood sheathing is used, corner bracing can be omitted. Large size panels save the time required for application and still provide a tight, draft-free installation of high insulation value. Minimum thicknesses of plywood wall sheathing is 5/16 inch for 16-inch stud spacing and 3/8 inch for 24-inch stud spacing. The panels should be installed with the face grain parallel to the studs. A little more stiffness can be gained by installing them across the studs, but this requires more cutting and fitting. Use 6-penny common nails for 5/16-, 3/8-, and 1/2-inch panels and 8-penny common nails for 5/8- and 13/16-inch panels. Space the nails not more than 6 inches on center at the edges of the panels and not more than 12 inches on center elsewhere.

c. *Vertical Wooden Siding.* This type of coverage is nailed to girts. The cracks are covered with wood strips called battens. The sheathing is nailed securely with 8- or 10-penny nails. The vertical sheathing requires less framing than siding since the sheathing acts as a support for the plate. To make this type of wall more weatherproof, some type of tar paper or light roll roofing may be applied over the entire surface and fastened with roofing nails and battens (fig. 35).

d. *Horizontal Wood Siding.* Wood siding is cut to various patterns and sizes to be used as the finished outside surface of a structure. The siding for outside wall coverings should be of a decay-resisting species that will hold tight at the joints and take and hold paint well. It should by all means be well seasoned lumber. Siding is made in sizes ranging from 1/2 inch to 3/4 inch by 12 inches. There are two principal types of siding (fig. 3): beveled siding and drop siding.

(1) *Beveled siding* (fig. 3). Beveled siding is made with beveled boards thin at the top edge and thick at the butt. It is the most common form of wood siding and comes in 1 inch for narrow widths, and 2 inches and over for the wide types. They are usually nailed at the butt edge and through the tip edge of the board below. Very narrow siding is quite often nailed near its thin edge like shingles. It is nailed to solid sheathing over which building paper has been attached. Window and door casings are first framed. The siding butts are put against the edges of these frames. Corners may be mitered, or the corner boards may be first nailed to the sheathing and then the siding is fitted against the edges.

(2) *Drop siding* (fig. 3). Drop siding is designed to be used as a combination of sheathing and siding, or with separate sheathing. It comes in a wide variety of face profiles and is either shiplapped or tongued and grooved. If used as a combined sheathing and siding material, tongue and grooved lumber is nailed directly to the studs with the tongue up. When sheathing is not used, the door and window casings are set after the siding is up. If sheathing is first used and then building paper is added, drop siding is applied like beveled siding, after the window and door casings are in place.

(3) *Corrugated metal sheets.* Corrugated metal is used extensively as a wall cover since little framing, time, and labor are required to install it. It is applied vertically and nailed to girts with the nails placed in the ridges. Sheathing can be used behind the iron with or without building paper. Since tar paper used behind metal will cause the metal to rust, a resin-sized paper should be used.

(4) *Building paper.*

(a) Building paper is of several types, the most common of which is the resin-sized. It is generally red or buff in color (sometimes black) and comes in rolls, usually 36 inches wide. Each roll contains 500 square feet and weighs from 18 to 50 pounds. Ordinarily, it is not waterproof. Another type is heavy paper saturated with a coaltar product, sometimes called sheathing paper. It is waterproof and protects against heat and cold.

(b) In wood-frame buildings to be covered with either siding, shingles, or iron, building paper is used to protect against heat, cold, or dampness. Building paper is applied horizontally along a wall from the bottom of the structure upward and nailed with roofing nails at the laps. Thus the overlapping of the paper helps water runoff. Care must be taken not to tear the paper. The waterproof type paper is used also in the built-up roof where the roof is nearly flat. Several layers are used with tar between each layer.

15. Interior Walls and Partitions

a. *Wall and Partition Coverings.* Wall and partition coverings are divided into two general types—wet wall material, generally plaster; and dry wall material including wood, plaster board, plywood, and fiberboard. Only dry wall material will be covered in this manual.

b. *Dry Wall Materials.* Dry wall material—

gypsumboard, fiberboard, or plywood, usually comes in sheets 1/2 inch thick and 4 x 8 feet in size, but may be obtained in other sizes. It is normally applied in either single or double thickness with panels placed as shown in figure 36. When covering both walls and ceilings, always start with the ceiling (para 17). Annular ringed nails should be used for applying finished-joint drywall to reduce nail popping.

(1) Apply dry wall as follows:

(*a*) Start in one corner and work around the room. Make sure that joints break at the centerline of a stud.

(*b*) Use 1/2-inch thick recessed-edge wallboard and span the entire height of the wall if possible.

(*c*) Use 13-gage nails, 1 5/8 inches long. Start nailing at the center of the board and work outward. Space the nails 3/8 inch in from the edge of the board and about 8 inches apart. Dimple nails below surface of panel with a ball-peen hammer. Be careful not to break the surface of the board by the blow of the hammer.

(*d*) Procedures for cutting and sealing wallboard are covered in (3) below.

(2) Fit dry wall materials to rough or uneven walls as follows:

(*a*) Place a piece of scrap material in the angle (fig. 37) and scribe (mark) it to indicate the surface peculiarities.

(*b*) Saw the scrap material along the scribed line.

(*c*) Place the scribed strip on the wallboard to be used. Keep the straight edge of the scrap material parallel with the edge of the wallboard. Scribe the good piece of wallboard.

(*d*) Saw the wallboard along the scribed line.

(3) Cut panels by sawing, or by scoring with an awl and snapping over a straight edge (fig. 38). *Cut with finish side up to avoid damaging surface.* Cut openings for pipe and electrical receptacles with a keyhole saw. Nail panels to wall studs with 13-gage nails, 8 inches on centers. *All panel end joints must center on studs.* Cover nails with cement. Joints may be left open, beveled, lapped, filled, covered with battens or moldings, or treated with cement and tape. The treatment of joints varies slightly with different materials. Generally, all cracks over 1/8 inch must be filled with special crack filler before joint cement is applied. The cement is spread over joints with a plasterer's trowel. Apply the cement evenly and thin (feather) edges on surface of wall panel. Fill channels in recessed edges with cement, carrying it 1 inch past channel edges. At corners, apply cement in a channel-wide band and feather edges. Press perforated tape into wet cement and smooth tape down with trowel. Clean off excess cement. At corners, fold tape down center before applying, and smooth each side of corner separately when applied. When cement is dry, apply a second coat of thinned cement to hide tape.

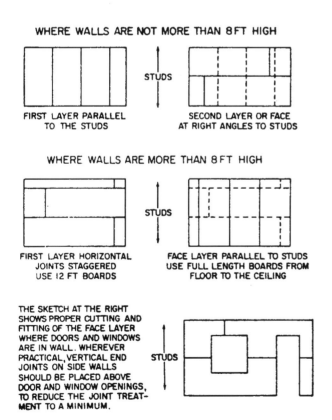

WHERE WALLS ARE NOT MORE THAN 8 FT HIGH

FIRST LAYER PARALLEL TO THE STUDS

SECOND LAYER OR FACE AT RIGHT ANGLES TO STUDS

STUDS

WHERE WALLS ARE MORE THAN 8 FT HIGH

FIRST LAYER HORIZONTAL JOINTS STAGGERED USE 12 FT BOARDS

FACE LAYER PARALLEL TO STUDS USE FULL LENGTH BOARDS FROM FLOOR TO THE CEILING

STUDS

THE SKETCH AT THE RIGHT SHOWS PROPER CUTTING AND FITTING OF THE FACE LAYER WHERE DOORS AND WINDOWS ARE IN WALL. WHEREVER PRACTICAL, VERTICAL END JOINTS ON SIDE WALLS SHOULD BE PLACED ABOVE DOOR AND WINDOW OPENINGS, TO REDUCE THE JOINT TREATMENT TO A MINIMUM.

STUDS

Figure 36. Placing wallboard.

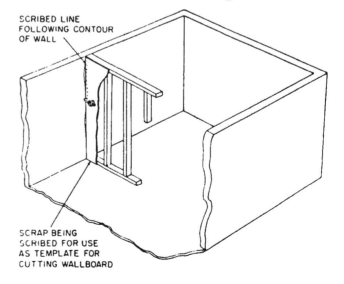

SCRIBED LINE FOLLOWING CONTOUR OF WALL

SCRAP BEING SCRIBED FOR USE AS TEMPLATE FOR CUTTING WALLBOARD

Figure 37. Fitting single-piece wallboard to uneven walls.

Feather the edges carefully to preserve flat appearance of wall. When the final coat is dry, smooth the joint with sandpaper.

c. *Sheetrock.* Sheetrock sheets are very brittle and require careful handling to prevent breakage. Approximately 1 1/4 inches of a sheet's edge is made 1/16 inch thinner than the body of the sheet. When two sheets are placed side by side, their edges form a recess to receive perforated paper tape and gypsum cement which conceals the joints between the sheets. A 1/8-inch space between the edges of the sheets helps to hold the filler cement in place. The sheets are usually fastened in place with blued nails which have an oversize head and are 1 1/2 inches long. The nails along the edges are covered with perforated tape and cement. Nails are spaced about 5 inches apart and 3/8 inch from the edge. Those in the middle of the sheets are spaced 8 or 9 inches apart and are set below the surface to receive the filler cement. It is common practice to strike the nailheads one extra blow for setting. This makes a slight depression (hammer mark) which holds the cement around the nailhead.

d. *Wood Paneling.* Plywood panels are used extensively as interior wall covering and can be obtained on the market in sizes from 1/4 to 3/4 inch thick; 36 to 48 inches wide; and 60, 72, 84, or 96 inches long. Plywood gives a wall a wood finish surface. If desired, the less expensive plywoods can be used and covered with paint or wallpaper or can be decorated in the same way as plastered surfaces. These panels are usually applied vertically from floor to ceiling and fastened with 4d finishing nails. Special strips or battens of either wood or metal may be used to conceal the joints when flush joints are used. Joints can also be treated with moldings, either in the form of battens fastened over the joints or applied as splines between the panels.

16. Moldings

The various interior trims of a building should have a definite architectural relationship in the design to that of the doors, windows, and the general architecture of the building.

a. *Base Molding.* Base molding serves as a finish between the finished wall and floor. It is available in several widths and forms. Two-piece base consists of a baseboard topped with a small base cap (A, fig. 39). When plaster is not straight and true, the small base molding will conform more closely to the variations than will the wider base alone. A common size for this type of baseboard is 5/8 by 3 1/4 inches or wider. One-piece baseboard is 5/8 by 3 1/4 inches or wider. One-piece base varies in size from 7/16 by 2 1/4 inches to 1/2 by 3 1/4 inches and wider (Band C, fig. 39). Although a wood member is desirable at the junction of the wall and carpeting to serve as a protective "bumper", wood trim is sometimes eliminated entirely. Most baseboards are finished with a base shoe, 1/2 by 3/4 inch in size (A, B, and C, fig. 39). A single-base molding without the shoe is sometimes placed at the wall-floor junction, especially where carpeting might be used.

b. *Installation of Base Molding.* Square-edged baseboard should be installed with a butt joint at inside corners and a mitered joint at outside corners (D, fig. 39). It should be nailed to each stud with two eightpenny finishing nails. Molded single-piece base, base moldings, and base shoe should have a coped joint at inside corners and

TO CUT PLASTERBOARD:

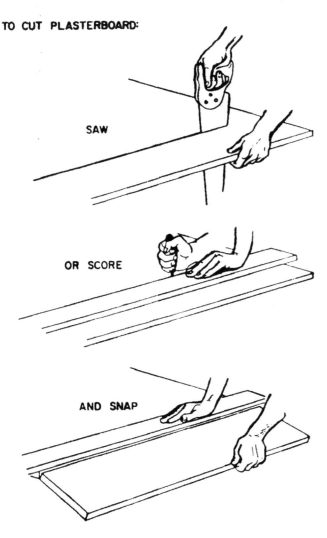

SAW

OR SCORE

AND SNAP

Figure 38. Cutting wallboard.

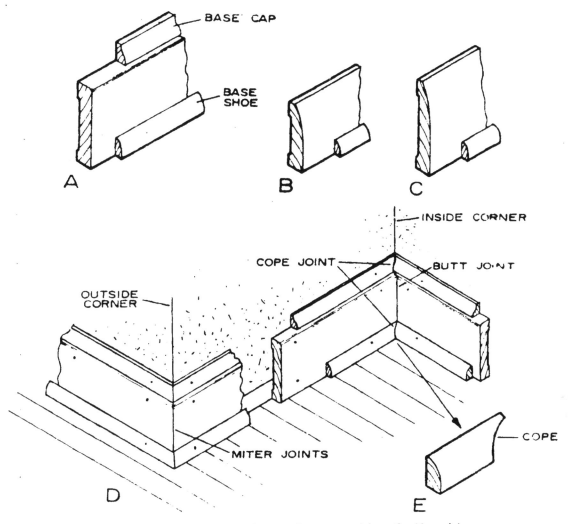

A, Square-edge base; B, narrow ranch base; C, wide ranch base;
D, installation; E, cope.

Figure 39. Base molding.

a mitered joint at outside corners. A coped joint is one in which the first piece is square-cut against the plaster or base and the second molding coped. This is done by sawing a 45° miter cut and with a coping saw trimming the molding along the inner line of the miter (E, fig. 39). The base shoe should be nailed into the subfloor with long slender nails and not into the baseboard itself. Thus, if there is a small amount of shrinkage of the joists, no opening will occur under the shoe.

17. Ceiling Covering

In present-day construction, dry, rigid wallboards are used instead of laths and plaster to cover ceilings, as well as walls (para 15). The most common drywall finishes are gypsumboard, fiberboard, and plywood. Sheets of gypsumboard and fiberboard are attached directly to the joists.

Smaller pieces of fiberboard (tiles) require furring strips (wooden strips nailed across joints) to which they are attached.

a. Gypsumboard.

(1) *Nailing to ceiling.* The 4-foot by 8-foot boards are nailed to the ceiling with 5-penny-nails through 1/2-inch thick gypsum or 4-penny nails through 3/8-inch gypsum. The nails are spaced 5 to 7 inches apart, off center, and driven about 1/16 inch below the surface of the board.

(2) *Cutting panels and treatment of joints.* The cutting of the panels and the treatment of joints are the same as those of walls and partitions (para 15b(3).

(3) *Brace for paneling ceiling.* A brace is constructed and used (fig. 40) to raise and hold a panel in place to aid in fitting and nailing

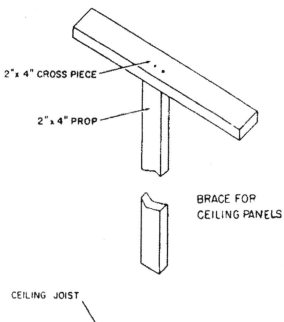

2" x 4" CROSS PIECE

2" x 4" PROP

BRACE FOR CEILING PANELS

CEILING JOIST

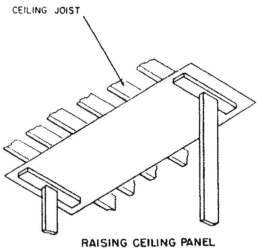

RAISING CEILING PANEL

Figure   40. Brace for raising and holding ceiling panels.

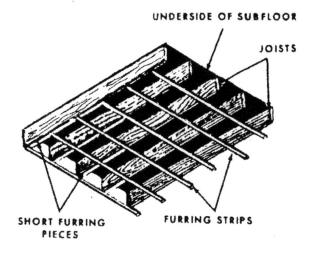

UNDERSIDE OF SUBFLOOR

JOISTS

SHORT FURRING PIECES

FURRING STRIPS

Figure   41. Furring strips on ceiling joists.

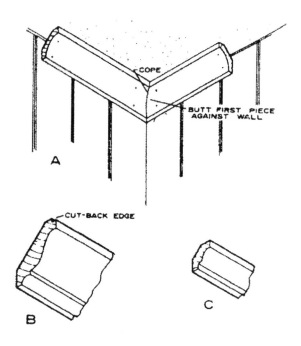

COPE

BUTT FIRST PIECE AGAINST WALL

A

CUT-BACK EDGE

B

C

Ceiling moldings; A, installation (inside corner); B, crown molding; C, small crown molding.

Figure   42. Ceiling molding.

the wallboard to the ceiling. Eight inch nail spacing is used in nailing the panels to the joists.

b. *Fiberboard.* Fiberboard sheets are obtained in thicknesses from 1/2 to 2 inches. The joints between the sheets may be covered with batten strips of either wood or fiberboard to further improve its appearance. When fiberboard sheets must be cut, a special fiberboard knife is recommended to obtain a smooth cut.

(1) *Tiles.* Fiberboard sheets are also made in small pieces called tiles which are often used for covering ceilings. These tiles may be square or rectangular to fit standard joist spacing. They may be made with a lap joint which permits blind nailing or stapling through the edge. They may also be of tongue-and-groove construction fastened in place with 2-penny box nails driven through special metal clips.

(2) *Furring strips.* For fiberboard tiles that need solid backing, furring strips are placed at right angles across the bottom of the joists and short furring pieces are placed along the joists between the furring strips, as shown in figure 41.

(3) *Tile installed in metal channels.* Metal channels are nailed to furring strips and the tiles are slid into them horizontally. In lowering ceilings, usually in older buildings, metal channels are suspended on wire to "drop" a ceiling below the original ceiling. Some large (2 x 4-ft) panels are installed in individual frames.

18. Ceiling Molding

Ceiling moldings are sometimes used at the junction of wall and ceiling for an architectural effect or to terminate dry-wall paneling of gypsumboard or wood (A, fig. 42). As in the base moldings, inside corners should also be cope-jointed. This insures a tight joint and retains a good fit if there are minor moisture changes. A cutback edge at the outside of the molding will partially conceal any unevenness of the plaster and make painting easier where there are color changes (B, fig. 42). For gypsum dry-wall construction, a small simple molding might be desirable (C, fig. 42). Finish nails should be driven into the upper wallplates and also into the ceiling joists for large moldings when possible.

Section III. DOOR FRAMES, WINDOW FRAMES, AND OTHER WALL OPENINGS

19. Doors

Door and window openings in exterior walls generally require headers. Regular studs are normally placed 16 inches on center apart. Extra studs are added at the sides of all such openings. Openings should allow 1/2 inch between the back at jambs and framing member for the plumbing and leveling of jambs.

a. Door Frames.

(1) Before the exterior covering is placed on the outside walls, the door openings are prepared for the frames. To prepare the openings, square off any uneven pieces of sheathing and wrap heavy building paper around the sides and top. Since the sill must be worked into a portion of the rough flooring, no paper is put on the floor. Position the paper from a point even with the inside portion of the stud to a point about 6 inches on the sheathed walls and tack it down with small nails.

(2) Outside door frames are constructed in several ways. In most hasty construction, the frames will be as shown in figure 43. This type requires no construction of frame because the studs on each side of the opening act as a frame. The outside finish is applied to the wall before the door is hung. The casing is then nailed to the sides of the opening which is set back the width of the stud. A 3/4- by 3/4-inch piece is nailed over the door to act as a support for the drip cap and is also set back the width of the stud. Hinge blocks are nailed to the casing where the hinges are to be placed. The door frame is now complete and ready for the door to be hung. Figure 43 shows the elevation of a single outside door.

(3) Inside door frames, like outside frames, are constructed in several ways. In most hasty construction, the type shown in figure 44 is used. The interior type is constructed like the outside type, except that no casing is used on inside door frames. Hinge blocks are nailed to the inside wall finish, where the hinges are to be placed, to provide a nailing surface for the hinge flush with the door. Figure 44 shows the elevation of a single inside door. Both the outside and inside door frames may be modified to suit climatic conditions.

b. Door Jambs. Door jambs (fig. 45) are the linings of the framing of door openings.

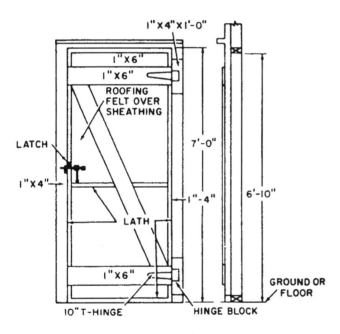

ELEVATION

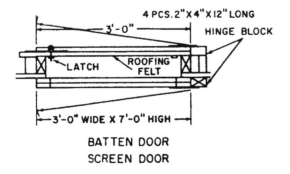

BATTEN DOOR
SCREEN DOOR

Figure 43. Single outside door.

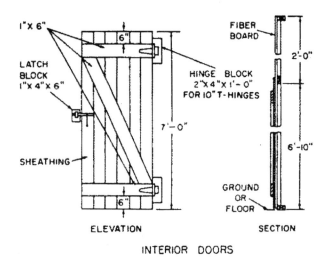

INTERIOR DOORS

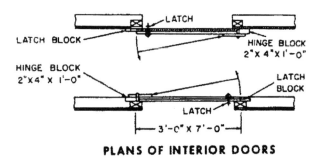

PLANS OF INTERIOR DOORS

Figure 44. Single inside door.

Casings and stops are nailed to the door jambs and the door is hung from them. Inside jambs are made of 3/4-inch stock and outside jambs of 1 3/8-inch stock. The width of the stock will vary with the thickness to the walls. Inside jambs are built up with 3/8- by 1 3/8-inch stops nailed to the jamb, while outside jambs are usually rabbeted out to receive the door. Jambs are made and set as follows:

(1) Regardless of how carefully rough openings are made, be sure to plumb the jambs and level the heads, when jambs are set.

(2) Rough openings are usually made 2 1/2 inches larger each way than the size of the door to be hung. For example, a 2-foot 8-inch by 6-foot 8-inch door would need a rough opening of 2 feet 10 1/2 inches by 6 feet 10 1/2 inches. This extra space allows for the jambs, the wedging, and the clearance space for the door to swing.

(3) Level the floor across the opening to determine any variation in floor heights at the point where the jambs rest on the floor.

(4) Now cut the head jamb with both ends square, having allowed width of the door plus the depth of both dadoes and a full 3/16 inch for door clearance.

(5) From the lower edge of the dado, measure a distance equal to the height of the door plus the clearance wanted under it. Mark and cut square.

(6) On the oposite jamb do the same, only make additions or subtractions for the variation in the floor, if any.

(7) Now nail the jambs and jamb heads together with 8-penny common nails through the dado into the head jamb.

(8) Set the jambs into the opening and place small blocks under each jamb on the sub-floor just as thick as the finish floor will be. This is to allow the finish floor to go under.

(9) Plumb the jambs and level the jamb head.

(10) Wedge the sides with shingles between the jambs and the studs, to aline, and then nail securely in place.

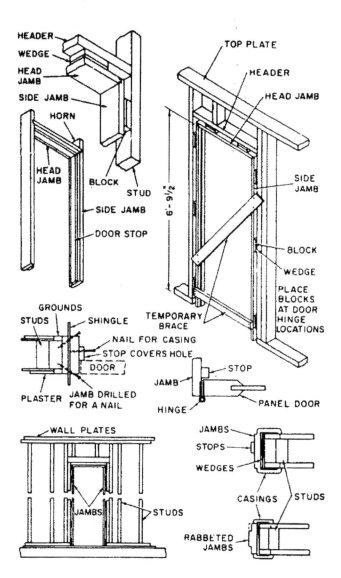

Figure 45. Door jamb and door trim.

(11) Take care not to wedge the jamb unevenly.

(12) Use a straightedge 5 or 6 feet long inside the jambs to help prevent uneven wedging.

(13) Check jambs and head carefully, because jambs placed out of plumb will have a tendency to swing the door open or shut, depending on the direction in which the jamb is out of plumb.

c. Door Trim. Door trim material is nailed onto the jambs to provide a finish between the jambs and the wall. It is frequently called "casing" (fig. 45). Sizes vary from 1/2 to 3/4 inch in thickness, and from 2 1/2 to 6 inches in width. Most trim has a concave back, to fit over uneven plaster. In mitered work, care must be taken to make all joints clean, square, neat, and well fitted. (If the trim is to be mitered at the top corners, a miter box, miter square, hammer nail set, and block plane will be needed.) Door openings are cased up as follows:

(1) Leave a margin of 1/4-inch from the edge of the jamb to the casing all around.

(2) Cut one of the side casings square and even at the bottom, with the bottom of the jamb.

(3) Cut the top or mitered end next, allowing 1/4-inch extra length for the margin at the top.

(4) Nail the casing onto the jamb and even with the 1/4-inch margin line, starting at the top and working toward the bottom.

(5) Use 4-penny finishing nails along the jamb side and 6-penny or 8-penny case nails along the outer edge of the casings.

(6) The nails along the outer edge will need to be long enough to go through the casing and into the studs.

(7) Set all nailheads about 1/8 inch below the surface of the wood with a nail set.

(8) Now apply the casing for the other side and then the head casing.

20. Windows

Windows are generally classified as sliding, double hung, and casement (fig. 46). All windows, whatever the type, consist essentially of two parts, the frame and the sash. The frame is made up of four basic parts: the head, the jambs (two), and the sill. The sash is the framework which holds the glass in the window. Where the openings are provided, studding must be cut away and its equivalent strength replaced by doubling the studs on each side of the opening to form trimmers and inserting a header at the top. If the opening is wide, the header should be doubled and trussed. At the bottom of the opening, the bottom header or rough sill is inserted.

a. Window Frames. These are the frames into which the window sashes are fitted and hung. They are set into the rough opening in the wall framing and are intended to hold the sashes in place. The rough window opening is made at least 10 inches larger each way (width and height) than the window glass (pane) size to be used. If the sash to be used is, for instance, a two-light window, 24 by 26 inches, add 10 inches to the width (24 inches) to obtain the total width of 34 inches for the rough opening. Add the upper and lower glasses (26 inches each) and an additional 10 inches for the total height of the rough opening, 62 inches. These allowances are standard and provide for weights, springs, balances, room for plumbing and squaring, and for regular adjustments.

b. Double-Hung Window. The double-hung window (fig. 47) is made up of two parts: an upper and a lower sash, which slide vertically past one another. Screens can be located on the outside of a double-hung window without interfering with its operation, and ventilators and window air conditioners can be placed with the window mostly closed. However, for full ventilation of a room, only one-half of the area of the window can be used, and any current of air

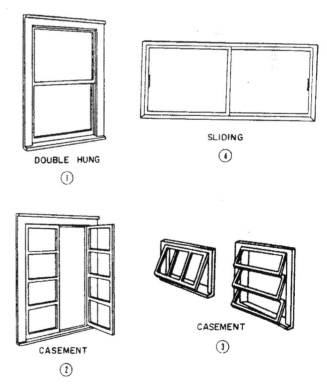

Figure 46. Types of windows.

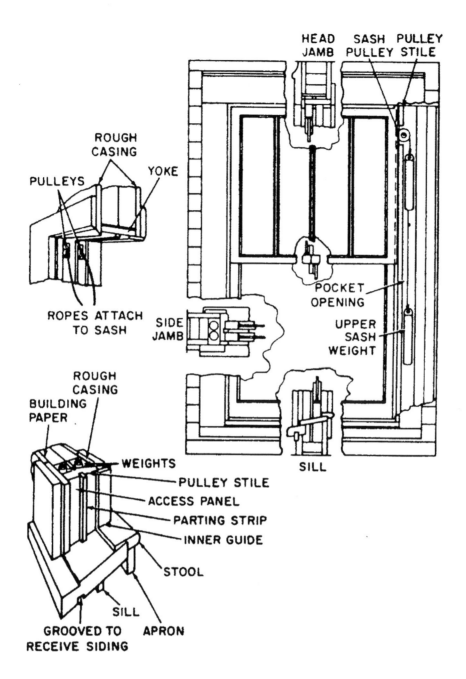

Figure 47. Double-hung window.

passing across its face is to some extent lost to the room.

(1) The box frame (fig. 47) consists of a top piece or yoke, two side pieces or jambs called pulley stiles, and the sill. The yoke and pulley stiles are dadoed into the inner and outer pieces (rough casing), forming an open box with the opening toward the studs and headers. The rough casing provides nailing surface to the studs and headers forming the plaster stop. The outside rough casing is also a blind stop for sheathing which should fit snugly against it, with building paper lapping the joint.

(2) The 2-inch space between the framing studs and the pulley stile forms the box for counterweights which balance the window sash. The weight box is divided by a thin strip known as the pendulum, which separates the weights for the two sash units. In the stiles near the sill is an opening for easy access to the weights. This opening has a removable strip which is part of the stile and channel for the lower sash (fig. 47).

(3) Yoke and stile faces are divided by a parting strip which is dadoed into them, but removable so that the upper sash can be taken out. The strip forms the center guide for the upper and lower sash, while the outerrough casing,

projecting slightly beyond the stiles and yoke, forms the outer guide. The inner guide for the sash is formed by a strip or stop, usually with a molding form on the inner edge. This stop is removable to permit the removal of the lower sash.

(4) At the upper parts of the stiles, two pulleys on each side (one for each sash) are mortised flush with the stile faces for the weight cord or chain.

(5) The sill is part of the box frame and slants downward and outward. It usually has one or two 1/4-inch brakes, one occurring at the point where the lower sash rests on the sill, and another near the outer edge to form a seat for window screens or storm sash. These brakes prevent water, dripping on the sill, from being blown under the sash. The underside of the sill, near its outer edge, is grooved to receive the edge of siding material to form a watertight seal.

(6) On the room side of the sill is another piece, the stool, which has a rabbet on its underside into which the sill fits. The stool edge projects from the will, forming a horizontal stop for the lower sash. The stool is part of the interior trim of the window, made up of side and top casings and an apron under the stool. The framed finished side and top casings are on the weather face. A drip cap rests on top of the outside head casing and is covered with metal flashing to form a watertight juncture with the siding material.

c. *Hinged or Casement Windows.* There are basically two types of casement windows, the outswinging and the inswinging types, and these may be hinged at the sides, top, or bottom. The casement window which opens out requires the window screen to be located on the inside with some device cut into its frame to operate the casement. Inswinging casements, like double-hung windows, are clear of screens, but they are extremely difficult to make watertight, particularly against a driving rainstorm. Casements have the advantage of their entire area being opened to air currents, with the added advantage of catching a parallel breeze and slanting it into a room.

(1) Casement windows are considerably less complicated in their construction, being simple frames and sash. The frames are usually made of planks 1 3/4 inch thick with rabbets cut in them to receive the sash. Usually there is an additional rabbet for screens or storm sash. The frames are rabbeted 1/2 inch deep and 1 1/2 or 1 7/8 inches wide for sash 1 3/8 or 1 3/4 inches

thick. The additional rabbet is usually 15/16 or 1 3/16 inches wide, depending on whether the screen or storm sash is 7/8 or 1 1/8-inch thick.

(2) Outswinging casement windows have the rabbet for the sash on the outer edges of the frame, the inner edge being rabbeted for the screen. Sill construction is like that for a double-hung window, with the stool much wider and forming a stop for the bottom rail. Casement-window frames are of a width to extend to the sheathing face on the weather side and to the plaster face on the room side (fig. 48).

(3) When there are two casement windows in a row in one frame, they may be separated by a vertical double jamb called a mullion, or the stiles may come together in pairs like a french door. The edges of the stiles may be a reverse rabbet; a beveled reverse rabbet with battens, one attached to each stile; or beveled astragals (T-shaped molding), one attached to each stile. The battens and astragals insure better weather-tightness. The latter are more resistant to loosening through use. Two pairs of casement sash in one frame are hinged to a mullion in the center (fig. 48).

(4) Inswinging casement-window frames are like the outswinging type with the sash rabbet cut in the inner edge of the frame (fig. 48). The sill construction is slightly different, being of one piece (similar to that of a door sill) with

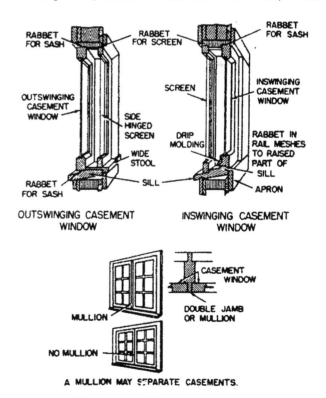

Figure 48. Casement windows.

a rabbet cut for a screen or storm sash toward the front edge, and the back raised where the sash rail seats. This surface is rabbeted at its back edge to form a stop for the rail which is also rabbeted to mesh.

(5) Sills in general have a usual slope of about 1 in 5 inches so that they shed water quickly. They are wider than the frames, extending usually about 1½ inches beyond the sheathing. They also form a base for the outside finished casing.

(6) The bottom sash rail of an inswinging casement window is constructed differently from the outswinging type. The bottom edge is rabbeted to mesh with the rabbet on the sill, and a drip molding is set in the weather face to prevent rain from being blown under the sash.

d. Window Frames In hasty construction, millwork window frames are seldom used. The window frames are mere openings left in the walls with the stops all nailed to the stud. The sash may be hinged to the inside or the outside of the wall or constructed so as to slide. The latter type of sash is most common in Army construction because it requires little time to install. Figure 49 shows the section and plan of a window and window frame of the type used in the field. After the outside walls have been finished, a 1 by 3 is nailed on top of the girt at the bottom of the window opening to form a sill. A 1 by 2 is nailed to the bottom of the plate and on the side studs which acts as a top for the window sash. One guide is nailed at the bottom of the opening flush with the bottom of the girt, and another is nailed to the plate with the top edge flush with the top of the plate. These guides are 1 by 3's, 8 feet long. Stops are nailed to the bottom girt and plate, between the next two studs, to hold the sash in position when open (fig. 49).

21. Other Wall Openings

a. Stovepipes. Stovepipes carried outside a building through a side wall eliminate the need for flashing and waterproofing around the pipe (fig. 50). The opening should be cut in an area selected to avoid cutting studs, braces, plates, and so on. Sheathing must be cut back in a radius 6 inches greater than that of the pipe. Safety thimbles or other insulation must be used on the inside and outside of the sheathing. Sheet metal insulation may be constructed and used as a single insulator on the outside. Make openings as follows:

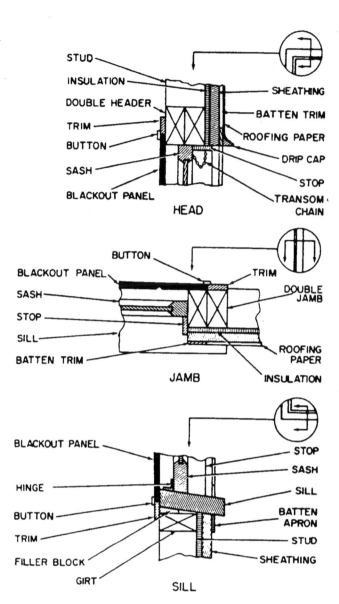

Figure 49. Detail of wall section with window frame and sash.

(1) Cut a hole through the sheet metal where the stovepipe is to penetrate.

(2) Mark a circle on the metal 1/2-inch larger in diameter than the pipe and then make another circle within this circle with a diameter 2 inches less than the diameter of the first.

(3) With a straightedge, draw lines through the center of the circle from the circumference. These marks should be from 1/2 to 3/4 inch apart along the outer circumference.

(4) Cut out the center circle, then cut to the outside of the circle along the lines drawn. After the lines have been cut, bend the metal strips outward at a 45° angle and force the pipe through the hole to the desired position. Very little water will leak around this joint.

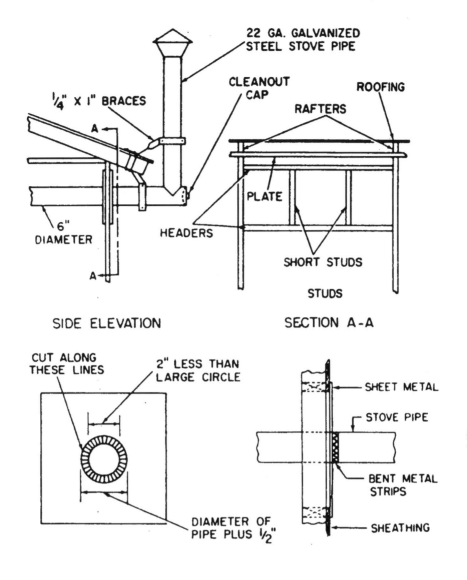

*Figure   50.   Preparation of wall opening for
stovepipe.*

b. Ventilators. Adequate ventilation is necessary to prevent condensation in buildings. Condensation may occur in the walls, in the crawl space under the structure, in basements, on windows, and so on. Condensation is most likely to occur in structures during the first 6 to 8 months after a building is built and in extreme cold weather when interior humidity is high. Proper ventilation under the roof allows moisture-laden air to escape during the winter heating season and also allows the hot dry air of the summer season to escape. The upper areas of a structure are usually ventilated by the use of louvers or ventilators.

(1) *Types of ventilators* (fig.   51). Types of ventilators used are as follows:

(a) Roof louvers (1).

(b) Cornice ventilators (2).

(c) Gable louvers (3).

(d) Flat-roof ventilators (4).

(e) Crawl-space ventilation (5).

(f) Ridge ventilators (6).

(2) *Upper structure ventilation.* One of the most common methods of ventilating is by the use of wood or metal louver frames. There are many types, sizes, and shapes of louvers. The following are facts to consider when building or installing the various kinds of ventilation:

(a) The size and number of ventilators are determined by the size of the area to be ventilated.

(b) The minimum net open area should be 1/4 square inch per square foot of ceiling area.

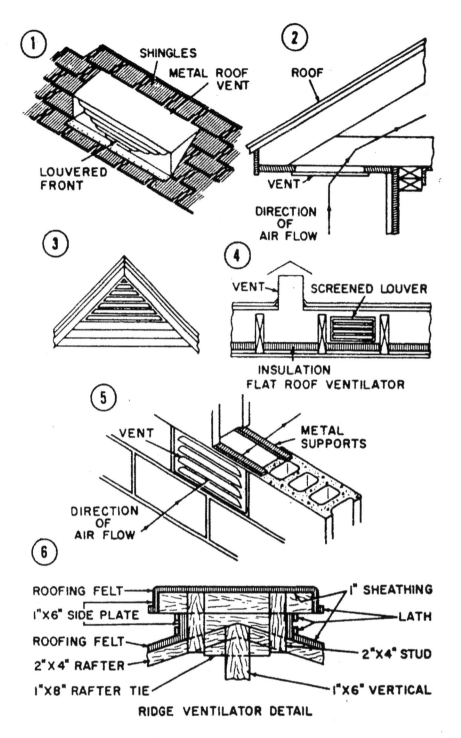

Figure   51. Types of ventilators.

(c) Most louver frames are usually 5 inches wide.

(d) Back edge should be rabbeted out for a screen or door, or both.

(e) Three-quarter-inch slats are used and spaced about 1 3/4 inches apart.

(f) Sufficient slant or slope to the slats should be provided to prevent rain from driving in.

(g) For best results, upper structure lou- vers should be placed as near the top of the gable as possible.

(3) *Crawl-space ventilation.* Crawl spaces under foundations of basementless structures should be well ventilated. Air circulation under the floors prevents excessive condensation that causes warping, swelling, twisting, and rotting of the lumber. These crawl-space ventilators are usually called "foundation louvers" (5, fig.   51). They are set into the foundation at the time it is

being built. A good foundation vent should be equipped with a copper or bronze screen and adjustable shutters for opening and closing the louver. The sizes for the louvers should be figured on the same basis as that used for upper structure louvers—1/4-inch for each square foot of under-floor space.

22. Steps and Stairs

Stairwork is made up of the framing on the sides, known as stringers or carriages, and the steps, known as treads. Sometimes pieces are framed into the stairs at the back of the treads; these pieces are known as risers. The stringers or carriages may consist of materials 2 or 3 inches thick and 4 or more inches wide which are cut to form the step of the stairs. Blocks (fig. 52) may also be nailed on to form the steps. There are usually three stringers to a stair, one at each of the two outer edges and one at the center. The floor joists must be properly framed around the stair well, or wellhole, in order to have enough space for the erection of the stair framing and the finished trim of the entire staircase.

a. The step or stair stringer may be made of 2 by 4's, with triangular blocks nailed to one edge to form the stringer. The blocks are cut from 2 by 6's and nailed to the 2 by 4, as shown in 1, figure 52. The step stringers are fastened at the top and bottom as shown in 2, figure 52. Figures 52 and 53 show the foundation and give the details of the sizes of the step treads, handrails, the methods of installing them, and the post construction. This type of step is most common in field construction.

b. When timbers heavier than 2 by 4's are used for stringers, they are laid out and cut as shown in figure 54.

23. Stairway Framing

a. To frame simple, straight string stairs, take a narrow piece of straight stock, called a story pole, and mark on it the distance from the lower

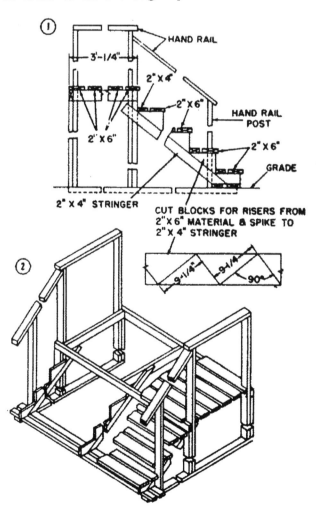

Figure 52. Step construction.

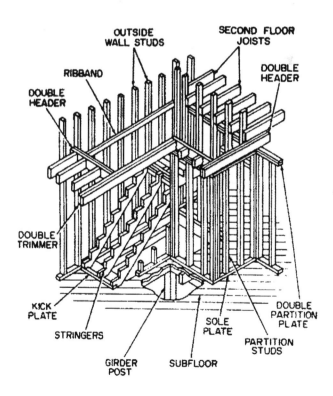

Figure 53. Details of complete stair construction.

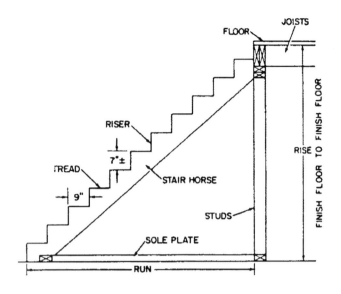

Figure 54. *Method of laying out stair stringers.*

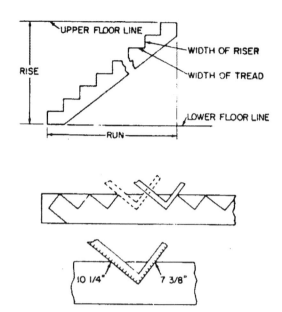

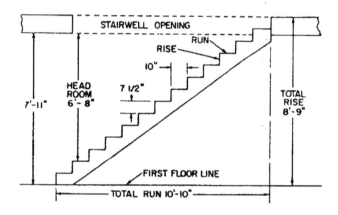

floor to the upper floor level. This is the lower room height, plus the thickness of the floor joists, and the rough and finished flooring. It is also the total rise of the stairs. If it is kept in mind that a flight of stairs forms a right angled triangle (fig. 55), with the rise being the height of the triangle, the run being the base of the triangle, and the length of the stringers being the hypotenuse of the triangle, it will help in laying out the stair distances. Set dividers at 7 inches, the average distance from one step to another, and step off this distance on the story pole. If this distance will not divide into the length of the story pole evenly, adjust the divider span slightly and again step off this distance on the story pole. Continue this adjusting and stepping off until the story pole is marked off evenly. The span of the dividers must be near 7 inches and represents the rise of each step. Count the number of spaces stepped off evenly by the dividers, on the story pole. This will be the total number of risers in the stairs.

b. Measure the length of the wellhole for the length of the run of the stairs. This length may also be obtained from the details on the plans. The stair well length forms the base of a right-angled triangle. The height of the triangle and the base of the triangle have now been obtained.

c. To obtain the width of each tread, divide the number of risers, less one—since there is always one more riser than tread—into the run of the stairs. The numbers thus obtained are to be used on the steel square in laying off the run and rise of each tread and riser on the

Figure 55. *Principal parts of stair construction.*

stringer stock (fig. 54). These figures will be about 7 inches and 10 inches, respectively, since the ideal run and rise totals 17 inches. Lay off the run and rise of each step on the stringer stock equal to the number of risers previously obtained by dividing the story pole into equal spaces. The distance of the height, base, and hypotenuse of a right-angled triangle are thus obtained.

24. Check on Design of Risers and Treads

a. Rules. The following are two rules of thumb that may be used to check the dimensions of risers and treads:

(1) Riser + tread = between 17 and 19 inches.

(2) Riser x tread = between 70 and 75 inches.

b. Check. If the sum of the height of the riser and the width of the tread ((1) above) falls between 17 and 19 inches, and the product of the height of the riser and the width of the tread equals between 70 and 75 inches, the design is satisfactory.

TABLE 1

SIZES OF BUILT—UP WOOD GIRDERS FOR VARIOUS LOADS AND SPANS

Based on Douglas Fir 4—SQUARE Guide—Line FRAMINIG

Deflection Not Over 1/360 Of Span—Allowable Fiber Stress 1600 lbs. per sq. in.

LOAD PER LINEAR FOOT OF GIRDER	LENGTH OF SPAN				
	6'-0''	7'-0''	8'-0''	9'-0''	10'-0''
	NOMINAL SIZE OF GIRDER REQUIRED				
750	6x8 in.	6x8 in.	6x8 in.	6x10 in.	6x10 in.
900	6x8	6x8	6x10	6x10	8x10
1050	6x8	6x10	8x10	8x10	8x12
1200	6x10	8x10	8x10	8x10	8x12
1350	6x10	8x10	8x10	8x12	10x12
1500	8x10	8x10	8x12	10x12	10x12
1650	8x10	8x12	10x12	10x12	10x14
1800	8x10	8x12	10x12	10x12	10x14
1950	8x12	10x12	10x12	10x14	12x14
2100	8x12	10x12	10x14	12x14	12x14
2250	10x12	10x12	10x14	12x14	12x14
2400	10x12	10x14	10x14	12x14	
2550	10x12	10x14	12x14	12x14	
2700	10x12	10x14	12x14		
2850	10x14	12x14	12x14		
3000	10x14	12x14			
3150	10x14	12x14			
3300	12x14	12x14			

The 6-in. girder is figured as being made with three pieces 2 in. dressed to 1-5/8 in. thickness

The 8-in. girder is figured as being made with four pieces 2 in. dressed to 1-5/8 in. thickness.

The 10-in. girder is figured as being made with five pieces 2-in. dressed to 1-5/8 in. thickness.

The 12-in. girder is figured as being made with six pieces 2 in. dressed to 1-5/8 in. thickness.

Note—For solid girders multiply above loads by 1.130 when 6-inch girder is used; 1.150 when 8-in. girder is used; 1.170 when 10-in. girder is used and 1.180 when 12-in. girder is used.

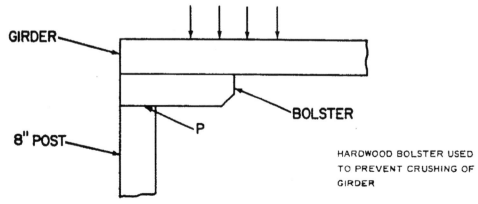

GIRDER

BOLSTER

P

8" POST

HARDWOOD BOLSTER USED TO PREVENT CRUSHING OF GIRDER

EXTERIOR FINISH

The FRAMING of a wood-frame structure consists of (1) the main supporting framework of joists, studs, rafters, and other structural members; and (2) the subflooring and the wall and roof sheathing, which strengthen and brace the framing. These structural elements constitute the ROUGH CARPENTRY in the structure.

The remainder of the work on the structure consists of the construction and/or installation of nonstructural elements. This work is called the FINISH. Most of the finish involves items of essential practical usefulness, such as the door and window frames, the doors and windows themselves, the roof covering, and the stairs. Some of the finish, however, such as the casings on doors and windows and the moldings on cornices and on inside walls, is purely ornamental. The part of the finish which is purely ornamental is called TRIM.

The finish is divided into EXTERIOR FINISH and INTERIOR FINISH. The principal parts of the exterior finish are the CORNICES, the ROOF COVERING, ASBESTOS-CEMENT SIDING, INSULATION, and the OUTSIDE-WALL COVERING. The order in which these parts are erected may vary slightly, but since the roof covering must go on as soon as possible, the cornice work is usually the first item in the exterior finish.

CORNICE WORK

The rafter-end edges of a roof are called EAVES. A hip roof has rafter-end edges all the way around, and all four edges of a hip roof are therefore eaves. The rafter-end or sidewall edges of a gable roof are eaves; the gable-end or end-wall edges are called RAKES.

The exterior finish at and just below the eaves is called the CORNICE. Purely ornamental parts of a cornice (consisting mainly of molding) are called CORNICE TRIM. Exterior finish which runs up the rakes of a gable roof is called GABLE CORNICE TRIM. Besides the main roof, the additions and dormers (if any) also have cornices and cornice trim.

TYPES OF CORNICES

The type of cornice required for a particular structure is indicated on the wall sections, and there are usually cornice detail drawings as well. A roof with no rafter overhang usually has the SIMPLE cornice shown in figure 12-1. This cornice consists of a single strip called a FRIEZE, which is beveled on the upper edge to fit close under the overhang of the eaves, and rabbeted on the lower edge to overlap the upper edge of the top course of siding. If trim is used it usually consists of molding placed as shown in the figure. Molding trim in this position is called CROWN molding.

A roof with a rafter overhang may have an OPEN cornice or a CLOSED (also called a BOX) cornice. The simplest type of open cornice is shown in figure 12-2. Like the simple cornice, it consists only of a frieze, which in this case must be notched to fit around the rafters. If trim is used, it usually consists of molding cut to fit between the rafters as indicated. Molding trim in this position is called BED molding.

A closed or box cornice is shown in figure 12-3. In this type the rafter overhang is entirely boxed in by the roof covering, the fascia, and a bottom strip called a PLANCIER. The plancier is nailed to the lower edges of a series of horizontal members called LOOKOUTS, which are cut to fit between the rafter ends and the face of the sheathing. The frieze, if any, is set just below the lookouts. The trim, if any, is placed and named as shown in the figure.

The gable cornice trim on a gable-roof structure with a simple or an open cornice is made by carrying the frieze and the crown molding up the rakes as shown in figure 12-4. Molding trim along the rakes, however, is called RAKE molding.

Figure 12-5 shows gable-end-wall cornice work on a gable-roof structure with a closed cornice. As you can see, the crown molding and the fascia are carried up the rakes to form the gable cornice trim.

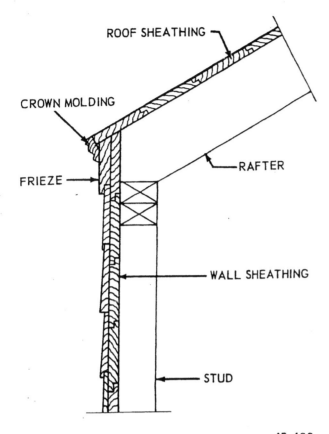

ROOF SHEATHING

CROWN MOLDING

FRIEZE

RAFTER

WALL SHEATHING

STUD

45.493

Figure 12-1.—Simple cornice.

CORNICE CONSTRUCTION

Most specifications call for BUILDING PA-PER between the sheathing and the siding. Building paper is impregnated with some waterproofing material such as asphalt or paraffin; it is used to make the walls water-tight and to keep out air and dust. It is usually applied horizontally, with a 2- to 4-in. overlap.

Before the cornice can be erected, the top course of building paper must be applied to the sheathing. For the open and closed cornice the paper must be cut to fit around the rafters.

Constructing a simple or an open cornice is simply a matter of laying out, beveling, rabbeting, notching (if required) and nailing on the frieze and the trim. Nails should be coated-casing, or finish; the size depends on the thickness of the piece being set in place. Carry a supply of 4-penny, 6-penny, and 8-penny nails, and drive nails in only part way until all the pieces of the cornice have been set in place. All joints should be planed smooth with a block plane and fitted together tightly. All members

must be mitered for joining on outside corners and mitered or coped for joining on inside corners.

The normal procedure for constructing a closed cornice is as follows:

1. Line up the tail plumb cuts and lower corners of the rafters by stretching a line and planing or sawing down any irregularities.

2. Lay out and cut the lookouts and nail them in place (if this was not done in the framing stage). Lookouts must be level, with bottom edges and outer ends in perfect alignment. Each lookout should be first nailed to the rafter and then toenailed against the ledger.

3. Lay out, cut, and rabbet the frieze, and nail it in place just below the lookouts.

4. Lay out and cut the plancier, and fit and nail it to the bottom edges of the lookouts.

5. Lay out, cut, and bevel the fascia, and nail it to the ends of the rafters and lookouts.

6. Lay out, cut, bevel (if necessary), and nail on the moldings.

ROOF COVERING

Roofs are covered with many different kinds of materials, such as slate, tile, wood shingles, asphalt, asbestos-cement, sheet metal, and BUILT-UP roofing. You are not likely to work with any specifications calling for slate, tile, sheet metal, or wood-shingle roofing. Built-up roofing is used mainly on flat or nearly flat roofs. On pitched-roof structures, asphalt and asbestos-cement are the types of roof covering most frequently used.

ASPHALT AND ASBESTOS-CEMENT ROOFING

Asphalt roofing comes in ROLLS (usually 36 in. wide, called ROLLED ROOFING), ROLLED STRIPS (usually 15 in. wide), FLAT STRIPS (usually 12 in. wide and 36 in. long), and as individual separate shingles. The type most commonly used is the flat strip, often called a STRIP SHINGLE.

A 12 x 36 SQUARE-BUTT strip shingle is shown in figure 12-6. This shingle should be laid 5 in. TO THE WEATHER, meaning that 7 in. of each course should be overlapped by the next higher course. The lower, exposed end of a shingle is called the BUTT; the shingle shown in figure 12-6 has a SQUARE BUTT,

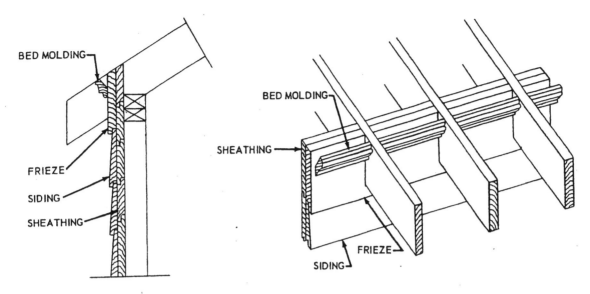

Figure 12-2.—Simplest type of open cornice.

45.494

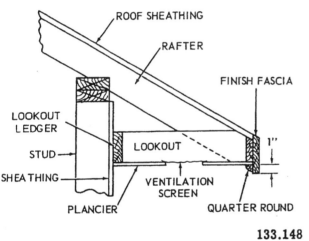

133.148

Figure 12-3.—Closed or box cornice.

45.497

Figure 12-4.—Gable cornice trim on gable-roof structure with simple cornice.

divided into 3 TABS. Various other butt shapes are manufactured.

Asbestos-cement roofing usually consists of individual shingles, 12 in. by 24 in. being the size most commonly used.

The first essential in covering a roof is to erect a scaffold extending to a height which will bring the eaves about waist-high to a man standing on the scaffold. Before any roof covering is applied, the roof sheathing must be swept clean and carefully inspected for irregularities, cracks, holes, or any other defects. No roofing should be applied unless the sheathing boards are absolutely dry. An UNDERLAY of ROOFING

FELT is first applied to the sheathing. Roofing felt usually comes in 3-ft-wide rolls, and it should be laid with a 4-in. lap as indicated.

Before work begins, bundles of shingles should be distributed along the scaffold. There are 27 strips in a bundle of 12 x 36 asphalt strip shingles, and 3 bundles will cover 100 sq ft. After the first course at the eaves (called the STARTER course) is laid by inverting the first course of shingles, you begin each course which follows by stretching

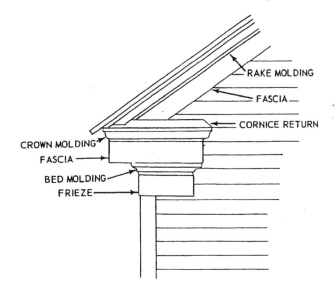

RAKE MOLDING
FASCIA
CORNICE RETURN
CROWN MOLDING
FASCIA
BED MOLDING
FRIEZE

45.496.0

Figure 12-5.—Gable-end-wall cornice work on a gable-roof structure with a closed cornice.

An asbestos-cement roof is laid in about the same manner.

SHINGLES AT HIPS AND VALLEYS

One side of a hip or valley shingle must be cut at an angle to obtain an edge line which will match the line of the hip or valley rafter. One way to cut these shingles is to use a pattern made as follows:

Select a piece of 1 x 6 about 3 ft long. Determine the UNIT LENGTH of a common rafter in the roof (if you don't already know it); set the framing square back-up on the piece to the unit run of a common rafter on the tongue and the unit length of a common rafter on the blade, as shown in the top view of figure 12-8. Draw a line along the tongue; saw the piece along this line, and use it as a pattern to cut the shingles as shown in the bottom view of figure 12-8.

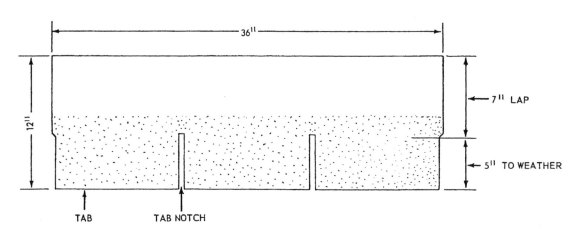

36"

12"

7" LAP

5" TO WEATHER

TAB   TAB NOTCH

29.120

Figure 12-6.—A 12 x 36 square-butt asphalt strip shingle.

a guide line or snapping a chalk line from edge to edge to position the course.

Figure 12-7 shows the method of laying a 12 x 36 asphalt strip-shingle roof.

Strip shingles should be nailed with 1-in. copper or hot-dipped galvanized roofing nails, 2 to each tab; this means 6 nails to each full strip. Nails should be placed about 6 1/2 in. from the butt edges, to ensure that each nail will be covered by the next course, and driven through 2 courses. Placing a nail so that it will be covered by the next course is called BLIND NAILING.

FLASHING

Places especially liable to leakage in roofs and outside walls are made watertight by the installation of FLASHING. Flashing consists of sheets or strips of a watertight, rust-proof material (such as galvanized sheet or sheet copper alloy for valleys and felt for hips), installed so as to deflect water away from places that are liable to leakage. The places in a roof most liable to leakage are the lines along which adjoining roof surfaces intersect (such as the lines followed by ridge hips and valleys), and

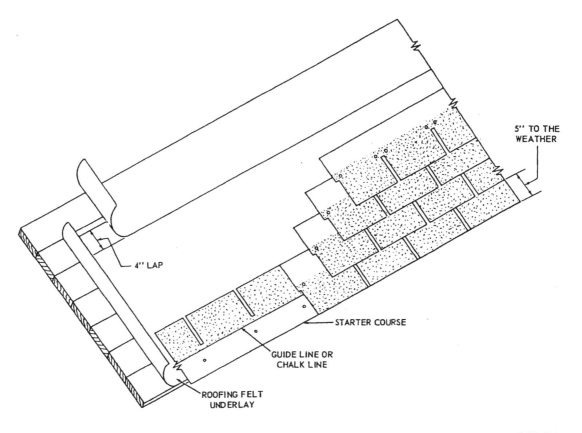

Figure 12-7.—Laying an asphalt shingle roof.

the lines of intersection between roof surfaces and the walls of dormers, chimneys and skylights.

Ridge lines and hip lines tend naturally to shed water, and these lines are therefore only moderately subject to leakage. A strip of felt paper, applied as shown in figure 12-9, usually makes a satisfactory flashing for a ridge or hip. The ridge or hip is then FINISHED. On an asphalt shingle roof a ridge or hip may be finished as shown in figure 12-9. A sufficient number of SQUARES are made by cutting shingles into thirds and the squares are then blind-nailed to the ridge or hip as shown.

Since water gathers in the valleys of a roof they are highly subject to leakage. Valley flashing varies with the manner in which the valley is to be finished. There are two common types of valley finish, known as the OPEN valley and the CLOSED valley.

In working with an open valley, always remember that the roof covering does not extend across the valley. The flashing consists of a prefabricated piece of galvanized iron, copper, or some similar metal, with a SPLASH RIB

or RIDGE down the center and a smaller CRIMP along each of the edges. The flashing is nailed down to the valley with nails driven in the edges, outside the crimps. Great care must be taken not to drive any nails through the flashing inside of the crimps. Puncturing the flashing inside the crimps is very likely to cause leaking.

In the closed valley the roof covering extends across the valley. Sheet metal flashing, cut into small sheets measuring about 18 in. x 10 in. and called SHINGLE TINS, is laid under each course of shingles, along the valley, as the course is laid. The first course of the double course at the eaves is laid, and the first sheet of flashing is placed on top of it. The second course is laid over the first course, and a sheet of flashing is then laid over this one so that the metal is partly covered by the next course. This procedure is continued all the way up the valley.

Shingle tins measuring about 5 in. x 7 in. are used in a similar manner to lay flashing up the side walls of dormers, chimneys, skylights, and the like. Each tin is bent at a right angle so that part of the tin extends up the side wall and the

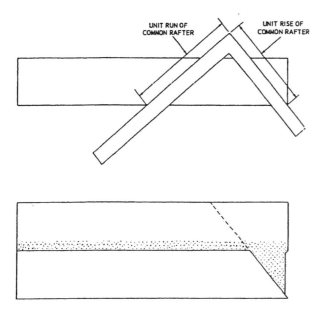

117.52

Figure 12-8.—Laying out pattern for cutting hip and valley shingle.

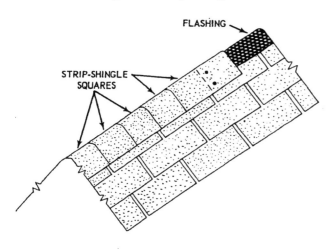

133.149

Figure 12-9.—Hip or ridge flashing and finish on asphalt strip-shingle roof.

rest lies flat on the roof covering. Flashing of this type is called SIDE FLASHING. In addition to the side flashing, a dormer, chimney, or skylight has a strip of flashing called an APRON along the bottom of the outer wall or face and a chimney or skylight has a similar strip, called the SADDLE flashing, along the bottom of the inner wall or face.

BUILT-UP ROOFING

Built-up roofing consists of several layers of tar-rag-felt, asphalt-rag-felt, or asphalt-asbestos-felt set in a hot BINDER of melted pitch or asphalt. A final layer of binder is spread on top and sprinkled with a layer of gravel, crushed stone, or slag. Built-up roofing is confined to roofs which are no steeper than about 4 in 12. On steeper roofs the binder tends to work down and clog gutters and drains. Pitch binder should not be used on a roof steeper than 3 in 12. Asphalt binder may be used on somewhat steeper roofs. For built-up roofing, roof sheathing should be tight-laid and, preferably, doubled.

Each layer of built-up roofing is called a PLY. In a 5-ply roof the first two layers are laid without binder; these are called the DRY NAILERS. Before they are nailed in place, a layer of building paper is tacked down to the roof sheathing.

Built-up roofing, like shingling, is started at the eaves, so that strips will overlap in the direction of the watershed. Figure 12-10 shows the manner of laying 32-in. material to obtain 5-ply coverage at all points on the roof. Nailing must be in accordance with a predetermined schedule, designed to distribute the nails in successive plys evenly among the nails already driven. The roofing shown in figure 12-10 is laid as follows:

1. Lay the building paper with a 2-in. overlap as shown. Spot-nail it down just enough to keep it from blowing away.

2. Cut a 16-in. strip of saturated felt and lay it along the eaves. Nail it down with nails placed 1 in. from the back edge, spaced 12 in. on centers.

3. Nail a full-width (32 in.) strip over the first strip, in the same nailing schedule.

4. Nail the next full-width strip with the outer edge 14 in. from the outer edges of the first two, to obtain a 2-in. overlap over the edge of the first strip laid. Continue laying full-width strips with the same exposure (14 in.) until the opposite edge of the roof is reached. Finish off with a half-strip along this edge. This completes 2-ply dry nailer.

5. The 3-ply starts with one-third of a strip, covered by two-thirds of a strip and then by a full strip, as shown. To obtain a 2-in. overlap of the outer edge of the second full strip over the inner edge of the first strip laid, the outer edge of the second full strip must be 8 2/3 in.

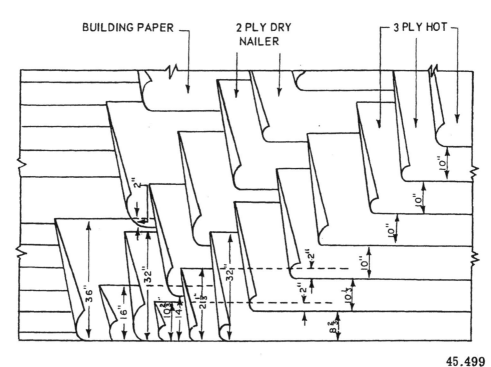

Figure 12-10.—Laying a 5-ply built-up roof.

from the outer edges of the first three strips laid. To maintain the same overlap, the outer edge of the third full strip must be 10 1/3 in. from the outer edge of the second full strip. Subsequent strips may be laid with an exposure of 10 in. Finish off at the opposite edge of the roof with a full strip, two-thirds of a strip, and one-third of a strip, to maintain 3 plys throughout.

The binder is melted and maintained at proper temperature in a pressure fuel kettle. The kettle must be set up and kept level. If it is not level it will heat unevenly, and this creates a hazard. The first duty of the kettle man is to inspect the kettle, especially to ensure that it is perfectly dry. Any accumulation of water inside will turn to steam when the kettle gets hot. This may cause the hot binder to bubble over, which creates a very serious fire hazard. Detailed procedure for lighting off operating, servicing, and maintaining the kettle is given in the manufacturer's manual.

The kettle man must maintain the binder at a steady temperature, as indicated by the temperature gage on the kettle. Correct temperature is designated in binder manufacturer's specifications; for asphalt it is about 400° F. The best way to keep an even temperature is to add material pro rata as melted material is tapped off. Pieces must not be thrown into the melted mass, but placed on the surface, pushed under slowly, and then released. If the material is not being steadily tapped off, it may eventually overheat, even with the burner flame at the lowest possible level. In that case, the burner should be withdrawn from the kettle and placed on the ground, to be re-inserted when the temperature falls. Prolonged overheating causes flashing and impairs the quality of the binder.

Asphalt or pitch must not be allowed to accumulate on the exterior of the kettle, because of the fire hazard. If the kettle catches fire, close the lid immediately, shut off the pressure and burner valves, and, if possible, remove the burner from the kettle. Never attempt to extinguish a kettle fire with water. Use sand, dirt, or a chemical fire extinguisher.

A hot roofing crew consists of a mop man and as many felt layers, broomers, nailers, and carriers as the size of the roof requires. The mop man is in charge of the roofing crew. It is his important responsibility to mop on only binder which is at the proper temperature. Binder which is too hot will burn the felt, and the layer it makes will be too thin. A layer which is too thin will eventually crack, and the felt may separate from the binder. Binder which is too cold goes on too thick, so that more material is used than is required.

The felt layer must get the felt down as soon as possible after the binder has been placed. If the interval between mopping and felt-laying is too long, the binder will cool to the point where it will not bond well with the felt. The felt layer should follow the mop man at an interval of not more than 3 feet. The broomer should follow immediately behind the felt layer, brooming out all air bubbles and imbedding the felt solidly in the binder.

Buckets of hot binder should never be filled more than three-fourths full, and they should never be carried at any speed faster than walking. Whenever possible, the mop man should work downwind from the felt layer and broomer, to reduce the danger of spattering. He must take every precaution against spattering at all times. He should LIFT his mop out of the bucket, not drag it across the rim. Dragging the mop in this manner may upset the bucket, and the hot binder may quickly spread to the feet, or, worse still, to the knees, of nearby members of the roofing crew.

OUTSIDE WALL COVERING

After the door and window frames, the outside-wall covering is the next major item in the exterior finish. On an all-wood structure the principal parts of the outside-wall covering are the WATER TABLE, the CORNER COVERING, and the SIDING, usually erected in that order.

WATER TABLE

The term water table may be applied to anything that is used to keep the water from running down the face of the foundation wall. A water table may also be used to form a starting point for the siding material and to improve the exterior appearance of the building. Figure 12-12 shows two common types of water tables.

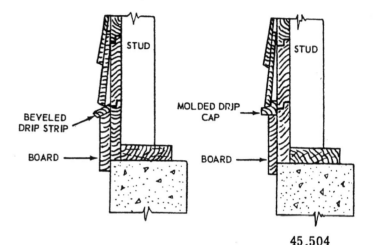

45.504

Figure 12-12.—Common types of water table.

In general, any type of assembled water table should be flashed with metal at the drip cap. There should be a quirk (curve) provided in the underside of the drip cap to prevent water from working into the joints of the assembled water table and causing decay.

CORNER COVERING

The outside corners of a wooden frame structure can be finished in several ways. Siding boards can be miter-joined at the corners. Shingles can be edge-lapped alternately, first from one side, then from the other. Ends of siding boards can be butted and the corner then covered with a metal cap. A type of corner finish which can be used with almost any kind of outside-wall covering is called a CORNER BOARD. This corner board can be applied to the corner, with the siding or shingles end-or edge-butted against the board.

A corner board usually consists of 2 pieces of 1 1/8-in. stock, one piece 3 in. wide, the other 4 in. wide if an edge-butt joint between boards is used. The boards, cut to a length which will extend from the top of the water table to the bottom of the frieze, are edge-butted and nailed together before they are nailed to the corner, a procedure which ensures a good tight joint. (See fig. 12-13.) A strip of building paper should be tacked over the corner before the corner board is nailed in position (always allow an overlap of paper to cover the subsequent crack formed where the ends of the siding butts against the cornerboard).

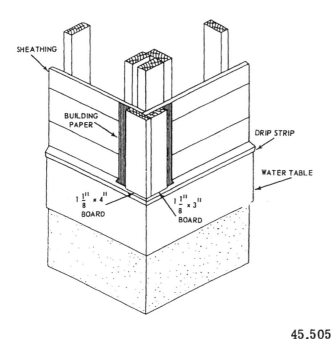

45.505

Figure 12-13.—Corner board.

SIDING

When the cornices, door and window frames, water table, and corner boards (if any) have been installed, the application of the siding begins. For wood siding the specifications usually contain such language as the following:

All exterior sheathing is to be covered with one layer of waterproof building paper before finished material is applied. Paper is to be placed horizontally with at least a 2-in. lap.

Care must be taken to ensure that the building paper overlaps the drip caps or drip strips on the water table, or the flashing on the table if there is any. As the application of either shingle or board siding begins at the water table, the first strip of paper is applied there. The next strip is not applied until the major part of the first strip has been covered with siding.

The type of siding to be used is indicated in the wall sections, and also, as a rule, in the specification, which may state something like the following:

Exterior walls to be covered with the best grade of clear vertical grain shingles laid 10 in. to the weather,
or:
Exterior walls to be covered with 1 x 8 clear cypress shiplap.

The first course of shingle siding is doubled, as in roof shingling, or even tripled. When the first course has been laid, a careful study of the rest of the wall should be made, with consideration given to the total height and the size and height of window openings. Theoretically, all courses should have the exposure specified. Actually, however, in order to make courses line up as nearly as possible with the top and bottom lines of door and window openings, slight adjustments in the amount of exposure are made. These must be evened out by distributing them over adjacent courses, so that the appearance of uniform exposure is maintained. When the heights of all the courses have been determined, they should be laid out on a story pole. Use the pole to mark the heights of courses at the ends of the wall, and use a straightedge or a chalk line between the marks to guide the course laying.

The same general procedure should be followed for bevel siding. Recommended minimum amounts of lap for this type of siding are as follows:

4-in. bevel siding . . . .   3/4 in.
5-in. bevel siding . . . .   7/8 in.
6-in. bevel siding . . . .   1 in.
8-in. bevel siding . . . . 1 1/4 in.
10-in. bevel siding . . . . 1 1/2 in.

In adjusting the exposures of courses, these minimums should be observed as closely as possible. Lay out a story pole for siding courses in the same manner as for shingle courses. Regular siding nails should be used: 6d for 1/2-in. siding, 8d for anything thicker. The lower edge of the first strip laid should be beveled to fit tightly on the drip strip or drip cap. End butt joints between strips should be

149

broken by as many strips as possible, never by less than 2. Ends should be smoothed with a block plane after cutting, to ensure tight-fitting joints which will keep out wind, dust, and water.

Much wood siding used nowadays consists of large plywood panels. For this type of siding horizontal girts must be nailed between the studs along the lines where horizontal joints between panels will occur. Both the horizontal and the vertical joints between panels must be made weathertight. There are several methods of this. Horizontal joints may be protected by flashing laid on the girts and shaped so as to protrude through the joint and overhang the upper edge of the lower panel. Or the horizontal edges of the panels may be rabbeted so they will join together in an overlapping joint like that between strips of shiplap.

Vertical joints may be closed by nailing vertical battens over them; by leaving a slight space between the edges of panels, rabbeting the edges, and gluing in a spline; by a vertical joint sealed by calking compound. The best way to calk a vertical joint is to bevel the edges of the panels as shown in figure 12-14, so that a V-shaped reservoir for the compound is made when the edges are brought together.

Wood siding of all kinds has been to a large extent superseded by various kinds of COMPOSITION siding. Manufacturers of each type include complete instructions for its application with their product, and the only way to ensure satisfactory results is to follow these instructions closely.

133.368
Figure 12-14.—Calking a vertical joint between plywood panels.

PREPARATION

Much time and expense can be saved by planning the job properly. Use safe scaffolding. Use competent and experienced mechanics. Make sure proper material storage facilities are on the job to protect the asbestos-cement siding from all hazards and damage.

Siding from different lots or factory runs may have slight and unavoidable differences in colors. All surfaces to which siding is applied should be supported adequately, be smooth, clean and dry, and provide an adequate nailing base and support. Provide a suitable sheathing or surface for the siding that will serve as an adequate nailing base, capable of developing the full holding power of nails or fasteners that must be used, and that is substantially level, plumb, and smooth. When men are working on a structure that has been or is being sided with asbestos-cement siding, they must be required to take adequate precautions not to damage, stain, or harm the exterior wall siding. This is especially important when painting or built-up roofing work is being done.

FLASHING AT OPENINGS AND CORNERS

Metal flashing should be applied properly at all door and window openings. (See fig. 12-15.)

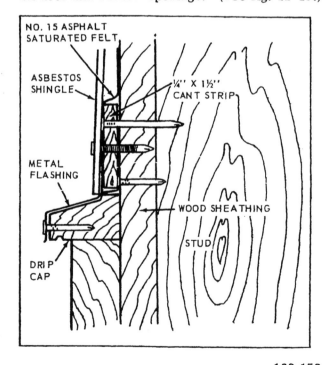

133.152
Figure 12-15.—Flashing cap mold on doors and windows.

Flash all outside corners and inside corners with a 12-inch-wide strip of underlay material centered in or around the corner when corner boards are used. (See fig. 12-16.)

In other corner treatments, carry the underlayment felt around the corner of each sidewall so that a double thickness of felt results over the corner, and use folded backer strips at each course of shingles at the corner. (See fig. 12-16.)

Asbestos-cement siding should be bedded in nonshrinking calking compound at all corners and wherever it butts against wooden trim, masonry, or other projections. Care must be taken in applying the compound to avoid smearing the face of the shingles. Avoid applying visible or exposed calking compound.

CORNER FINISHING

Where wall surfaces join at inside corners, the courses of siding are generally butted, although metal molding or wood corner strip may be used. Outside corners can be handled by any one of the following methods.

For lapped adjoining courses at outside corners, temporarily place a whole shingle against each adjoining wall, so that they meet and join at the corner. Scribe and cut the adjoining vertical edges of the siding units at the proper angle to form a lapped or woven corner joint.

Corner joints should be lapped to the left and right in alternate courses. Courses on adjoining walls should meet and match at corners.

Wood corner boards are made of two pieces of nominal one inch lumber. A 1 by 3 member is nailed to the backside of the 1 by 4 member. This will form a face surface of equal dimension on each side of the corner. Corner boards, as well as all other exterior trim, should be face and back primed before assembly to the structure.

Several styles of nonstaining metal corner finish moldings are available. Apply as recommended by the manufacturer.

APPLICATION OF SIDING TO WALL

The following is based on applying 12- by 24-inch asbestos-cement siding over nominal 1 inch-thick wood lumber sheathing. For applying other sizes of siding, follow the manufacturer's recommendations. For application over nonlumber sheathing, including plywood, the following instructions may require modification as described in other applicable areas of this paragraph. Methods of applying asbestos-cement siding over nonlumber sheathing are detailed later in this paragraph. Very few buildings are true and parallel. Therefore, it is necessary to watch the relationship of the courses to the eave lines, and make sure adjustments as may be needed so that the final course is not too narrow or wedgeshaped. Some uniform adjustments of the exposure of each course may be necessary.

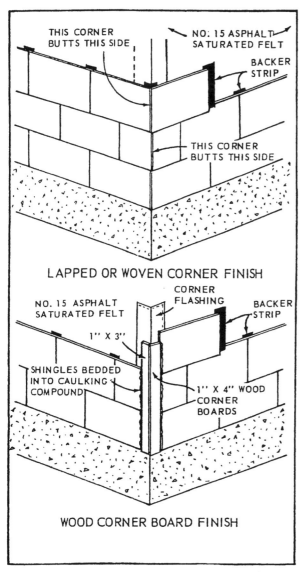

LAPPED OR WOVEN CORNER FINISH

WOOD CORNER BOARD FINISH

133.153

Figure 12-16.—Flashing corners.

Determine where the bottom edge of the first course is to be. Make sure that all courses meet and match at corners and are level all around the building. Determine the total number of courses to complete one wall and lay out the job so that top courses under the eaves will not be too narrow or wedgeshaped. Determine how all corners are to be finished and how openings and other places are to be flashed properly and trimmed. Remove all unnecessary projections from the wall. Snap a level chalkline all around the building to fix the location of the top edge of the first course of siding as shown in figure 12-17. The siding will overhang the bottom edge of the cant strip 1/4 inch to provide a drip edge. Snap additional horizontal chalklines to mark the top of the cant strip and each succeeding course. Space the lines the distance necessary to provide the required exposure for the type of _____ cement siding being used.

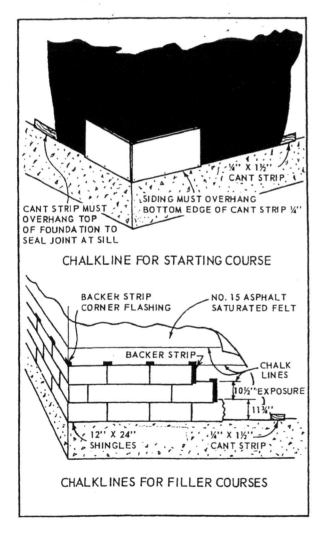

CHALKLINE FOR STARTING COURSE

CHALKLINES FOR FILLER COURSES

133.154

Figure 12-17.—Use of chalklines.

CANT STRIP

Nail a 1/4- by 1-1/2-inch wood strip along the bottom edge of the sheathing so that it is level and overhangs the top of the foundation enough to seal the joint between the top of the foundation, the wood sill, and the bottom of the sheathing. This strip gives a necessary cant or pitch to the first course of shingles and should always be used.

FIRST AND ODD-NUMBERED COURSES

Start at the outside corner of the wall with a full-size siding unit. Make sure this unit is placed plumb and level, and aligned with the chalkline, because it guides the lay of all other units. All siding units in this course must overhang the bottom edge of the cant strip 1/4 inch to provide a drip edge. Use the proper face nails supplied with the siding for the type of sheathing and application method being used. Drive nails snug but not too tight. Before driving the last nail at the right-hand end of the unit, insert a backer strip in place and secure it with the last nail. Backer strips must always be used and placed centered at the joint between siding units, and with the lower end overlapping the head of the cant strip or lower course. Continue to apply full-size siding units in the first course, with their top edges aligned with the chalkline. The last unit in a course or at an opening should not be less than 6 inches wide, and if a smaller space will remain to be filled, a few inches should be cut from the units applied earlier in the course. Punch any necessary facenail holes in short pieces of siding. Do not leave spaces between ends of units. Wedgeshaped spaces between the ends of siding units are proof of incorrect application. Butt units tightly together end to end.

SECOND AND SUCCEEDING EVEN-NUMBERED COURSES

When using 12- by 24-inch siding, succeeding courses should have their vertical joints break on "halves." Start the second course with a half unit. When using 32 inch-long units, break on "thirds." Start the second course of 48 inch-long units with a 2/3 unit. Some bundles of siding contain units shorter than full length to provide the necessary shorter pieces for starting courses. Starting at the left-hand corner with a partial unit, having its head edge aligned with the chalkline and its lower edge overlapping the head of the next lower course the correct distance to provide the necessary head-lap between courses, insert a nail in a face-nail hole, making sure the shank of the nail is resting on the top edge of the next lower course, thus establishing the proper amount of head-lap. Then nail in place, and continue to work with full size units.

INSULATION

Exterior wall insulation is normally installed at the time a building or structure is built, according to area climatic conditions and building occupancy. The economic feature of saving and equalizing heat and/or air conditioning is of primary importance. Insulation also serves a valuable purpose in moisture control, which prevents rot and fungus growth. In buildings and structures without adequate insulation, or where insulation has deteriorated or been displaced, it should be installed or replaced after a study of the best type and method of application for prevailing conditions. The fireproofing and verminproofing qualities of insulation should also be considered.

TYPES OF INSULATION

Roll or batt blankets may be used where access to the space between studs allows their placement and fastening. Loose material (pellets or wool) may be used where areas are accessible from a limited opening only, such as around windows and doors and in wall utility compartments. Other types of insulation include rigid and semirigid composition board, which is generally used around concrete slabs and as sheathing under the siding. Utility batts may be used where no vapor barrier is required or where a separate vapor barrier has been provided.

Roll or batt insulation is most satisfactorily placed when either the inside or outside surface of a building or structure is uncovered. Replacement of insulation should be considered when the outer face of a wall is resheathed or when an inner surface is replaced. When both wall faces are covered it is necessary to pour loose insulation from the top or force it in by compressed air from some opening in the wall. In any case, care should be exercised to fill all small crevices and to place material into confined spaces and around piping and wiring. The vapor barrier side of insulation should face toward the warm side of the wall. In placing any type or kind of insulation, follow the manufacturer's recommendations for proper thickness, form, and fastening. Figure 12-18 illustrates application of insulating batts, blankets, and utility batts to standard wood-constructed walls. Figure 12-19 shows methods of placing insulated material on masonry and metal sidewalls.

Batts and Blankets

In figure 12-18 the following steps are demonstrated for batts and blankets.

Cut insulation to stud height plus 3 inches for top and bottom nailing flanges. Foot and inch markings along the edge of the blanket simplify

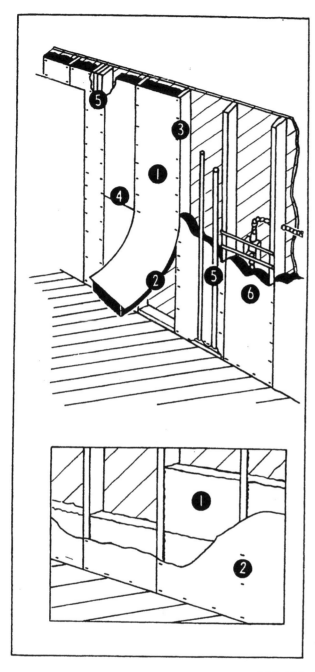

133.158

Figure 12-18.—Placing batts, blankets, and utility batts in exterior wood frame wall.

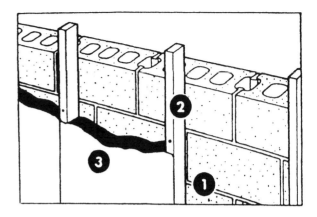

MASONRY SIDEWALLS

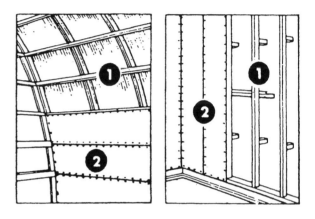

METAL SIDEWALLS

133.159

Figure 12-19.—Placing insulation inside masonry and metal sidewalls.

measuring. Insulation may also be applied from a roll and cut off at bottom to fit.

Fluff the blanket to full thickness, open the nailing flanges, and press back the insulation to leave an end nailing flange exposed. Make sure vapor barrier faces the building interior (warm-in-winter side).

Start at the top of the stud space and work down if roll blankets are used. Batts can be installed from the floor up. Staple or nail flanges to the stud at 5- to 6-inch spacing.

Press insulation closely together at joints so that no voids are left. Make sure the vapor barrier is not broken by spaces at joints.

Insulate with special care on the cold side of pipes and drains. Compress insulation behind pipes where possible, or pack with utility batts or pouring wool.

Hand-pack narrow spaces with utility batts, pouring wool, or scraps from batts or blankets. Cut and apply the vapor barrier to provide vapor protection.

Utility Batts

In figure 12-19 the following steps are described for utility batts.

1. Stack 15- by 10-inch utility batts between studs. If the 15-inch dimension is placed horizontally, batts fit between studs placed 16 inches on center. With the 15-inch dimension vertical, 2 batts can be packed into the space between studs on 20-inch centers.

2. Tack the vapor barrier paper over the insulation to prevent condensation. For complete vapor protection, the vapor barrier must be continuous at joints.

Masonry Sidewalls

For masonry sidewalls, take the following steps (fig. 12-19):

1. Dampproof the inner face of the masonry with a vapor-porous material such as a water-emulsion asphalt or fibrated mastic.

2. Attach furring strips slightly thicker than normal to provide space for economy (1-1/2-inch) or medium (2-inch) roll blankets.

3. Apply roll or batt blankets to furring strips, following directions given for wood sidewalls.

Metal Sidewalls

For metal sidewalls, take the following steps (fig. 12-19):

1. Attach furring strips to purlins or grits of the metal building on a standard spacing to take roll blanket insulation.

2. Staple or nail roll blankets to furring strips. Make sure the vapor barrier is continuous to prevent condensation on steel sheets. Cover with the desired finish.

INTERIOR FINISH

The interior finish consists mainly of the finish covering applied to the rough walls, ceilings, and floors. Other major interior finish items are the inside door frames, the doors, the window sash, and the stairs.

Interior-finish items whose function is principally ornamental are classified under the general heading of INTERIOR TRIM. Interior trim includes inside door and window casings, window stools and aprons, baseboards, and molding trim.

The usual order of construction for the interior finish is as follows:

1. Ceiling covering
2. Wall covering
3. Stairs
4. Window sash
5. Window inside casings, stools, and aprons
6. Finish flooring
7. Inside door frames and casings
8. Baseboards
9. Molding trim.

WALL AND CEILING COVERING

The two major types of wall and ceiling covering are PLASTER and DRY-WALL COVERING. Dry-wall covering is a general term applied to sheets or panels of wood, plywood, fiberboard, and the like.

PLASTER

A PLASTER wall and/or ceiling covering requires the construction of a PLASTER BASE, or surface on which the plaster can be spread and to which it will adhere. A surface of this kind was formerly constructed by nailing wooden LATHS (thin, narrow strips usually 48 in. long) to the edges of studs and joists, or to wooden FURRING STRIPS anchored to concrete or masonry walls. In modern construction, wooden lath has been almost entirely superseded by GYPSUM lath, FIBERBOARD lath and METAL lath.

Gypsum lath usually consists of 16 in. by 48 in. sheets of GYPSUM BOARD, either solid or perforated and usually squared-edged. It is applied horizontally to studs and at right angles to joists, and nailed to studs, joists, or furring strips with 1 1/8-in. flat-headed GYPSUM-LATH NAILS, 5 to each stud, joist or strip crossing.

Fiberboard lath consists of sheets of fiberboard, also usually 16 in. by 48 in. in size. It may be either square-edged or shiplap edged. It is applied in much the same manner as gypsum lath, except that 1 1/4-in. blued FIBERBOARD-LATH NAILS are used.

Metal lath consists of screen-like sheets of MESHED or RIBBED metal, usually 27 in. by 96 in. in size. To walls it is applied horizontally; to ceilings with the long dimension perpendicular to the line of the joists. It may be nailed to studs or to furring strips with regular metal-lath STAPLES, or with 8-penny nails driven part-way in and then hammered over. It may be similarly nailed to ceiling joists, or it may be tied up with wire ties to nails driven through the joists about 2 in. above the lower edges.

Before lath is applied to walls and ceilings, PLASTER GROUNDS are installed as called for in the working drawings. Plaster grounds are wood strips of the same thickness as the combined thickness of the lath and plaster. They are nailed to the framing members around doors and windows and to the studs along floor lines. They serve as a guide to the plasterers, to ensure that the plaster behind door casings, window casings, and baseboards will be of uniform and correct thickness. They also serve as nailing bases for the trim members mentioned.

Plastering is usually done in three coats, which form a combined thickness of about 5/8 in. The first coat is called the SCRATCH coat, because it is usually scored when partially set to improve the adhesion of the second coat. The second coat is called the BROWN coat, and the third the WHITE (also the SKIM or FINISH) coat. As gypsum or fiberboard lath provides the equivalent of a scratch coat, only the brown and finish coats of plaster are applied when these types of lath are used.

The basic ingredients for scratch-coat and brown-coat plaster are lime and sand. Proportions vary, but a scratch coat usually has about 1 part of lime to 2 parts of sand, by volume. The proportion of lime to sand in a brown coat is slightly smaller.

Plaster for an ordinary white coat usually consists of lime putty mixed with plaster-of-paris; a little marble dust may be included. Plaster for a high grade finish coat contains calcium sulphate instead of lime. KEENE's CEMENT is a well-known variety of calcium sulphate finish plaster. A very superior hard-finish coat can be obtained by mixing 4 parts of Keene's cement with 1 part of lime putty.

Manufacturers of plaster usually furnish instruction sheets which set forth the recommended ingredient proportions and methods of application for their products. Follow these instructions closely. The actual application of plaster, especially to ceilings, is a skill which can be acquired only through practice. Additional information on plaster work may be found in chapter 14.

DRY-WALL FINISH

DRY-WALL FINISH is a general term applied to sheets or panels of various materials used for inside-wall and ceiling covering. The most common dry-wall finishes are GYPSUM-BOARD, PLYWOOD, FIBERBOARD, and WOOD.

Gypsum Board

Gypsum board usually comes in a standard size of 4' by 8'. However, on notice it can be obtained in any length up to 16 ft. It can be applied to walls, either vertically or horizontally. A 4-ft wide sheet applied vertically to studs 16 in. O.C. will cover 3 stud spaces. Five-penny cement-coated nails should be used with 1/2-in.-thick gypsum, 4-penny nails with 3/8-in.-thick gypsum. Nails should be spaced 6 to 8 in. O.C. for walls and 5 to 7 in. O.C. for ceilings.

Nail heads should be driven about one-sixteenth inch below the face of the board; this set can be obtained by using a crowned hammer. The indentations around nails away from edges are concealed by applying JOINT CEMENT. The nail indentations along edges are concealed with a perforated fiber JOINT TAPE set in joint cement. Edges are slightly recessed to bring the tape flush with the faces. Besides concealing the nail indentations, the tape also conceals the joint.

The procedure for taping a joint is as follows:

1. Spread the joint cement along the joint with a 4- to 6-in. putty knife. Joint cement comes in powder form; the powder is mixed with water to about the consistency of putty.
2. Lay the tape against the joint and press it into the recess with the putty knife. Press until some of the joint cement is forced out through the holes in the tape.
3. Spread joint cement over the tape, and FEATHER (taper off) the outer edges.
4. Allow the cement to dry, then sand lightly. Apply a second coat, and again feather the edges.
5. Allow the cement to dry, and then sand the joint smooth.

For nail indentations away from edges, fill the indentations with cement, allow the cement to dry, and sand lightly. Apply another coat, allow to dry, and sand smooth.

Plywood

Plywood finish comes in sheets of various sizes which can be applied either vertically or horizontally. With horizontal application, lengths of stud stock called NAILERS are framed between the studs along the lines of horizontal joints. Panels can be nailed directly to studs and nailers, but a better method is to nail 2-in. furring strips to the studs and nailers and then glue and nail the panels to the strips. This method reduces joint movements caused by swelling or shrinking of the studs and nailers.

Joints between plywood panels can be finished in a variety of ways. For a tight butt joint, spread enough glue on the furring strip, stud, or nailer to provide a SQUEEZE of glue between the edges, allow the glue to dry, and then block-sand the joint smooth. Another smooth joint can be obtained by rabbeting the edges for shiplap.

Edges of panels can be smoothed and the joints left open for ornamental effect; or the edges can be beveled to form a V-groove joint when brought together; or joints can be left open and then filled with glued-in wooden splines. Outside corners between panels can be miter-joined, or the right angle between square edges at outside corners can be filled with quarter-round molding. Inside corners can be butted or mitered.

One-half inch plywood finish is nailed on with 1 1/4 in. finish nails spaced 6 in. O.C.

Fiberboard

Fiberboard wall finish comes in 2 ft by 8 ft sheets which are applied horizontally. The long edges are usually rabbeted or tongue-and-grooved for joining. Fiberboard is nailed in place with finish nails, brads, or cadmium plated fiberboard nails. Use 1 1/2-nails for 1/2-inch thick boards and 2-inch nails for 1-inch thick boards.

Fiberboard in small squares or rectangles is called TILEBOARD and each piece of tileboard is called a TILE. Common sizes are 12 inches by 12 inches, 12 inches by 24 inches, 16 inches by 16 inches, and 16 inches by 32 inches. Tiles can be nailed to studs, joists, and furring strips; usually, however, they are glued to a continuous surface of wood or plasterboard with a special type of adhesive.

STAIRS

There are many different kinds of stairs, but all have two main parts in common: the TREADS people walk on, and the STRINGERS (also called STRINGS, HORSES, and CARRIAGES) which support the treads. A very simple type of stairway, consisting only of stringers and treads, is shown in the left-hand view of figure 13-1. Treads of the type shown here are called PLANK treads, and this simple type of stairway is called a CLEAT stairway, because of the cleats attached to the stringers to support the treads.

A more finished type of stairway has the treads mounted on two or more sawtooth-edged stringers, and includes RISERS, as shown in the right-hand view of figure 13-1. The stringers

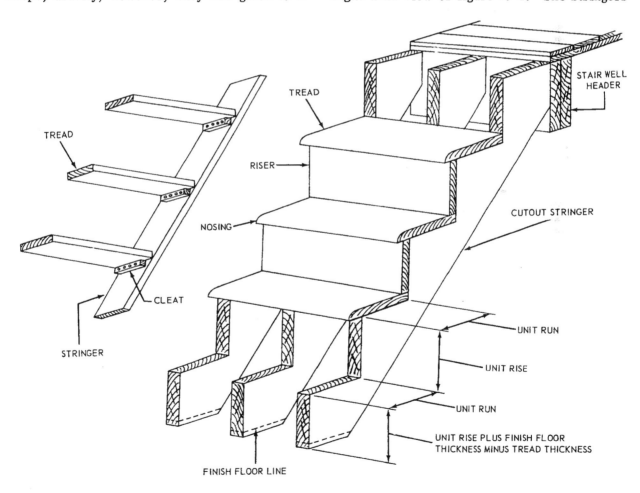

45.507

Figure 13-1.—Stairway nomenclature.

shown here are cut out of solid pieces of dimension lumber (usually 2 x 12), and are therefore called CUTOUT or SAWED stringers.

STAIRWAY LAYOUT

The first step in stairway layout is to determine the UNIT RISE and UNIT RUN shown in figure 13-1. The unit rise is calculated on the basis of the TOTAL RISE of the stairway, and the fact that the customary permissible unit rise for stairs is in the vicinity of 7 inches.

The total rise is the vertical distance between the lower finish floor level and the upper finish floor level. This may be shown in the elevations; however, since the actual vertical distance as constructed may vary slightly from what it should have been, and since it is the actual distance you are dealing with, the distance should be measured.

At the time the stairs are to be laid out, the subflooring is laid but the finish flooring isn't. If both the lower and the upper floor are to be covered with finish flooring of the same thickness, the measured vertical distance from lower subfloor surface to the upper subfloor surface will be the same as the eventual distance between the finish floor surfaces, and therefore equal to the total rise of the stairway. But if you are measuring up from a finish floor (such as a concrete basement floor, for instance), then you must add to the measured distance the thickness of the upper finish flooring to get the total rise of the stairway. If the upper and lower finish floors will be of different thicknesses, then you must add the difference in thickness to the measured distance between subfloor surfaces to get the total rise of the stairway. Use a straight piece of lumber plumbed in the stair opening with a spirit level, or a plumb bob and cord, to measure the vertical distance.

Assume that the total rise measures 8 ft 11 in., as shown in figure 13-2. Knowing this, you can determine the unit rise as follows. First, reduce the total rise to inches—in this case it comes to 107 in. Next, divide the total rise in inches by the average permissible unit rise, which is 7 in. The result, disregarding any fraction, is the number of RISERS the stairway will have—in this case it is 107/7, or 15. Now divide the total rise in inches by the number of risers—in this case, this is 107/15, which comes to 7.13 in., or, rounded off to the nearest 1/16 in., 7 1/8 in. This, then, is the unit rise, as shown in figure 13-2.

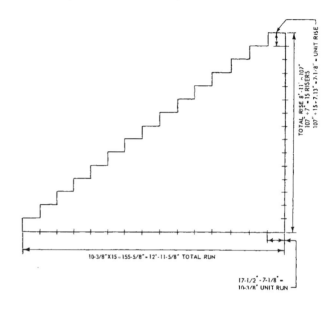

117.54

Figure 13-2.—Stairway layout computations.

The unit run is calculated on the basis of (1) the unit rise, and (2) a general architects' rule that the sum of the unit run and unit rise should be 17 1/2 in. In view of (2), if the unit rise is 7 1/8 in., the unit run is 17 1/2 in. minus 7 1/8 in., or 10 3/8 in.

You can now calculate the TOTAL RUN of the stairway. The total run is obviously equal to the product of the unit run times the total number of treads in the stairway. However, the total number of treads depends upon the manner in which the upper end of the stairway will be anchored to the header.

In figure 13-3, three methods of anchoring the upper end of a stairway are shown. In the first view there is a complete tread at the top of the stairway. This means that the number of complete treads will be the same as the number of risers. For the stairway shown in figure 13-1, there are 15 risers and 15 complete treads. Therefore, the total run of the stairway will be the product of the unit run times 15, or 10 3/8 in. x 15, or 155 5/8", or 12 ft 11 5/8 in., as shown.

In figure 13-3, second view, there is only part of a tread at the top of the stairway. If this method were used for the stairway shown in figure 13-2, the number of complete treads would be ONE LESS than the number of risers, or 14. The total run of the stairway would be the product of 14 x 10 3/8, PLUS THE RUN OF

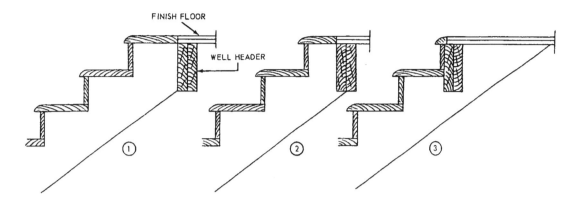

45.508

Figure 13-3.—Three methods of anchoring upper end of a stairway.

THE PARTIAL TREAD AT THE TOP. Suppose this run were 7 inches. Then the total run would be 14 x 10 3/8 + 7, or 152 1/4 in., or 12 ft 8 1/4 in.

In figure 13-3, third view, there is no tread at all at the top of the stairway; the upper finish flooring serves as the top tread. In this case the total number of complete treads is again 14, but since there is no additional partial tread, the total run of the stairway is 14 x 10 3/8, or 145 1/4 in., or 12 ft 1 1/4 in.

When you have calculated the total run of the stairway, drop a plumb bob from the well head to the floor below and measure off the total run from the plumb bob. This locates the anchoring point for the lower end of the stairway.

Cutout stringers for main stairways are usually made from 2 x 12 stock. The first question is: About how long a piece of stock will you need? Let's assume that you are to use the method of upper-end anchorage shown in the first view of figure 13-3 to lay out a stringer for the stairway shown in figure 13-2. This stairway has a total rise of 8 ft 11 in. and a total run of 12 ft 11 5/8 in. The stringer must be long enough to form the hypotenuse of a triangle with sides of those two lengths. For an approximate length estimate, call the sides 9 and 13 ft long. The length of the hypotenuse, then, will equal the square root of $9^2 + 13^2$, or the square root of 250, or about 15.8 ft, or about 15 ft 9 1/2 in.

Figure 13-4 shows the layout at the lower end of the stringer. Set the framing square to the unit run on the tongue and the unit rise on the blade, and draw the line AB. This line represents the bottom tread. Then draw AD perpendicular to AB, in length equal to the unit rise.

This line represents the bottom riser in the stairway. Now, you've probably noticed that, up to this point, the thickness of a tread in the stairway has been ignored. This thickness is now about to be accounted for, by making an allowance in the height of this first riser, a process which is called DROPPING THE STRINGER.

As you can see in figure 13-1, the unit rise is measured from the top of one tread to the top of the next for ALL RISERS EXCEPT THE BOTTOM ONE. For this one, the unit rise is measured FROM THE FINISHED FLOOR SURFACE TO THE SURFACE OF THE FIRST TREAD. If AD were cut to the unit rise, the actual rise of the first step would be the sum of the unit rise plus the thickness of a tread. Therefore, the length of AD is shortened by the thickness of a tread, as shown in figure 13-4— or by the thickness of a tread less the thickness of the finish flooring. The first is done if the stringer will rest on a finish floor, such as concrete basement floor. The second is done if the stringer will rest on subflooring.

When you have shortened AD to AE, as shown, draw EF parallel to AB. This line represents the bottom horizontal anchor-edge of the stringer. Then proceed to lay off the remaining risers and treads to the unit rise and unit run, until you have laid off 15 risers and 15 treads. Figure 13-5 shows the layout at the upper end of the stringer. The line AB represents the top—that is, the 15th—tread. BC, drawn perpendicular to AB, represents the upper vertical anchor-edge of the stringer, which will butt against the stairwell header.

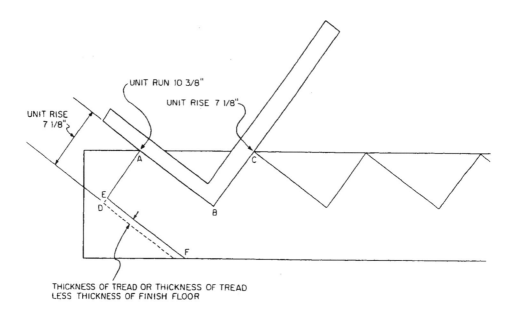

Figure 13-4.—Layout of lower end of cutout stringer.

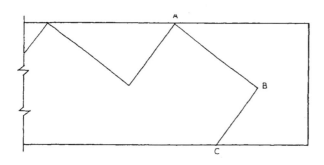

Figure 13-5.—Layout at upper end
of cutout stringer.

STAIRWAY CONSTRUCTION

We have been dealing with a common **STRAIGHT-FLIGHT** stairway, meaning one which follows the same direction throughout. When floor space is not extensive enough to permit construction of a straight-flight stairway, a **CHANGE** stairway is installed—meaning, one which changes direction one or more times. The most common types of these are 90-**DEGREE** change and 180-**DEGREE** change. These are usually **PLATFORM** stairways—that is, successive straight-flight lengths, connecting platforms at which the direction changes 90 degrees, or doubles back 180 degrees. Such a stairway is laid out simply as a succession of straight-flight stairways.

The stairs in a structure are broadly divided into **PRINCIPAL** stairs and **SERVICE** stairs. Service stairs are porch, basement, and attic stairs. Some of these may be simple cleat stairways; others may be **OPEN-RISER** stairways. An open-riser stairway has treads anchored on cut-out stringers or stair-block stringers, but no risers. The lower ends of the stringers on porch, basement, and other stairs anchored on concrete are fastened with a **KICK-PLATE** like the one shown in figure 13-6.

A principal stairway is usually more finished in appearance. Rough cutout stringers are concealed by **FINISH** stringers like the one shown in figure 13-7. Treads and risers are often rabbet-joined as shown in figure 13-8. To prevent squeaking, triangular blocks may be glued into the joints, as shown in the same figure.

The vertical members which support a stairway handrail are called **BALUSTERS**. Figure 13-9 shows a method of joining balusters to treads. For this method, dowels shaped on the lower ends of the balusters are glued into holes bored in the treads.

Stringers should be toenailed to well headers with 10-penny nails, three to each side of the stringer. Those which face against trimmer joists should be nailed to the joist with at least three 16-penny nails apiece. At the bottom a

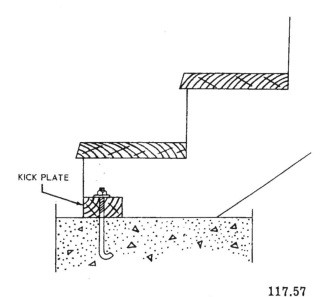

117.57

Figure 13-6.—Kick-plate for anchoring stairs to concrete.

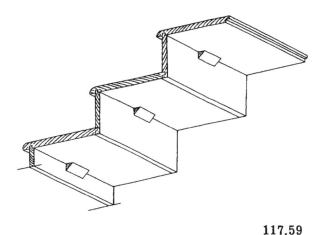

117.59

Figure 13-8.—Rabbet-joined treads and risers.

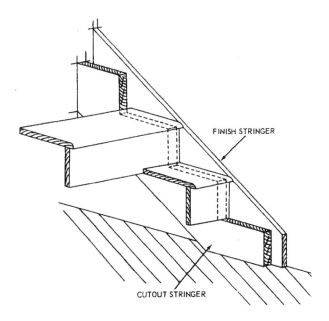

117.58

Figure 13-7.—Finish stringer.

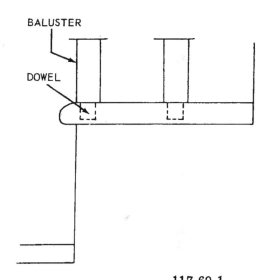

117.60.1

Figure 13-9.—One method of joining a baluster to the tread.

stringer should be toenailed with 10-penny nails, 4 to each side, driven into the subflooring and if possible into a joist below.

Treads and risers should be nailed to stringers with 6-penny, 8-penny, or 10-penny finish nails, depending on the thickness of the stock.

WINDOW SASH

A window frame is built to the dimensions of the window, as given on the window schedule. To prevent the sash from binding in the frame, it is necessary to apply a CLEARANCE ALLOWANCE when laying out the sash. Sash for a double-hung window is made 1/8 in. narrower and 1/16 in. shorter than the finished opening size; sash for wooden casements is made 1/8 in. narrower and 1/32 in. shorter than the opening size. Wooden sash is usually made from 1 3/8-in.-thick stock.

INSTALLING WINDOW SASH

Casement sash is hung in about the same manner that a door is hung.

Double-hung sash consists of an upper and a lower sash, each of which can be slid up and down in a separate vertical runway. The upper sash slides in the outer runway, the lower sash in the inner runway. The inner side of the outer runway is formed by the parting stop, the outer side by the blind stop, or by a SIDE STOP nailed to the faces of the jambs. The outer side of the inner runway is formed by the parting stop, the inner side by a side stop nailed to the faces of the side jambs. All this is shown in figures 13-10 and 13-11.

The weight of a double-hung sash may be counterbalanced by a couple of SASH WEIGHTS,

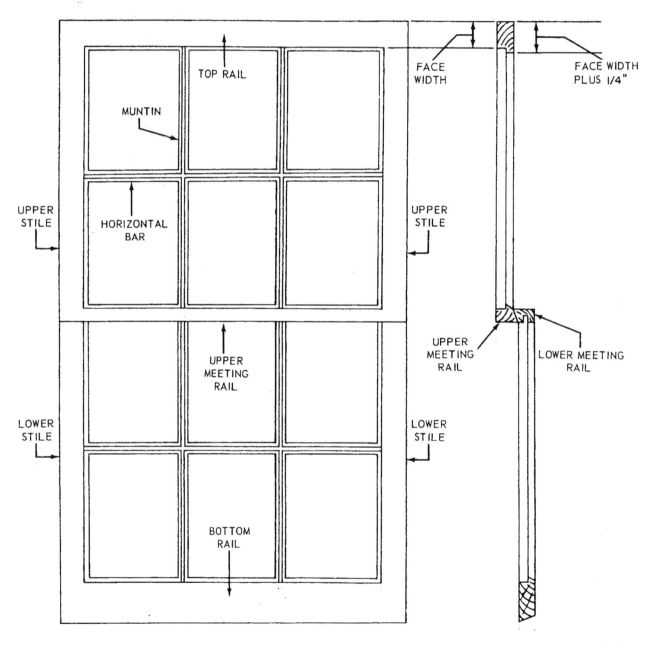

45.509

Figure 13-10.—Parts of a double-hung window sash.

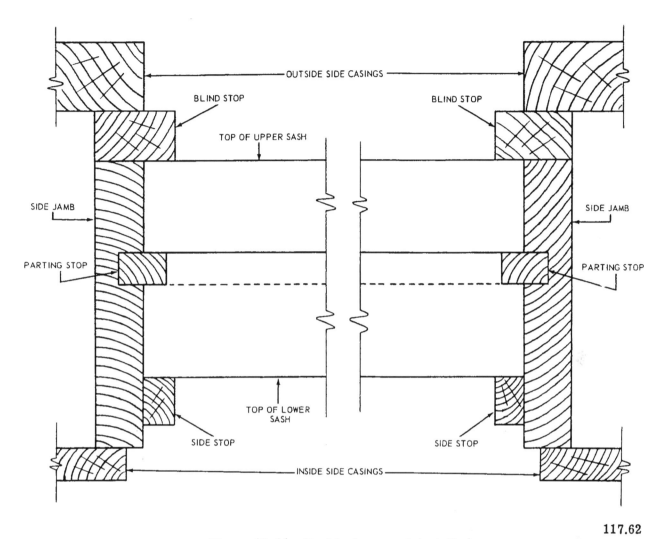

Figure 13-11.—Double-hung sash installed.

which hang in PULLEY POCKETS on either side of the frame, and which are connected to the tops of the upper and lower sash by lengths of SASH CORD running up and over pulleys at the top of the frame. SASH WEIGHTS HAVE BEEN LARGELY REPLACED, HOWEVER, BY VARIOUS SPRING DEVICES WHICH LIE INSIDE THE JAMBS AND DO NOT REQUIRE PULLEY POCKETS. For sash cord the outer edges of the stiles must be grooved about one-third of the way down from the top, and a hole must be cut at the end of each groove to contain a knot in the end of the cord. For some types of spring balances the stiles are not grooved; other types require a groove the full length of the stile.

Steps in fitting and hanging double-hung sash are as follows:

1. Try the upper sash in the frame for a fit; if necessary, plane down the stiles to get a clearance of 1/8 in.

2. Notch the ends of the meeting rails so the rails will fit around the parting stop as shown in figure 13-12. The depth of the notch is equal to the thickness of the parting stop, plus a 1/16-in. allowance for clearance. The width of the notch is the width of the parting stop, less the depth of the parting stop groove, plus a 1/16-in. allowance for clearance.

3. Remove the parting stop from the jambs, set the upper sash in its runway, and replace the parting stop. Run the upper sash all the way up and fasten it there with a nail tacked into each of the side jambs.

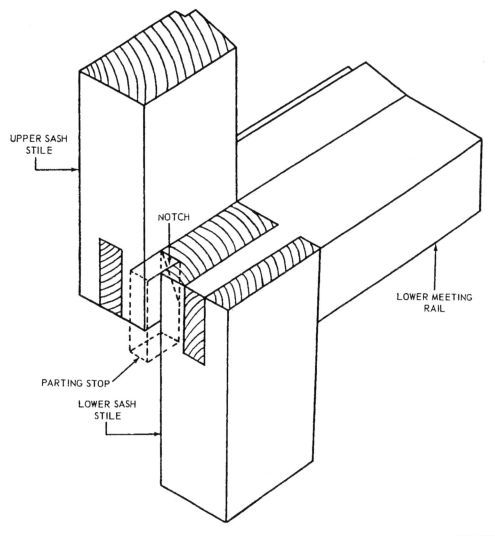

UPPER SASH
STILE

NOTCH

LOWER MEETING
RAIL

PARTING STOP

LOWER SASH
STILE

117.63

Figure 13-12.—Notching meeting rails for parting stop.

4. Try the lower sash for a fit, planing down the stiles as necessary.

5. Set the angle of the sill on the T-bevel by lining the handle of the bevel up with the parting stop and the blade with the sill. Lay off this angle on the bottom of the bottom rail and bevel the bottom of the rail to the angle.

6. Set the lower sash in its runway, all the way down, and measure the amount that the tops of the meeting rails are out of flush with each other. This is the amount that must be planed off the bottom rail to ensure that the meeting rails will be exactly flush when the window is closed. Plane down the bottom rail until the meeting rails come flush.

7. Remove the sash and the parting stop, and install or attach the counterbalance for the upper sash. Manufacturer's instructions for installing are usually included with SPRING BALANCES. To attach a sash weight, first run the end of the sash cord over the pulley into the sashweight pocket. Place the weight in the pocket and bend the cord to it with a round turn and two half-hitches through the eye of the weight. Set the sash in its runway, all the way down, and haul down on the sash cord until the weight is up to the pulley. Bring the cord against the stile, and cut it off about 4 in. below the hole at the end of the groove in the stile. This 4 in. is about the amount required to tie a figure-of-eight knot to set in the hole at the end of the groove.

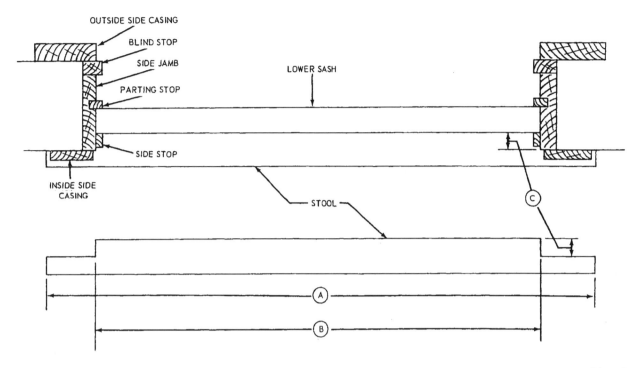

Figure 13-13.—Window stool layout.

When the counterbalances have all been prepared, set the upper sash in its runway, all the
way up, and nail the parting stop into its groove
with 8-penny finish nails spaced 12 in. O.C.

The side stop and the inside casings cannot
be installed until after the STOOL and APRON
have been installed. Figure 13-13 shows the
general layout of a window stool; whereas figure 13-14 shows the assembled window stool
and apron.

METAL WINDOWS

Either aluminum or steel windows will most
likely be installed in a permanent type of building. Information on construction requirements
and pointers on installing metal windows are
given below.

Regardless of the type of window used, it
should be of the size, combination, and type indicated or specified. Windows should be constructed to produce the results specified and
to assure a neat appearance. Permanent joints
should be formed by welding or by mechanical
fastenings, as specified for each type window.

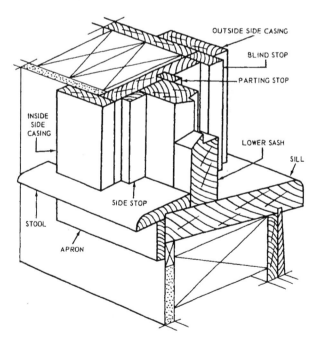

Figure 13-14.—Window stool
and apron.

Joints should be of sufficient strength to maintain the structural value of members connected. Welded joints should be solid, have excess metal removed, and be dressed smooth on exposed and contact surfaces. The dressing should be done so that no discoloration or roughness will show after finishing. Joints formed with mechanical fastenings should be closely fitted and made permanently watertight. Frames and sash, including ventilators, come assembled as a unit with hardware unattached.

Hardware should be of suitable design and should have sufficient strength to perform the function for which it is used. It should be attached securely to the windows with noncorrosive bolts or machine screws; sheet metal screws should not be used. Where fixed screens are specified, the hardware should be especially adapted to permit satisfactory operation of ventilators.

Make sure you exercise care in handling windows to avoid dropping them. In addition, store windows upright on pieces of lumber to keep them off the ground, and cover them thoroughly to protect them from the elements.

Windows should be installed and adjusted by experienced and qualified Builders. Aluminum windows in concrete or masonry walls should be set in prepared openings. Unless indicated or specified otherwise, all other windows should be built-in as the work progresses, or they should be installed without forcing into prepared openings. Windows should be set at the proper elevation, location, and reveal. They should be set plumb, square, level, and in alignment. They should also be braced, strutted, and stayed properly to prevent distortion and misalignment. Ventilators and operating parts should be protected against accumulation of cement, lime, and other building materials, by keeping ventilators tightly closed and wired fast to the frame. Screws or bolts in sill members, joints at mullions, and contacts of windows with sills, built-in fins, or subframes should be bedded in mastic sealant of a type recommended by the window manufacturer. Windows should be installed in a manner that will prevent entrance of water.

Ample provision should be made for securing units to each other, to masonry, or to other adjoining or adjacent construction. Windows that are to be installed in direct contact with masonry must have head and jamb members designed to enter into masonry not less than 7/16 inch. Where windows are set in prepared masonry openings, the necessary anchorage or fins should be placed during progress of wall construction. Anchors and fastenings should be built into, anchored, or bolted to the jambs of openings, and should be fastened securely to the windows or frames and to the adjoining construction. Unless indicated otherwise, anchors should be spaced not more than 18 inches apart on jambs and sills. Anchors and fastenings should have sufficient strength to hold the member firmly in position.

After windows have been installed and upon completion of glazing and painting, all ventilators and hardware should be adjusted to operate smoothly and to be weathertight when ventilators are closed and locked. Hardware and parts should be lubricated as necessary. Adjustments and tests should be as follows:

(a) Double-hung windows should have balances adjusted to proper tension, and guides waxed or lubricated.

(b) Casements equipped with rotary operators should be adjusted so that the top of the ventilator makes contact with the frame approximately 1/4 inch in advance of the bottom.

(c) Casements equipped with friction hinges, or friction holders, should be adjusted to proper tension.

(d) Projected sash should have arms or slides lubricated and adjusted to proper tension.

(e) Awning windows should have arms to ventilators adjusted so that the bottom edge of each ventilator makes continuous initial contact with frames when closed.

(f) Where windows are weatherstripped, the weatherstripping should make weathertight contact with frames when ventilators are closed and locked. The weatherstripping should not cause binding of sash, or prevent closing and locking of the ventilator.

After adjustment, all non-weatherstripped steel and aluminum windows, except security and commercial projected steel windows, should comply with prescribed feeler gage tests. Windows failing to comply with the tests should be removed and replaced with new windows, or should be corrected and restored to approved condition meeting the required tests. When ventilators are closed and locked, the metal-to-metal contacts between ventilators and their frames should conform to the following requirements:

Whenever conducting the feeler gage test on SIDE-HUNG VENTILATORS, the Builder should remember that it should not be possible to freely insert a steel feeler gage, 2 inches wide by 0.031 inch thick, at any point between the outside contacts of ventilator and frame; nor to freely insert a similar feeler gage, 0.020 inch thick, between more than 40 percent of such contacts.

Remember that for PROJECTED-OUT HORIZONTAL VENTILATORS, it should not be possible to freely insert a steel feeler gage, 2 inches wide by 0.031 inch thick, between the top rail inside contacts, or between the bottom and side rail outside contacts; nor to freely insert a similar feeler gage, 0.020 inch thick, between more than 40 percent of such contacts.

For PROJECTED-IN HORIZONTAL VENTILATORS, it should not be possible to freely insert a steel feeler gage, 2 inches wide by 0.031 inch thick, between the bottom rail outside contacts, or between the top and side rail inside contacts; nor to freely insert a similar feeler gage, 0.020 inch thick, between more than 40 percent of such contacts.

GLAZING

Glazing wood and metal sashes and doors consists of sash conditioning and placement of glass. Maintenance often involves only replacement of loose, deteriorated, or missing putty. When replacing glazing items in buildings and structures, use the same type materials as were used in the original work. Use replacement materials of improved quality only when justified by obvious inadequacy of the materials that have failed or by planned future utilization of the building or structure.

Wood sash may be glazed at the factory or on the job. In some instances it will reduce breakage and labor costs to have glazing done at the job site after sash is fitted. When a large number of stock-size wood sash are used, it is generally cheaper to have glazing done at the factory.

Steel sash are generally furnished open and glazing is performed on the job.

Cost of material varies with the size and kind of glass and whether glass is bedded in putty and face puttied, face puttied only, or set with wood or metal beads.

TYPES OF GLASS

Single strength glass is approximately 1/10 inch thick and used for small areas, never to exceed 400 square inches. Double strength glass is approximately .133 thick and is used where high wind resistance is necessary. Window glass comes in three grades, (AA) or superior grade, (A) or very good, and (B) for general or utility grade.

Heavy sheet glass comes in various thicknesses from 3/16 inch to 1/4 inch and in sheet sizes up to 76 inches x 120 inches. Sheet glass is sometimes used for windows but is usually used for greenhouses. It is slightly wavy and may cause a slight distortion of images viewed through it.

Plate glass is manufactured in a continuous ribbon and cut into large sheets. Plate glass is ground and polished for high quality. It comes in thicknesses from 1/8 inch to 1 1/4 inches and is usually used for large windows, such as store fronts.

Tempered glass is glass that has been reheated to just below its melting point and suddenly cooled by oil bath method.

By cooling against metallic surface. Tempered glass cannot be cut or drilled after tempering and must be ordered to exact size. It will withstand heavy impacts and great pressures but if tapped near edge, will disintegrate into small pieces.

Heat strengthened glass is made of polished plate or patterned glass and is reheated and cooled to strengthen it.

It is used in curtain wall design as spandrel glazing of multistoried buildings.

Patterned glass is a rolled flat glass with an impressioned design on one or both sides.

Wire glass is a regular rolled flat glass with either a hexagonal twisted or a diamond shaped welded continuous wire mesh as near as possible in the center of the sheet. The surface may be either patterned, figured or polished.

Heat absorbing glass is usually a heavy sheet glass, 1/8 inch or 1/4 inch thick, either a bluish or greenish color, has the ability to absorb the infra-red rays from the sun. More than 35 percent of the heat is excluded.

Insulating glass units are comprised of two or more sheets of glass separated by either 3/16 inch, 1/4 inch, or 1/2 inch air space. These units are factory sealed and the captive air is hydrated at atmospheric pressure. They are made of either window glass or polished plate glass. Special units may be obtained of varying combinations of heat absorbing, laminated patterned or tempered glass.

Glare reducing glass is available in double strength, in panes up to 60 inches x 80 inches, and 3/16 inch, 7/32 inch and 1/4 inch in panes up to 72 inches x 120 inches in size. It is light gray in color, gives clear vision and is also slightly heat absorbent. One-fourth inch glass will exclude about 21 percent of the sun's heat rays.

Laminated glass is comprised of two or more sheets of glass with one or more layers of transparent vinyl plastic sandwiched between the glass. An adhesive applied with heat and pressure cements the layers into one unit. The elasticity of the plastic cushions any blow against the glass, preventing sharp pieces from flying. There is also laminated glare reducing glass where the pigment in the vinyl plastic laminated provides the glare control quality.

SASH PREPARATION

Attach the sash to structure so it will withstand the design load and to comply with the specifications. Adjust, plumb and square the sash to within 1/8 inch of nominal dimensions on shop drawings. Remove all rivet, screw, bolt or nail heads, welding fillets and other projections from specified clearances. Seal all sash corners and fabrication intersections to make the sash watertight. Primer paint all sealing surfaces of wood sash and carbon steel sash. Use appropriate solvents to remove grease, lacquers and other organic protecting finishes from sealing surfaces of aluminum sash.

GLASS CUTTING

Insofar as possible, glass should be purchased and stocked in sizes that can be used without cutting. Glass of special sizes is cut in the shop. For glass sizes, measure all four sides of the sash and deduct 1/16 to 1/8 inch in the light size for irregularities in the sash. Minimum equipment required for glass cutting consists of a table, a common wood or metal T-square, and a glass cutter. The table should be about 4 feet square, with front and left-hand edges square. Mark off the surface of the table vertically and horizontally in inches. A thin coating of turpentine or kerosene on the glass line to be cut is helpful in lubricating the action of the cutter wheel. A sharp cutter must be carefully drawn only ONCE along the line of the desired cut. Additional strokes of the cutter may result in breakage.

Check dimensions related to sash openings to be sure that adequate clearances are maintained on all four sides of the perimeter. No attempt should be made to change the size of heat strengthened, tempered or doubled glazed units since any such effort will result in permanent damage. All heat absorbing glass must be clean cut. Nipping to remove flares or to reduce oversized dimensions of heat-absorbing glass is not permitted.

PREPARATION BEFORE GLAZING

Old wood sash. Clean all putty runs of broken glass fragments and glazier's points. Remove loose paint and putty by scraping. Wipe the surface clean with cloth saturated in mineral spirits or turpentine, prime the putty runs, and allow them to dry.

New wood sash. Remove dust, prime the putty runs, and allow them to dry. All new wood sash should be pressure treated for decay protection.

Old metal sash. Remove loose paint or putty by scraping. Use steel wool or sandpaper to remove rust. Clean the surfaces thoroughly with a cloth saturated in mineral spirits or turpentine. Prime bare metal and allow it to dry thoroughly.

New metal sash. Wipe the sash thoroughly with a cloth saturated in mineral spirits or turpentine to remove dust, dirt, oil, or grease. Remove rust with steel wool or sandpaper. If the sash is not already factory primed, prime it with rust-inhibitive paint and allow it to dry thoroughly.

SETTING GLASS IN WOOD AND METAL SASH

Do not glaze or reglaze exterior sash when the temperature is 40 degrees F or lower unless absolutely necessary. Sash and door members must be thoroughly cleaned of dust with a brush or cloth dampened with turpentine or mineral spirits. Lay a continuous 1/6-inch-thick bed of putty or compound in the putty run (fig. 13-15). The glazed face can be recognized as the size on which the glass was cut. If the glass has a bowed surface, it should be set with the concave side in. Wire glass is set with the twist vertical. Press the glass firmly into place so that the bed putty will fill all irregularities.

When glazing wood sash, insert two glazier's points per side for small lights and about 8 inches apart on all sides for large lights. When glazing metal sash, use the wire clips or metal glazing beads.

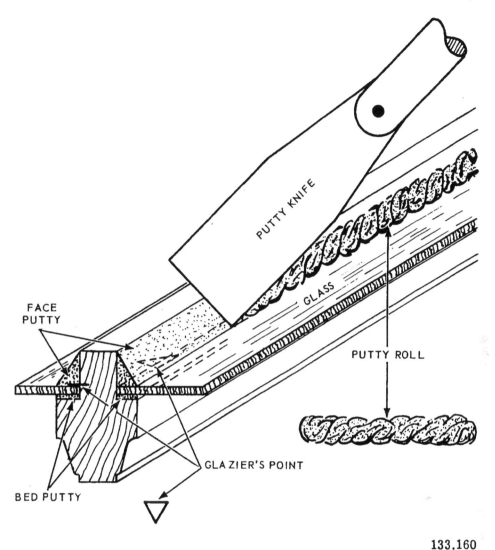

FACE PUTTY

PUTTY KNIFE

GLASS

PUTTY ROLL

GLAZIER'S POINT

BED PUTTY

133.160

Figure 13-15.—Setting glass with glazier's points and putty.

After the glass has been bedded, lay a continuous bead of putty against the perimeter of the glass-face putty run. Press the putty with a putty knife or glazing tool with sufficient pressure to ensure its complete adhesion to the glass and sash. Finish with full, smooth, accurately formed bevels with clean cut miters. Trim up the bed putty on the reverse side of the glass. When glazing or reglazing interior sash and transoms, whether fixed or movable, and interior doors, use wood or metal glazing beads. Exterior doors and hinged transoms should have glass secured in place with inside wood or metal glazing beads bedded in putty. When setting wire glass for security purposes, set wood or metal glazing beads, secured with screws, on the side facing the area to be protected. Wood sash putty should be painted as soon as it has surface-hardened. Do not wait longer than 2 months after glazing. Metal sash, Type I, elastic compound, should be painted immediately after a firm skin forms on the surface. Depending on weather conditions, the time for skinning over may be 2 to 10 days. Type II, metal sash putty, can usually be painted within 2 weeks after placing. This putty should not be painted before it has hardened because early painting may retard the set.

Clean the glass on both sides after painting. A cloth moistened with mineral spirits will remove putty stains. Ammonia, acid solutions, or water containing caustic soaps must not be used.

When scrapers are used, care should be exercised to avoid breaking the paint seal at the putty edge.

Handling and cutting glass creates a serious cutting hazard. Appropriate gloves and other personal protective equipment must be provided and adequate procedures for the disposal of cuttings and broken glass established.

FINISH FLOORING

Before any finish flooring is laid the rough floor must be thoroughly cleaned. All plaster droppings must be removed, all protruding nail-heads driven flush, and all irregularities planed down or otherwise smoothed. The rough floor should then be carefully inspected for any loose boards or other imperfections.

WOOD-STRIP FINISH FLOORING

Most wood-strip finish flooring is SIDE-MATCHED (tongue-and-grooved on the edges), and some is END-MATCHED (tongue-and-grooved on the ends) as well. Softwood flooring comes in face widths ranging from 2 1/4 to 5 in. The most widely used standard pattern of hardwood flooring has a face width of 2 1/4 in. Most wood-strip flooring is recessed on the lower face as shown in figures 13-16 and 13-17.

Wood subfloors are covered with building paper or with a layer of heavy felt before wood-strip finish flooring is applied. If the specifications call for furring strips between the subflooring and the finish flooring, the strips are nailed on top of the paper or felt. Furring strips are laid at right angles to the line of the finish flooring; they are usually spaced 12 or 16 in. O.C.

Wood-strip flooring is laid at right angles to the line of direction of the joists under the largest room on the floor. The first strip laid (which is called the STARTER strip) is laid parallel to and 5/8 in. away from the outer joist-end wall in the key room. This strip is placed with the side groove toward the wall, and face-nailed down with nails placed where they will be concealed by the SHOE MOLDING (molding placed in the angle between the baseboard and the floor) as shown in figure 13-16.

Subsequent strips are cut, fitted, and laid ahead of the nailing, about 6 or 8 courses (continuous wall-to-wall strips) at a time. A 3-man crew is convenient for wood-strip flooring, with one man cutting, the second fitting, and the third nailing. The cutter cuts strips of random

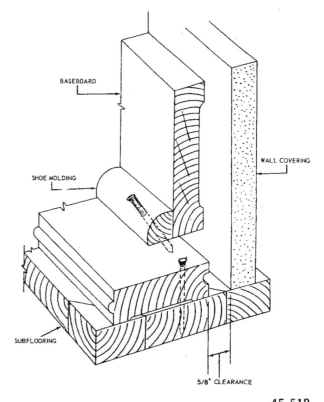

45.512

Figure 13-16.—Blind-nailing starter strip of wood finish flooring.

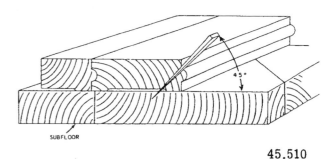

45.510

Figure 13-17.—Toenailing wood-strip flooring.

(various) lengths. The fitter lays out wall-to-wall strips, taking care to stagger end-joints in as uniform a manner as possible. The nailer drives strips up hard against previously nailed strips, using a piece of scrap flooring for the purpose, and then nails the strips down.

Courses which follow the starter course are toenailed down as shown in figure 13-17. Nails should be driven into joists, and it is a good idea to chalk-mark the lines of the joists on the building paper before the floor-laying is started. For 25/32-in.-thick flooring use 8-penny cut flooring nails; for 1/2-in.-thick flooring use 6-penny wire casing nails; for 3/8-in.-thick flooring use 4-penny wire casing nails. Drive each nail down to the point where another blow or two might cause the hammer to damage the edge of the strip; then use a nail set to drive the nail the rest of the way home. Best nailing procedure is to stand on the strip, with toes in line with the outer edge, and strike the nail from a stooping position which will bring the hammer head square against the nail.

Sanding

Power-operated sanding machines are the most satisfactory means of preparing wood floors for finishing. The operator should wear an approved respirator or dust mask while sanding. Abrasive paper, commonly called sandpaper, is made with paper of fabric backing. For machine use, a fabric-backed or fabric-reinforced paper backing is recommended. The mineral cutting agent glued to the face of the paper may be flint, garnet, or silicon carbide. Cutting surfaces are designated close coat (grits covering the entire face) or open coat (covering about half the cutting surface). Opencoat paper is recommended for sanding over materials, such as paint and varnish, that tend to clog spaces between the grits. Flint papers are made in at least 12 grades: 5/0 (very fine), 4/0, 3/0, 2/0, 0, 1/2, 1, 1 1/2, 2, 2 1/2, 3, 3 1/2 (very coarse). Flint (sand) papers having glue binders must not be stored where they will be subject to oil, moisture, or extreme heat and cold. Brittle paper can be softened by dampening the backing. The following table is a guide to sandpaper selection for floor furnishing.

Grade	Type	Use
3 1/2	Open	Preliminary roughing off of stubborn varnish, shellac, floor oil, wax, and deep penetrating filler compounds. Not to be used for cutting into wood surfaces.

Grade	Type	Use
3	Open	Used in place of No. 3 1/2 for surfaces of less resistance; is preferred if it does the required work.
2 1/2	Open	Preliminary roughing off of floor finishes such as shellac, wax, floor oils, alcohol stains, and lacquered surfaces. Use as followup paper for floors roughed off with No. 3 1/2.
2	Close	Use instead of No. 2 and No. 2 1/2 open coat where surface permits cutting without gumming. Closed coat should be used in preference to open coat whenever practicable.
1 1/2	Close	Use as a first paper on all new floors.
1	Open	Use as a followup for No. 2 and No. 2 1/2 in all cases.
1	Close	Use the same as No. 1 open coat to provide a smooth floor finish.
1/2	Close	Use a final finish on most floor work.
1/0 & 2/0	Close	Use as a final finish on best hardwood floor work.
3/0 & 4/0	Close	Use for finishing fine woodwork, such as furniture, and for rubbing down paint and varnish finishes.

In exceptional cases, when old floor finishes cannot be removed by sanding or scraping with an abrasive, highly volatile liquids may be used. These liquids, as well as those used in floor finishing, include paint and varnish remover, varnish, liquid paint, and shellac, which have flashpoints as low as 40 degrees F. Finishing should be done only under expert supervision.

Sealing

Seal wood floor by sealing and waxing them in the following manner: Apply liberally a sealer of light varnish. Spread or spray it along the grain of the wood. After the sealer has dried completely, buff the floor with a floor-polishing machine, using No. 1 steelwool pads. If portions of the floor look lusterless, dry, or dead after the buffing, continue sealing and polishing until the floor surface has a uniform appearance. Apply two thin coats of water emulsion wax that conforms to Federal Specification P-W-155. Buff the wax after each application has thoroughly dried.

RESILIENT FLOORING

In construction, wood-strip flooring has been largely replaced by various types of RESILIENT flooring, most of which is applied in the form of 6 x 6-, 9 x 9-, or 12 x 12-in. squares called TILES. The types most frequently used are ASPHALT, VINYL, LINOLEUM, CORK, and RUBBER.

Manufacturers recommend that wood subfloors have an underlayment for resilient flooring, or that sheets of synthetic wood, such as plywood or tempered hardboard, be nailed over single subfloors. The subsurface must be carefully cleaned, smoothed, and inspected, and any cracks wider than 1/8 in. or holes larger than 1/4 in. must be filled. The subsurface is then covered with a felt backing, cemented down with adhesive. The tile is then laid on the felt.

Asphalt, and vinyl tile is set in an asphalt tile EMULSION, linoleum and cork tile in linoleum cement, and rubber tile in waterproof rubber cement. The manufacturer's instructions on proper methods of applying adhesive and laying tile are provided and should be carefully followed. All floors subjected to excessive moisture should be applied with a waterproof adhesive.

ASPHALT AND VINYL TILES

Asphalt tile is a blended composition of asphaltic and/or resinous binders, asbestos fibers, and inert fillers or pigments. It can be installed satisfactorily over concrete floors in direct contact with the ground without the need to completely waterproof the concrete slab. It is quiet and safe to walk on, durable, and resistant to abrasion from foot traffic and common abuses such as scuffing and cigarette burns. The tile is low in maintenance cost. Tiles are available in sizes of 4 by 4 inches, 9 by 9 inches, and 12 by 12 inches, in thicknesses of 1/8 and 3/16 inch. Tiles 9 by 9 inches are most commonly used in military construction.

Vinyl tiles are available in two types: vinyl asbestos tile, Federal Specification L-T-345, and flexible vinyl, Federal Specification L-F-450. Tiles are available in sizes of 6 by 6 inches, 9 by 9 inches, and 12 by 12 inches, and in thicknesses of 1/8 and 3/32 inch. Vinyl is also available in 54-inch sheets. Vinyl tile may be laid on a concrete floor in direct contact with the ground only if the slab is membrane-waterproofed. Vinyl tiles are durable and easy to keep clean. Vinyl plastic floorings have good resistance to abrasion, are impervious to water, and are outstanding in resistance to grease, oils, and alkalies.

Asphalt and vinyl tiles should be laid according to the manufacturer's recommendations, with or without lining felt as suitable for the application. Before the tile is laid, the floor area should be squared and the best method of laying the tile determined, depending on the shape of the room, location of fixed furnishings and equipment, and doorways. Tile should always be laid from the center of the room toward the walls so that border widths can be adjusted accordingly. Tiles should be stored for 24 hours before installation in a room heated to at least 70 degrees. Cold tiles may cause condensation on the underside and break down the cement bond. Cement should be spread at a uniform consistency ahead of the work and allowed to dry to a tacky state before tile is laid in it.

CERAMIC AND QUARRY FLOOR TILE

Ceramic floor tile is glazed or unglazed, manufactured in small square, hexagonal, rectangular, and circular shapes about 1/4 inch thick, and often arranged in mosaic patterns. The pieces are usually factory-assembled (face side up) on paper sheets in the required pattern, laid on a mortar setting bed, pressed firmly on the mortar, and tamped true and even with the finished floor line. Grout is then forced into the joints, filling them completely, and is finished flush and level with the floor line.

Quarry tile is usually unglazed and manufactured in square and rectangular shapes, ranging from 2 3/4 inches to 9 inches in width, from 2 3/4 inches to 12 inches in length, and of varying thicknesses. Tiles are laid individually on a mortar setting bed with joints about 1/2 inch wide.

In locations such as galleys and food preparation areas, where the floor is directly exposed to the effects of corrosion agents, use acid-resistant joint material to fill the joints. The acid-resistant mortars are proprietary products and should be mixed in accordance with the manufacturer's recommendations. They should be composed of powdered resin and liquid resin cement and be resistant to the effects of oils, fats, greases, organic and inorganic acids, salts, alkalies, and mineral solvents.

DOORS

Inside door frames are constructed in several ways. The interior type is constructed like the outside type except that no casing is used on inside door frames. Hinge blocks are nailed to the inside wall finish, where the hinges are to be placed, to provide a nailing surface for the hinge flush with the door. Both the outside and inside door frames may be modified to suit a climatic condition.

DOOR JAMBS

Door jambs (fig. 13-18) are the linings of the framing of door openings. Casings and stops are nailed to the door jambs and the door is hung from them. Inside jambs are made of 3/4-inch stock and outside jambs of 1 3/8-inch stock. The width of the stock will vary in accordance with the thickness of the walls. Inside jambs are built up with 3/8- by 1 3/8-inch stops nailed to the jamb, while outside jambs are usually rabbeted out to receive the door. Jambs are made and set in the following manner:

Regardless of how carefully rough openings are made, be sure to plumb the jambs and level the heads, when jambs are set.

Rough openings are usually made 2 1/2 inches larger in width and height than the size of the door to be hung. For example, a 2-foot 8-inch by 6-foot 8-inch door would need a rough opening of 2 feet 10 1/2 inches by 6 feet 10 1/2 inches. This extra space allows for the jambs, the wedging, and the clearance space for the door to swing.

Level the floor across the opening to determine any variation in floor heights at the point where the jambs rest on the floor.

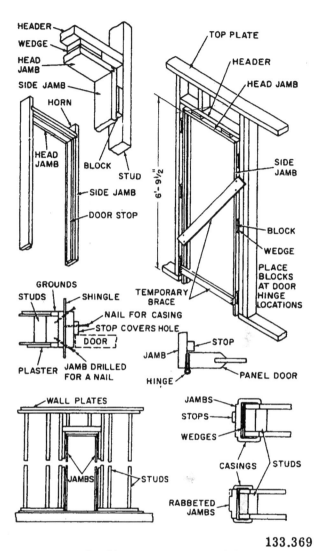

133.369

Figure 13-18.—Door jamb and door trim.

Now cut the head jamb with both ends square, having allowed width of the door plus the depth of both dadoes and a full 3/16 inch for door clearance.

From the lower edge of the dado, measure a distance equal to the height of the door plus the clearance wanted under it. Mark and cut square.

On the opposite jamb do the same, only make additions or subtractions for the variation in the floor, if any.

Now nail the jambs and jamb heads together with 8-penny common nails through the dado into the head jamb.

Set the jambs into the opening and place small blocks under each jamb on the subfloor just as thick as the finish floor will be. This is to allow the finish floor to go under.

Plumb the jambs and level the jamb head.

Wedge the sides with shingles between the jambs and the studs, to align, and then nail securely in place.

Take care not to wedge the jamb unevenly.

Use a straightedge 5 or 6 feet long inside the jambs to help prevent uneven wedging.

Check jambs and head carefully, because jambs placed out of plumb will have a tendency to swing the door open or shut, depending on the direction in which the jamb is out of plumb.

DOOR TRIM

Door trim material is nailed onto the jambs to provide a finish between the jambs and the plastered wall. It is frequently called "casing" (fig. 13-18). Sizes vary from 1/2 to 3/4 inches in thickness, and from 2 1/2 to 6 inches in width. Most trim has a concave back, to fit over uneven plaster. In mitered work, care must be taken to make all joints clean, square, neat, and well fitted. (If the trim is to be mitered at the top corners, a miter box, miter square, hammer nail set, and block plane will be needed.) Door openings are cased up in the following manner:

Leave a margin of 1/4-inch from the edge of the jamb to the casing all around.

Cut one of the side casings square and even at the bottom, with the bottom of the jamb.

Cut the top or mitered end next, allowing 1/4-inch extra length for the margin at the top.

Nail the casing onto the jamb and even with the 1/4-inch margin line, starting at the top and working toward the bottom.

Use 4-penny finish nails along the jamb side and 6-penny or 8-penny case nails along the outer edge of the casings.

The nails along the outer edge will need to be long enough to go through the casing and plaster and into the studs.

Set all nailheads about 1/8 inch below the surface of the wood with a nail set.

Now apply the casing for the other side and then the head casing.

FITTING A DOOR

If a number of doors are to be fitted and hung, a DOOR JACK like the one shown in figure 13-19 should be constructed, to hold doors upright for the planing of edges and the installation of HARD-WARE (hinges, locks, knobs, and other metal fittings on a door or window).

NOTE: The edge of the door can be beveled to prevent binding and to give a tighter fit.

The first step in fitting a door is to determine from the floor plan which stile is the hinge stile and which the lock stile, and to mark both the stiles and the corresponding jambs accordingly. Next, carefully measure the height of the finished opening ON BOTH SIDE JAMBS and the width of the opening AT BOTH TOP AND BOTTOM. The finished opening should be perfectly rectangular; but IT MAY NOT BE. Your job now is to fit the door accurately to the opening, regardless of the shape of the opening.

A well-fitted door, when hung, should conform to the shape of the finished opening, less a clearance allowance of 1/16 in. at the sides and on top. For an interior door without sill or threshold there should be a bottom clearance above the finished floor of from 3/8 to 1/2 in. This clearance is required to ensure that the door will swing clear of carpeting; if the carpeting is to be extra-thick, the bottom clearance will have to be greater than 1/2 in. For a door with a sill and no threshold, the bottom clearance should be 1/16 in. above the sill. For a door with a threshold, the bottom clearance should be 1/16 above the threshold. The sill and threshold, if any, should be set in place before the door is hung.

Lay off the measured dimensions of the finished opening, less allowances, on the door. Check the door jambs for trueness, and if you find any irregularities, transfer them to the door lines. Place the door in the jack and plane the edges to the lines, setting the door in the opening frequently to check the fit.

HANGING A DOOR

You will be dealing mainly with doors equipped with SIDE hinges (hinges located on the edges of one stile or the other). There are various types of side hinges, but yours will be mostly LOOSE-PIN BUTT MORTISE hinges like the one shown in figure 13-20. A loose-pin butt hinge consists of two rectangular LEAVES, pivoted on a PIN which is called a LOOSE PIN because it can be removed by simple extraction. The hinge is called a MORTISE hinge because the leaves are MORTISED into gains cut in the hinge stile of the door and the hinge jamb of the door frame.

The first step in hanging a door is to lay out the locations of the hinges on the hinge stile and the hinge jamb. Set the door in the frame, and

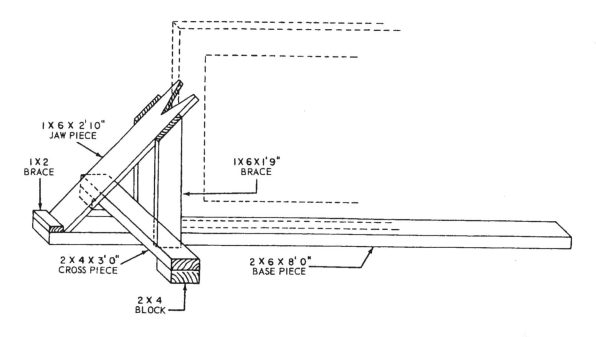

Figure 13-19.—Door jack.

117.68

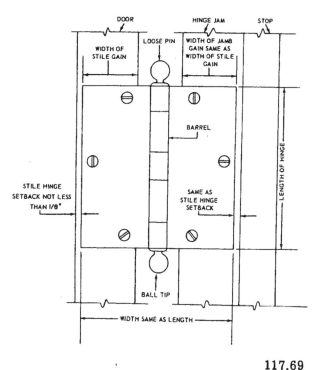

117.69

Figure 13-20.—Loose-pin butt
mortise hinge.

force the hinge stile against the hinge jamb with the wedge marked A in figure 13-21. Then insert a 4-penny finish nail between the top rail

and the head jamb, and force the top rail up against the nail with the wedge marked B in the figure. Since a 4-penny finish nail has a diameter of 1/16 in. (which is the standard top clearance for a door), the door is now at the correct height.

Exterior doors usually have 3 hinges, interior doors, as a rule, only 2. The vertical distance between the top of the door and the top of the top hinge, and between the top of the finish floor and the bottom of the bottom hinge, may be specified. If not, the distances customarily used are those shown in figure 13-21. The middle hinge, if there is one, is usually located midway between the other two.

The size of a loose-pin butt mortise hinge is designated by the length (height) and by the combined width of the leaves in inches (height is always given first). The width varies with the requirements of setback, clearance, door thickness, etc., and is calculated individually for each door. Doors 1 1/8 to 1 3/8 in. thick and up to 32-in. wide take a 3 1/2-in. hinge. Doors 1 1/8 to 1 3/8 in. thick and from 32 to 37-in. wide take a 4-in. hinge. Doors more than 1 3/8 in. but not more than 1 7/8 in. thick and up to 32-in. wide take a 4 1/2 in. hinge; if more than 32 but not more than 37-in. wide they take a 5-in. hinge; if from 37 to 43-in. wide they take a 5-in. EXTRA HEAVY hinge. Doors thicker than 1 7/8

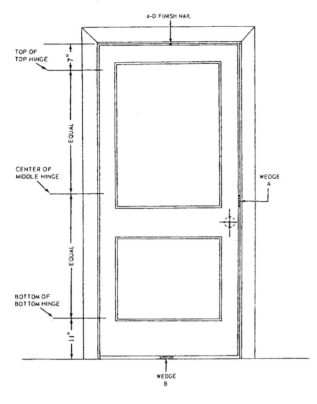

117.70

Figure 13-21.—Laying out hinge
locations on a door.

in. and up to 43-in. wide take a 5-in. extra heavy
hinge. Doors thicker than 1 7/8 in. and wider
than 43-in. take a 6-in. extra heavy hinge.

Place the door in the door jack and lay off
the outlines of the gains on the edge of the hinge
stile, using a hinge leaf as a marker. The
STILE HINGE SETBACK (shown in fig. 13-20)
should be not less than 1/8-in. and is usually
made about 1/4-in. Lay out gains of exactly the
same size on the hinge jamb, and then chisel
out the gains to a depth exactly equal to the
thickness of a leaf.

Separate the leaves on the hinges by extract-
ing the loose pins, and screw the leaves into the
gains, taking care to ensure that the loose pin
will be up when the door is hung in place. Hang
the door in place, insert the loose pins, and
check the clearances at the side jambs. If the
clearance along the hinge jamb is too large
(more than 1/16-in.) and that along the lock
jamb too small (less than 1/16), remove the
door, remove the hinge leaves from the gains,
and slightly deepen the gains. If the clearance
along the hinge jamb is too small and that along

the lock jamb too large, the gains are too deep.
This can be corrected by shimming up the leaves
with strips of cardboard placed in the gains.

INSTALLING A CYLINDER LOCK

The parts of an ordinary cylinder LOCK for
a door are shown in figure 13-22. The procedure for installing a lock of this type is as
follows:

Open the door to a convenient working position and check it in place with wedges under the
bottom near the outer edge.

Measure up 36 in. from the floor (the usual
knob height), and square a line across the face
and edge of the lock stile.

Use the template that is usually supplied
with cylinder lock; place the template on the
face of the door (at proper height and alignment
with layout lines) and mark the centers of holes
to be drilled. (See fig. 13-23.)

Drill the holes through the face of the door
and then the one through the edge to receive the
latch bolt. It should be slightly deeper than the
length of the bolt.

Cut a gain for the latch-bolt mounting plate,
and install the latch unit.

Install interior and exterior knobs.

Find the position of the strike plate and install it in the jamb.

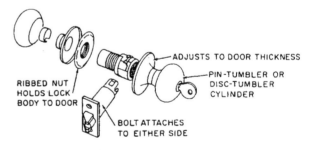

133.161

Figure 13-22.—Parts of a cylinder lock.

INTERIOR TRIM

The casing around the doors and windows,
the baseboard with its base mold and shoe mold,
the picture mold, chair rail, cornice mold, and
panel mold are the various trim members used
in finishing the interior of a building.

Various types of wood can be used for interior
trim, such as birch, oak, mahogany, walnut,
white and yellow pine, and other available woods.

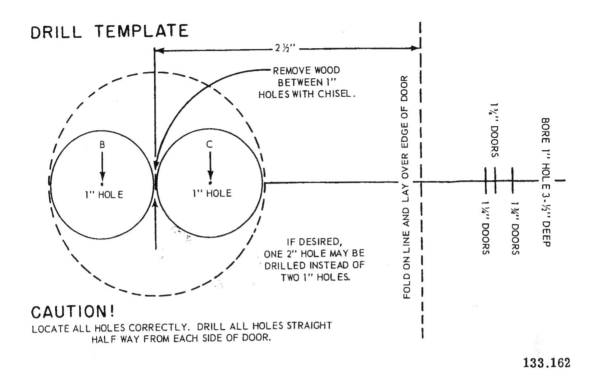

Figure 13-23.—One type of template.

A close-grain wood should be used when the trim is to be painted. However, harder woods free from pitch will provide a better paint sur-face.

BASEBOARDS

A trim member called a BASEBOARD is usu-ally installed on the line along which the walls join the floors. Baseboard is nailed to the studs with two 6-penny finish nails at each stud crossing. The first step in installing baseboard, therefore, is to locate all the studs in the wall and mark the locations on the floor with light pencil marks.

Baseboard is miter-joined at outside corners and butt-joined at inside corners. Where base-boards cannot be miter-joined or butt-joined at corners, they should be capped. Since the walls at corner baseboard locations may not be per-fectly vertical, inside and outside corners should be joined as follows:

To butt-join a piece of baseboard to another piece already in place at an inside corner, set the piece to be joined in position on the floor, bring the end against or near the face of the other piece, and take off the line of the face with a scriber as shown in figure 13-24. Use the same procedure when butting ends of baseboard against the side casings of doors.

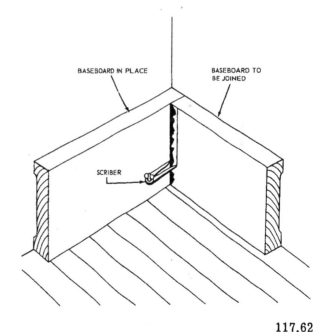

117.62

Figure 13-24.—Butt-joining baseboard at an inside corner.

BASIC FUNDAMENTALS OF HAMMERS

At some time or other, every mechanic, gardener, or home handyman comes to blows with a hammer. The general frustration isn't surprising since many householders and do-it-yourselfers own only one hammer - usually a nail or claw hammer,

A claw hammer is fine for the work it is designed to do but when it is misused, it is dangerous. Besides, poor workmanship is more likely when you use the wrong tools, or the right tools incorrectly.

There are at least 13 different types of hammers, each designed for a specific use.

KINDS OF HAMMERS

Nail or claw hammers, the kind you probably have, are designed for driving common and finishing nails and nail sets, using the center of the hammer face. The claws are for pulling common and finishing nail and ripping woodwork, and should never be struck against metal.

Ballpeen hammers are most commonly used for striking cold chisels, punches, and star drills, and for riveting, shaping, and straightening metal. Every mechanic, amateur or professional should have a light ballpeen hammer and a heavy ballpeen, blacksmith's, or hand drilling hammer. A nail hammer should never be used in place of a ballpeen hammer -- the face could chip, damaging the tool and possibly injuring the user.

Riveting and setting hammers are used by machinists and tinners for driving and spreading rivets and various sheet metal work.

Chipping hammers are for chipping welds, rust, paint, from metal.

Bricklayers' hammers are for setting and cutting bricks, masonry tile and concrete blocks and for chipping mortar from bricks.

Soft-face hammers and mallets are for striking blows where steel hammers would mar or damage the tool or surface being struck.

Other types of hammers include magnetic hammers (for holding and driving tacks), body and fender hammers, engineer's hammers and sledges, stone sledges and spalling hammers, hand drilling or mash hammers, bush hammers, axes, and hatchets.

RULES FOR WORKING WITH HAMMERS

1. Strike a hammer blow with the hammer face parallel to the surface being struck. Always avoid glancing blows and over and under strikes.

2. When striking another tool (cold chisel, punch, wedge, etc.), make sure the face of the hammer is larger than the head of the tool. For example, a half-inch cold chisel requires at least a one-inch hammer face.

3. Always use a hammer of suitable size and weight for a job. Don't use a tack hammer to drive a spike, nor a sledge to drive a tack.

4. Never use one hammer to strike another hammer.

5. Never use a striking or struck tool with a loose or damaged handle.

6. Discard any striking or struck tool if the face shows excessive wear, dents, chips, mushrooming, or faulty redressing.

7. Never redress hammers without proper instructions.

ABBREVIATIONS AND SYMBOLS
CONTENTS

Page

———

ABBREVIATIONS AND SYMBOLS

1. Abbreviations

The following abbreviations in connection with lumber are used by the carpenter:

AD - - - - - - - - - -air-dried
al - - - - - - - - - - -all length
av - - - - - - - - - - -average
avw - - - - - - - - -average width
avl - - - - - - - - - -average length
bd - - - - - - - - - -board
bd ft - - - - - - - -board foot
bdl- - - - - - - - - -bundle
bev - - - - - - - - -beveled
bm - - - - - - - - -board (foot) measure
btr - - - - - - - - - -better
clg- - - - - - - - - -ceiling
clr - - - - - - - - - -clear
CM - - - - - - - - -center matched; that is, tongue-and-groove joints are made along the center of
              the edge of the piece
Com - - - - - - - -common
Csg - - - - - - - - -casing
Ctg - - - - - - - - -crating
cu ft- - - - - - - - -cubic foot
D & CM - - - - - -dressed (one or two sides) and center matched
D & M - - - - - - -dressed and matched; that is, dressed one or two sides and tongue and
              grooved on the edges. The match may be center or standard
DS - - - - - - - - -drop siding
D & SM - - - - - -dressed (one or two sides) and standard matched
D 2S & CM- - - -dressed two sides and center matched
D 2S & M- - - - -dressed two sides and (center of standard) matched
D 2S & SM- - - -dressed two sides and standard matched
Dim - - - - - - -dimension
E- - - - - - - - - - -edge
FAS- - - - - - - -firsts and seconds, a combined grade of the two upper grades of hardwoods
fbk- - - - - - - - - -flat back
fcty - - - - - - - -factory (lumber)
FG - - - - - - - - -flat grain
Flg - - - - - - - - -flooring
fok- - - - - - - - -free of knots
Frm - - - - - - - -framing
ft - - - - - - - - - - -foot or feet
Hdl - - - - - - - - -handle (stock)
Hdwd- - - - - - -hardwood
Hrt - - - - - - - - -heart
Hrtwd - - - - - -heartwood
in - - - - - - - - - -inch or inches

KD - - - - - - - - - -kiln-dried
kd - - - - - - - - - -knocked down
lbr - - - - - - - - - -lumber
lgr - - - - - - - - -longer
lgth - - - - - - - - -length
linft - - - - - - - - -linear foot, that is, 12 inches
LR- - - - - - - - - -log run
Lr MCO - - - - - -log run, mill culls out
M - - - - - - - - - -thousand
MFBM - - - - - - -thousand (feet) board measure
MCO - - - - - - - -mill culls out
Merch - - - - - - -merchantable
MR - - - - - - - - -mill run
msm - - - - - - - -thousand (feet) surface measure
mw - - - - - - - -mixed width
No- - - - - - - - - -number
1s & 2s - - - - - -ones and twos, a combined grade of the hardwood grades of firsts and sec-
                   onds
Ord - - - - - - - -order
P- - - - - - - - - - -planed
Pat - - - - - - - - -pattern
Pky - - - - - - - -picky
Pln - - - - - - - - -plain, as in plain sawed
Pn- - - - - - - - - -partition
Qtd - - - - - - - -quartered (with reference to hardwoods)
rd - - - - - - - - - -round
rdm - - - - - - -random
res - - - - - - - - -resawed
rf g - - - - - - - - -roofing
Rfrs- - - - - - - - -roofers
rip - - - - - - - - -ripped
rl - - - - - - - - - -random length
rw - - - - - - - - -random width
S & E - - - - - - -surfaced one side and one edge
S2S & M - - - - -surfaced two sides and standard or center matched
S2S & SM - - - -.surfaced two sides and standard matched
Sap - - - - - - -sapwood
S1E - - - - - - - -surfaced one edge
S1S1E - - - - - -surf aced one side and one edge
S1S2E - - - - - -surfaced one side and two edges
S2E - - - - - - - -surfaced two edges
S4S - - - - - - - -.surfaced four sides
S & CM - - - - -surfaced one or two sides and center matched
S & M - - - - - -surfaced and matched; that is, surfaced one or two sides and tongued and
                   grooved on the edges. The match may be center or standard.
S & SM - - - - -surfaced one or two sides and standard matched
S2S & CM - - - -surfaced two sides and center matched
Sap - - - - - - -sapwood
SB - - - - - - - -standard bead
Sd- - - - - - - - -seasoned

Sdg -------siding
Sel --------select
SESd-------square-edge siding
sf ---------surface foot; that is, an area of 1 square foot
Stfwd-------softwood
ShD -------shipping dry
Ship -------shiplap
Sm --------standard matched
sm --------surface measure
snd --------sap no defect
snd --------sound
sq ---------square
sq E -------square edge
sq E & S -----square edge and sound
sqrs-------squares
Std --------standard
stk---------stock
SW ---------sound wormy
T & G ------tongued and grooved
TB & S -----top, bottom, and sides
tbrs --------timbers
VG ---------vertical grain
wal --------wider, all length
wdr --------wider
wt ---------weight
wth --------width

2. Symbols

Symbols commonly used in carpentry are given below. For additional information on the various symbols used in construction plans and blueprints, refer to TM 5-704.

a. *Architectural*

Tile -	
Earth -	
Plaster -	
Sheet metal -	
Built-in cabinet -	
Outside door: Brick wall - - - - - - - - - - - - - - -	
Frame wall - - - - - - - - - - - - - - -	
Inside door: Frame wall - - - - - - - - - - - - - - - -	
Brick -	
Firebrick -	
Concrete -	
Cast concrete block - - - - - - - - - - - - - - - - - - -	
Insulation : Loose fill - - - - - - - - - - - - - - - - - - -	
Board or quilts - - - - - - - - - - - - - - -	
Cut stone -	
Ashlar -	
Shingles (siding) -	
Wood, rough -	
Wood, finished -	
Cased or arched openings - - - - - - - - - - - - - - -	
Single caseinent window - - - - - - - - - - - - - - - -	
Double hung windows - - - - - - - - - - - - - - - - - - -	
Double casement window - - - - - - - - - - - - - - - -	

b. Plumbing

Bathtubs:

Corner - - - - - - - - - -

Free standing - - - - - -

Floor drain- - - - - - - - -

Shower drain - - - - - - - -

Hot-water tank - - - - - - - - ◯ H.W.T.

Grease trap - - - - - - - - -

Hose bibb or sill cock - - -

Lavatories:

Pedestal - - - - - - - - - -

Wall-hung - - - - - - - - -

Corner. - - - - - - - - - -

Toilets:

Tank - - - - - - - - - - - -

Flush valve - - - - - - - -

Urinals:

Stall-type - - - - - - - - -

Wall-hung. - - - - - - - -

Laundry trays - - - - - -

Built-in shower - - - - -

Shower - - - - - - - - - - -

Sinks:

Single drain board.

Double drain board.

C. *Electrical*

Pull switch- - - - - - - - - - ●

Single-pole switch - - - - - S₁

Double-pole switch- - - - - S₂

Triple-pole switch - - - - - - S₃

Buzzer - - - - - - - - - - - -

Floor outlet - - - - - - - - -

Bell- - - - - - - - - - - - - -

Drop cord - - - - - - - - - - Ⓓ

Ceiling outlet- - - - - - -

Wall bracket - - - - - - -

Single convenience out-

let - - - - - - - - - - - -

Double convenience out-

let - - - - - - - - - - - -

Ceiling outlet. gas & elec-

tric - - - - - - - - - - - -

Motor - - - - - - - - - - -

Light outlet with wir-

ing and switches indi-

cated - - - - - - - - - - -

GLOSSARY OF CARPENTRY AND BUILDING CONSTRUCTION TERMS

TABLE OF CONTENTS

GLOSSARY OF CARPENTY AND BUILDING CONSTRUCTION TERMS

Anchor - Irons of special form used to fasten together timbers or masonry.

Anchor bolts - Bolt which fastens columns, girders, or other members to concrete or masonry.

Backing - The bevel on the top edge of a hip rafter that allows the roofing board to fit the top of the rafter without leaving a triangular space between it and the lower side of the roof covering.

Balloon frame - The lightest and most economical form of construction, in which the studding and corner posts are set up in continuous lengths from first-floor line or sill to the roof plate.

Baluster- A small pillar or column used to support a rail.

Balustrade - A series of balusters connected by a rail, generally used for porches, balconies, and the like.

Band - A low, flat molding.

Base - The bottom of a column; the finish of a room at the junction of the walls and floor.

Batten (cleat) - A narrow strip of board used to fasten several pieces together.

Batter board - A temporary framework used to assist in locating the corners when laying a foundation.

Batter pile - Pile driven at an angle to brace a structure against lateral thrust.

Beam - An inclusive term for joists, girders, rafters, and purlins.

Bedding - A filling of mortar, putty, or other substance in order to secure a firm bearing.

Belt course - A horizontal board across or around a building, usually made of a flat member and a molding.

Bent -A single vertical framework consisting of horizontal and vertical members supporting the deck of a bridge or pier.

Bevel board (pitch board) - A board used in framing a roof or stairway to lay out bevels.

Board - Lumber less than 2 inches thick.

Board foot - The equivalent of a board 1 foot square and 1 inch thick.

Boarding in - The process of nailing boards on the outside studding of a house.

Bollard - Steel or cast iron post to which large ships are tied.

Braces - Pieces fitted and firmly fastened to two others at any angle in order to strengthen the angle thus treated.

Bracket - A projecting support for a shelf or other structure.

Break joints - To arrange joints so that they do not come directly under or over the joints of adjoining pieces, as in shingling, siding, etc.

Bridging - Pieces fitted in pairs from the bottom of one floor joist to the top of adjacent joists, and crossed to distribute the floor load; sometimes pieces of width equal to the joists and fitted neatly between them.

Building paper - Cheap, thick paper, used to insulate a building before the siding or roofing is put on; sometimes placed between double floors.

Built-up member - A single structural component made from several pieces fastened together.

Built-up timber - A timber made of several pieces fastened together, and forming one of larger dimension.

Carriages - The supports or the steps and risers of a flight of stairs.

Casement - A window in which the sash opens upon hinges.

Casing - The trimming around a door or window opening, either outside or inside, or the finished lumber around a post or beam, etc.

Ceiling - Narrow, matched boards; sheathing of the surfaces that inclose the upper side of room.

Center-hung sash - A sash hung on its centers so that it swings on a horizontal axis.

Chamfer - A beveled surface cut upon the corner of a piece of wood.

Checks - Splits or cracks in a board, ordinarily caused by seasoning.

Chock - Heavy timber fitted between fender piles along wheel guard of a pier or wharf.

Chord - The principal member of a truss on either the top or bottom.

Clamp - A mechanical device used to hold two or more pieces together.

Clapboards - A special form of outside covering of a house; siding.

Cleats - Metal arms extending horizontally from a relatively low base used for securing small ships, tugs, and work boats.

Column - A square, rectangular, or cylindrical support for roofs, ceilings, and so forth, composed of base, shaft, and capital.

Combination frame - A combination of the principal features of the full and balloon frames.

Concrete - An artificial building material made by mixing cement and sand with gravel, broken stone, or other aggregate, and sufficient water to cause the cement to set and bind the entire mass.

Conductors - Pipes for conducting water from a roof to the ground or to a receptacle or drain; downspout.

Cornice - The molded projection which finishes the top of the wall of a building.

Counterflashings - Strips of metal used to prevent water from entering the top edge of the vertical side of a roof flashing; they also allow expansion and contraction without danger of breaking the flashing.

Cross brace - Bracing with two intersecting diagonals.

Deadening - Construction intended to prevent the passage of sound.

Decking - Heavy plank floor of a pier or bridge.

Diagonal - Inclined member of a truss or bracing system used for stiffening and wind bracing.

Drip - The projection of a window sill or water table to allow the water to drain clear of the side of the house below it.

Fascia - A flat member of a cornice or other finish, generally the board of the cornice to whic the gutter is fastened.

Fender pile - Outside row of piles that protects a pier or wharf from damage by ships.

Fitter - Piece used to fill space between two surfaces.

Flashing - The material used and the process of making watertight the roof intersections and other exposed places on the outside of the house.

Flue - The opening in a chimney through which smoke passes.

Flush - Adjacent surfaces even, or in same plane (with reference to two structural pieces).

Footing - An enlargement at the lower end of a wall, pier, or column, to distribute the load.

Footing form - A wooden or steel structure, placed around the footing that will hold the concrete to the desired shape and size.

Foundation - That part of a building or wall which supports the superstructure.

Frame - The surrounding or inclosing woodwork of windows, doors, etc., and the timber skeleton of building.

Framing - The rough timber structure of a building, including interior and exterior walls, floor, roof, and ceilings.

Full frame - The old fashioned mortised-and-tenoned frame, in which every joint was mortised and tenoned. Rarely used at the present time.

Furring - Narrow strips of board nailed upon the walls and ceilings to form a straight surface upon which to lay the laths or other finish.

Gable - The vertical triangular end of a building from the eaves to the apex of the roof.

Gage - A tool used by carpenters to strike a line parallel to the edge of a board.

Gambrel - A symmetrical roof with two different pitches or slopes on each side.

Girder - A timber used to support wall beams or joists.

Girt (ribband) - The horizontal member of the walls of a full or combination frame house which supports the floor joists or is flush with the top of the joists.

Grade - The horizontal ground level of a building or structure.

Groove - A long hollow channel cut by a tool, into which a piece fits or in which it works. Two special types of grooves are the *dado,* a rectangular groove cut across the full width of a piece, and the *housing,* a groove cut at any angle with the grain and part way across a piece. Dados are used in sliding doors, window frames, etc.; housings are used for framing stair risers and threads in a string.

Ground - A strip of wood assisting the plasterer in making a straight wall and in giving a place to which the finish of the room may be nailed.

Hanger - Vertical-tension member supporting a load.

Header - A short joist into which the common joists are framed around or over an opening.

Headroom - The clear space between floor line and ceiling, as in a stairway.

Heel of a rafter - The end or foot that rests on the wall plate.

Hip roof - A roof which slopes up toward the center from all sides, necessitating a hip rafter at each corner.

Jack rafter - A short rafter framing between the wall plate; a hip rafter.

Jamb - The side piece or post of an opening; sometimes applied to the door frame.

Joint-butt - Squared ends or ends and edges adjoining each other:

    Dovetail - Joint made by cutting pins the shape of dovetails which fit between dovetail upon another piece.

    Drawboard - A mortise-and-tenon joint with holes so bored that when a pin is driven through, the joint becomes tighter.

    Fished - An end butt splice strengthened by pieces nailed on the sides.

    Glue - A joint held together with glue.

    Halved - A joint made by cutting half the wood away from each piece so as to bring the sides flush.

    Housed - A joint in which a piece is grooved to receive the piece which is to form the other part of the joint.

    Lap - A joint of two pieces lapping over each other.

    Mortised - A joint made by cutting a hole or mortise, in one piece, and a tenon, or piece to fit the hole, upon the other.

    Rub - A flue joint made by carefully fitting the edges together, spreading glue between them, and rubbing the pieces back and forth until the pieces are well rubbed together.

    Scarfed - A timber spliced by cutting various shapes of shoulders, or jogs, which fit each other.

Joists - Timbers supporting the floorboards.

Kerf - The cut made by a saw.

Knee brace - A corner brace, fastened at an angle from wall stud to rafter, stiffening a wood or steel frame to prevent angular movement.

Laths - Narrow strips to support plastering.

Lattice - Crossed wood, iron plate, or bars.

Ledgerboard - The support for the second-floor joists of a balloon-frame house, or for similar uses; ribband.

Level - A term describing the position of a line or plane when parallel to the surface of still water; an instrument or tool used in testing for horizontal and vertical surfaces, and in determining differences of elevation.

*Lintel (cap -)*A horizontal structural member spanning an opening, and supporting a wall load.

Lookout - The end of a rafter, or the construction which projects beyond the sides of a house to support the eaves; also the projecting timbers at the gables which support the verge boards.

Louver - A kind of window, generally in peaks of gables and the tops of towers, provided with horizontal slots which exclude rain and snow and allow ventilation.

Lumber - Sawed parts of a log such as boards, planks, scantling, and timber.

Matching, or tonguing and grooving - The method used in cutting the edges of a board to make a tongue on one edge and a groove on the other.

Meeting rail - The bottom rail of the upper sash of a double-hung window. Sometimes called the check-rail.

Member - A single piece in a structure, complete in itself.

Miter - The joint formed by two abutting pieces meeting at an angle.

Molding Base - The molding on the top of a baseboard.

> *Bed* – A molding used to cover the joint between the plancier and frieze (horizontal decorative band around the wall of a room); also used as a base molding upon heavy work, and sometimes as a member of a cornice.
>
> *Lip* - A molding with a lip which overlaps the piece against which the back of the molding rests.
>
> *Picture* - A molding shaped to form a support for picture hooks, often placed at some distance from the ceiling upon the wall to form the lower edge of the frieze.
>
> *Rake* - The cornice upon the gable edge of a pitch roof, the members of which are made to fit those of the molding of the horizontal eaves.

Mortise - The hole which is to receive a tenon, or any hole cut into or through a piece by a chisel; generally of rectangular shape.

Mullion - The construction between the openings of a window frame to accommodate two or more windows.

Muntin - The vertical member between two panels of the same piece of panel work. The vertical sash-bars separating the different panels of glass.

Newel - The principal post of the foot of a staircase; also the central support of a winding flight of stairs.

Nosing - The part of a stair tread which projects over the riser, or any similar projection; a term applied to the rounded edge of a board.

Pad eyes - Metal rings mounted vertically on a plate for tying small vessels.

Partition - A permanent interior wall which serves to divide a building into rooms.

Pier-(a) Timber, concrete, or masonry supports for girders, posts, or arches. (b) Intermediate supports for adjacent ends of two bridge spans. (c) Structure extending outward from shore into water used as a dock for ships.

*Piers-*Masonry supports, set independently of the main foundation.

Pilaster - A portion of a square column, usually set within or against a wall.

Piles - Long posts driven into the soil in swampy locations or whenever it is difficult to secure a firm foundation, upon which the footing course of masonry or other timbers are laid.

Piling - Large timbers or poles driven into the ground or the bed of a stream to make a firm foundation.

Pitch - Inclination or slope, as for roofs or stairs, or the rise divided by the span.

Pitch board - A board sawed to the exact shape formed by the stair tread, riser, and slope of the stairs and used to lay out the carriage and stringers.

Plan - A horizontal geometrical section of a building, showing the walls, doors, windows, stairs, chimneys, columns, etc.

Plank - A wide piece of sawed timber, usually 1 1/2 to 4 1/2 inches thick and 6 inches or more wide.

Plaster - A mixture of lime, hair, and sand, or of lime, cement, and sand, used to cover outside and inside wall surfaces.

Plate - The top horizontal piece of the walls of a frame building upon which the roof rests.

Plate cut - The cut in a rafter which rests upon the plate; sometimes called the seat cut.

Plow - To cut a groove running in the same direction as the grain of the wood.

Plumb cut - Any cut made in a vertical plane; the vertical cut at the top end of a rafter.

Ply - A term used to denote a layer or thickness of building or roofing paper as two-ply, three-ply, etc.

Porch - An ornamental entrance way.

Post - A timber set on end to support a wall, girder, or other member of the structure.

Pulley stile - The member of a window frame which contains the pulleys and between which the edges of the sash slide.

Purlin - A timber supporting several rafters at one or more points, or the roof sheeting directly.

Rabbet or rebate - A corner cut out of an edge of a piece of wood.

Rafter - The beams that slope from the ridge of a roof to the eaves and make up the main body of the roof's framework.

Rafters, common - Those which run square with the plate and extend to the ridge.

    Cripple - Those which cut between valley and hip rafters.

    Hip - Those extending from the outside angle of the plates toward the apex of the roof.

    Jacks - Those square with the plate and intersecting the hip rafter.

    Valley - Those extending from an inside angle of the plates toward the ridge or center line of the house.

Rail - The horizontal members of a balustrade or panel work.

Rake - The trim of a building extending in an oblique line, as rake dado or molding.

Return - The continuation of a molding or finish of any kind in a different direction.

Ribband - (See Ledgerboard.)

Ridge - The top edge or corner formed by the intersection of two roof surfaces.

Ridge cut - (See Plumb cut.)

Rise - The vertical distance through which anything rises, as the rise of a roof or stair.

Riser - The vertical board between two treads of a flight of stairs.

Roofing - The material put on a roof to make it wind and waterproof.

Rubble - Roughly broken quarry stone.

Rubble masonry - Uncut stone, used for rough work, foundations, backing, and the like.

Run - The length of the horizontal projection of a piece such as a rafter when in position.

Saddle board - The finish of the ridge of a pitch-roof house. Sometimes called comb board.

Sash - The framework which holds the glass in a window.

Sawing, plain - Lumber sawed regardless of the grain, the log simply squared and sawed to the desired thickness; sometimes called slash or bastard sawed.

Scab - A short piece of lumber used to splice, or to prevent movement of two other pieces.

Scaffold or staging - A temporary structure or platform enabling workmen to reach high places.

Scale - A short measurement used as a proportionate part of a larger dimension. The scale of a drawing is expressed as 14 inch = 1 foot.

Scantling - Lumber with a cross-section ranging from 2 by 4 inches to 4 by 4 inches.

Scarfing - A joint between two pieces of wood which allows them to be spliced lengthwise.

Scotia - A hollow molding used as a part of a cornice, and often under the nosing of a stair tread.

Scribing - The marking of a piece of wood to provide for the fitting of one of its surfaces to the irregular surface of another.

Seat cut or plate cut - The cut at the bottom end of a rafter to allow it to fit upon the plate.

Seat of a rafter -The horizontal cut upon the bottom end of a rafter which rests upon the top of the plate.

Section - A drawing showing the kind, arrangement, and proportions of the various parts of a structure. It is assumed that the structure is cut by a plane, and the section is the view gained by looking in one direction.

Shakes -Imperfections in timber caused during the growth of the timber by high winds or imperfect conditions of growth.

Sheathing -Wall boards, roofing boards; generally applied to narrow boards laid with a space between them, according to the length of a shingle exposed to weather.

Sheathing paper -The paper used under siding or shingles to insulate in the house; building papers.

Siding -The outside finish between the casings.

Sills -The horizontal timbers of a house which either rest upon the masonry foundations or, in the absence of such, form the foundations.

Sizing - Working material to the desired size; a coating of glue, shellac, or other substance applied to a surface to prepare it for painting or other method of finish.

Sleeper - A timber laid on the ground to support a floor joist.

Span - The distance between the bearings of a timber or arch.

Specifications - The written or printed directions regarding the details of a building or other construction.

Splice - Joining of two similar members in a straight line.

Square - A tool used by mechanics to obtain accuracy; a term applied to a surface including 100 square feet.

Stairs, box -Those built between walls, and usually with no support except the wall.

Standing finish - Term applied to the finish of the openings and the base, and all other finish work necessary for the inside.

Stringer - A long horizontal timber in a structure supporting a floor.

Stucco -A fine plaster used for interior decoration and fine work; also for rough outside wall coverings.

Stud - An upright beam in the framework of a building.

Studding - The framework of a partition or the wall of a house; usually referred to as 2 by 4@s.

Sub floor - A wood floor which is laid over the floor joists and on which the finished floor is laid.

Threshold - The beveled piece over which the door swings; sometimes called a carpet strip.

Tie beam (collar beam) - A beam so situated that it ties the principal rafters of a roof together and prevents them from thrusting the plate out of line.

Timber - Lumber with cross-section over 4 by 6 inches, such as posts, sills, and girders.

Tin shingle - A small piece of tin used in flashing and repairing a shingle roof.

Top plate - Piece of lumber supporting ends of rafters.

To the iveather - A term applied to the projecting of shingles or siding beyond the course above.

Tread - The horizontal part of a step.

Trim - A term sometimes applied to outside or interior finished woodwork and the finish around openings.

Trimmer -The beam or floor joist into which a header is framed.

Trimming - Putting the inside and outside finish and hardware upon a building.

Truss - Structural framework of triangular units for supporting loads over long spans.

Valleys - The internal angle formed by the two slopes of a roof.

Verge boards - The boards which serve as the eaves finish on the gable end of a building.

Vestibule - An entrance to a house; usually inclosed.

Wainscoting - Matched boarding or panel work covering the lower portion of a wall.

Wale - A horizontal beam.

Wash - The slant upon a sill, capping, etc., to allow the water to run off easily.

Water table - The finish at the bottom of a house which carries water away from the foundation.

Wharf - A structure that provides berthing space for vessels, to facilitate loading and discharge of cargo.

Wind ("i" pronounced as in "kind") - A term used to describe the surface of a board when twisted (winding) or when resting upon two diagonally opposite corners, if laid upon a perfectly flat surface.

Wooden brick - Piece of seasoned wood, made the size of a brick, and laid where it is necessary to provide a nailing space in masonry walls.
